GROWTH MANAGEMENT AND PUBLIC LAND ACQUISITION

Growth Management and Public Land Acquisition

Balancing Conservation and Development

Edited by
TIMOTHY S. CHAPIN AND CHRISTOPHER COUTTS
Florida State University, USA

Routledge
Taylor & Francis Group
LONDON AND NEW YORK

First published 2011 by Ashgate Publishing

Published 2016 by Routledge
2 Park Square, Milton Park, Abingdon, Oxon OX14 4RN
711 Third Avenue, New York, NY 10017, USA

Routledge is an imprint of the Taylor & Francis Group, an informa business

British Library Cataloguing in Publication Data
Growth management and public land acquisition : balancing conservation and development. -- (Urban planning and environment)
1. Real estate development--Environmental aspects--United States. 2. Real estate development--Environmental aspects--United States--Case studies. 3. Cities and towns--Growth--Environmental aspects--United States. 4. Cities and towns--Growth--Environmental aspects--United States--Case studies. 5. Public lands--United States--Management. 6. Public lands--United States--Management--Case studies.
I. Series II. Chapin, Timothy Stewart. III. Coutts, Christopher.
333.7'315'0973-dc22

Library of Congress Cataloging-in-Publication Data
Chapin, Timothy Stewart.
Growth management and public land acquisition : balancing conservation and development / by Timothy S. Chapin and Christopher Coutts.
p. cm. -- (Urban planning and environment)
Includes index.
ISBN 978-0-7546-7941-7 (hardback)
1. Public lands--United States. 2. Natural areas--United States. 3. Sustainable development--United States. I. Coutts, Christopher. II. Title.
HD216.C43 2011
333.1'1--dc22

2010046576

ISBN 9780754679417 (hbk)

Contents

List of Figures *vii*
List of Tables *ix*
Acknowledgments *xi*
List of Contributors *xiii*

1 Introduction: Balancing Conservation and Development 1
Timothy S. Chapin and Christopher Coutts

PART I LINKING GROWTH MANAGEMENT AND LAND CONSERVATION

2 Land Preservation: An Essential Ingredient in Smart Growth 7
Tom Daniels and Mark Lapping

3 Farmland Preservation as a Growth Management Strategy: Lessons for State and Local Governments 33
Tom Daniels

4 Florida Forever: Conserving Land and Guiding Growth in the Sunshine State 55
Andrew H. McLeod

5 Balancing Land Conservation and Land Development: The Rise and Fall of Florida's Rural Land Stewardship Areas Program 79
Timothy S. Chapin and Harrison Higgins

PART II CHALLENGES AND OPPORTUNITIES

6 Preservation Backfired? Open Space Acquisition and Its Impacts on Land Markets 101
Yan Song

7 Green Infrastructure and Public Health: An Evaluation of the Florida Communities Trust Public Land Acquisition Program 117
Christopher Coutts

8 The Role of Local Governments in Open Space Preservation and Land Acquisition in Florida 143
SeJin Lee and Richard C. Feiock

9 Understanding Public Support for Land Acquisition and Growth Management: The Case of Florida 159
Timothy S. Chapin

10 Incorporating Land Values to Improve Targeting Schemes for Land Acquisition: An Application to Maryland's GreenPrint Program 173
Karen Palm Szobota and Lori Lynch

11 A Case Study of Wisconsin's Knowles–Nelson Stewardship Program 201
W. David Clutter

12 Conclusion: Evaluating the Prospects for Integrating Land Conservation and Growth Management 219
Timothy S. Chapin and Christopher Coutts

Index *225*

List of Figures

3.1	Preserved farmland, agricultural zoning, and urban growth areas in Lancaster County, PA, 2008	52
6.1	Land conversion in proximity areas of conserved open space	111
7.1	Green infrastructure	127
7.2	Proportion of positive responses to questions with public health significance in funded versus unfunded FCT applications 2001–2006	129
10.1	Green infrastructure identified and protected in southern Maryland counties	177

List of Tables

3.1 Leading state farmland preservation programs, 2008 40
3.2 Leading counties in farmland acres preserved, 2009 45
3.3 Population and farmland change in 12 leading farmland preservation counties 46
3.4 Growth boundaries in four metro counties 48
3.5 Agricultural zoning in five metro counties 48
4.1 Milestones in state land conservation 57
4.2 Preservation 2000 funding allocations, 1990–99 58
4.3 Florida Forever funding allocations, 2001–08 60
4.4 Florida Forever funding allocations, 2009 70
4.5 Types of Florida Forever purchases, 2001–08 72
4.6 Florida managed conservation lands, 2008 72
6.1 Results from spatial hedonic analysis for transactions, 2000 107
6.2 Results from estimating land in alternative residential use, 2000 110
6.3 Probit analysis of land conversion decision 110
7.1 FCT questions with public health significance 130
7.2 Summary of funded and unfunded FCT applications, 2001–2006 132
7.3 Differences in questions with public health significance between funded and unfunded groups 133
8.1 Land acquisition applications by jurisdiction 150
8.2 Comparisons of governments with and without land acquisition applications 151
8.3 Logit regression of FCT land acquisitions 152
9.1 Summary of variables influencing citizen attitudes towards land conservation and growth management 163
9.2 Summary of primary independent variables of interest 165
9.3 Support for increased environmental funding and growth management 166
9.4 Regression results for support for increased environmental spending 168
9.5 Regression results for support for growth management 169
10.1 Description of model data 180
10.2 Estimated coefficient explaining the value for 10+ acre parcels in three southern Maryland counties 184
10.3 Scoring parameters and weights for desktop ecological scores 188
10.4 Overall targeting packages for GreenPrint for three counties: benefit, acreage and erodible soils 191

10.5 Overall alternative targeting strategy for three counties: benefits or benefits per dollar 191
10.6 Disaggregate targeting practices for GreenPrint for three counties with $16 million budget: Benefit, acreage, and erodible soils 194
11.1 Matland's ambiguity-conflict matrix: policy implementation process 205
11.2 Assessment of program implementation 207
11.3 Factors that affect program implementation positively 208
11.4 Factors that affect program implementation positively, by cohort 209
11.5 Factors that affect program implementation negatively, by cohort 210
11.6 Summary of key findings from the Delphi analyses 212

Acknowledgments

In January 2008 a symposium entitled "Achieving Growth Management through Public Open Space Acquisition: Realities and Prospects" was held on the campus of Florida State University in Tallahassee, Florida. At this symposium we brought together leading conservation and growth management scholars, planning practitioners, and conservation advocates to discuss the role that land acquisition might play in promoting growth management efforts in Florida (and elsewhere). The original intent of the event was deceptively simple: to evaluate the role that the Florida Forever land acquisitions have had in promoting the state's growth management goals. We had hoped that this event might help in the push to have Florida Forever expanded in the coming decades as Florida deals with its ongoing development–preservation struggle.

However, as the event progressed it became clear to all involved that public policy in the areas of growth management and land acquisition is often shaped by what we *think* is effective policy, rather than what we *know* to be effective policy. Our discussions during the event led the participants to conclude that there is much to be learned about the opportunities and challenges faced by planners and policymakers at the nexus of growth management and land conservation. While there clearly are strong connections between the two initiatives, little empirical investigation has been undertaken at this nexus. Ultimately, this recognition of our wide gap in knowledge and the general quality of the presentations at the symposium led us to pursue this edited volume.

It is worth noting that this symposium was yet another in a long line of events sponsored by the *DeVoe Moore Center for the Study of Critical Issues in Economic Policy and Government* at Florida State University (http://www.coss.fsu.edu/dmc/). The mission of the DeVoe Moore Center is to increase knowledge and public understanding about the role of government in a market economy and to study how government rules, regulations, and programs affect the economy. The Center has been a great resource for faculty in the Department of Urban and Regional Planning, the institutional home of the editors, and for the state of Florida as it wrestles with the many problems associated with its usually fast growing economy. We greatly appreciate the financial support from the DeVoe Moore Center, spearheaded by Center Director Keith Ihlanfeldt, and also thank Keith for his suggestions that we market the event to both scholarly and practitioner audiences.

An edited volume like this one cannot proceed without effort from a great number of people whose names are not attached to chapters in the book. Most notably, Kathy Makinen of the DeVoe Moore Center provided outstanding copyediting services for the book. Every chapter in this volume is better because of her excellent work and her suggestions for simpler and more direct language. We also thank the wonderful staff at Ashgate Publishing for their help in seeing us through the publication process.

Lastly, we offer thanks to the many planners and environmental advocates that contributed indirectly to this volume. A great many individuals took time to answer questions from the various chapter authors, provided input via interviews or surveys, or read and commented on paper drafts. The book is far better for their input.

List of Contributors

The Editors

Timothy S. Chapin is Associate Professor and Chair of the Department of Urban and Regional Planning at Florida State University. Dr. Chapin's research interests are in the areas of growth management/comprehensive planning and downtown redevelopment. He was lead editor and chief contributor to *Growth Management in Florida: Planning for Paradise* (Ashgate Publishing), a book that evaluates the effectiveness of the state's 1985 Growth Management Act. Chapin's work has been supported by the Century Commission for a Sustainable Florida, the Lincoln Institute for Land Policy, and the Department of Housing and Urban Development. He earned a PhD in urban design and planning from the University of Washington.

Christopher Coutts is an Assistant Professor in the Department of Urban and Regional Planning and a Research Associate in the Center for Demography and Population Health at Florida State University. His research focuses on the influence of the built environment and ecologically-sensitive land use practices on community health and health behavior. His Peace Corps work in Malawi is what spurred his ongoing investigation of the fundamental role of the environment on health. He earned a graduate degree in Public Health from New Mexico State University and a Ph.D. in Urban, Technological, and Environmental Planning from the University of Michigan.

The Contributors

W. David Clutter is currently the Director of Lands Programs for the Natural Resources Foundation of Wisconsin. He has over sixteen years' experience in protecting natural resources and biological diversity in Texas, New Mexico, Alaska, Illinois and Wisconsin. He has served with county and federal agencies, as well as statewide and national nonprofits to assist with wildlife research, implement land protection and stewardship, facilitate regional land trust collaborations, conservation planning and nonprofit development and secure funds necessary to implement an array of projects and programs. For much of his career his work has focused on engaging citizens and local, regional, statewide and federal organizations and agencies to develop and implement collaborative conservation initiatives.

Tom Daniels is a Professor in the Department of City and Regional Planning at the University of Pennsylvania. For nine years, he was Director of the Agricultural Preserve Board of Lancaster County, Pennsylvania, where he managed the county's nationally recognized purchase of development rights program. Daniels is the author of *When City and Country Collide: Managing Growth in the Metropolitan Fringe* and co-author of *Holding Our Ground: Protecting America's Farms and Farmland, The Environmental Planning Handbook for Sustainable Communities and Regions*, and *The Small Town Planning Handbook*. He often serves as a consultant to state and local governments.

Richard C. Feiock is Augustus B. Turnbull Professor of Public Administration and Policy at Florida State University. He directs Florida State University's newly established Sustainable Energy and Governance Center, and was founding director of the DeVoe Moore Center's Program in Local Governance. Feiock has lectured in Moscow (Russia and Idaho), Seoul, Beijing and throughout the U.S. and was a Fulbright Fellow in South Korea in 2006. He has written or edited six books and over one-hundred refereed journal articles. His work appears in the leading scholarly journals of political science, public administration, and urban affairs.

Harrison Higgins is currently Associate Director at cityLAB at UCLA. Higgins is a former Planner-in-Residence in the Department of Urban and Regional Planning at Florida State University. An urban designer and planner with more than fifteen years experience, Higgins has worked with a number of Florida communities to develop and implement their comprehensive plans. Higgins' planning practice has also included clients in Arizona, California, New Mexico, New York, Oregon, and Washington state.

Mark Lapping is a Distinguished Professor in the Department of Public Policy and Management at the University of Southern Maine. Lapping was Founding Dean of the Bloustein School of Planning and Public Policy at Rutgers University. Author of several books, he has also written well over 150 articles and monographs, and has been on the editorial boards of the *Journal of the American Planning Association*, the *Journal of Rural Studies*, *Agriculture and Human Value*, and the *Journal of Planning Research and Education*. He has been a consultant to governments and agencies throughout North America and in several other nations.

SeJin Lee is currently a doctoral student in the Askew School of Public Administration at Florida State University. Working with her major professor, Richard Feiock, she has undertaken research on the role of government structure in shaping local land use and land conservation strategies.

Lori Lynch is a Professor in the Agricultural and Resource Economics Department at the University of Maryland. She received her Ph.D. from U.C. Berkeley in 1996 and Master's Degree from U.C. Davis in 1989. Her research has focused on land use issues particularly land preservation. Her research program compares conservation techniques, evaluates programs' (TDR, PDR, auctions, donation, targeted areas) success, assesses the effect of easement restriction and down-zoning policies on land prices, explores the factors influencing participation in preservation programs, determines what land characteristics are rewarded through easement payments, tests for a critical mass of resource land, as well as explores whether preserved open space increases the value of adjacent properties.

Andrew H. McLeod is currently the Government Affairs Director of the Florida Chapter of The Nature Conservancy. He has also been appointed as a member of the Century Commission for a Sustainable Florida. McLeod has also worked as national conservation finance director for the nonprofit Trust for Public Land and as director of the Rhode Island Department of Environmental Management. McLeod holds a M.A. from Georgetown University and M.P.A. from the Kennedy School of Government at Harvard University.

Yan Song is an Associate Professor in the Department of City and Regional Planning of the University of North Carolina at Chapel Hill. Her research interests includes urban economics, land use planning, growth management, economics of land use regulations, urban form, impacts of urban growth, and GIS and other computer-aided planning tools. Her research projects have been supported by the National Science Foundation (NSF), US Environmental Protection Agency (EPA), U.S. Department of Housing and Urban Development (HUD), and Lincoln Institute of Land Policy.

Karen Palm Szobota gained environmental economics consulting experience at Triangle Economic Research, Durham, NC before earning her Master's degree from the University of Maryland's graduate program in Agricultural and Resource Economics. Working under the direction of Lori Lynch, she used predicted market values for ecologically valuable natural lands to develop optimal target schemes for land preservation programs for her thesis. Szobota now lives in Richmond, VA and works as an analytic consultant.

Chapter 1
Introduction: Balancing Conservation and Development

Timothy S. Chapin and Christopher Coutts

In his book *Garden Cities of Tomorrow* (originally published in 1898), Ebenezer Howard articulated a vision for future development that still shapes our thinking about cities, suburbs, and undeveloped lands. Howard's Garden Cities model called for a development pattern in which a large central city is established as the hub of the region's economy and surrounding this central city are a constellation of smaller towns, all separated quite visibly and deliberately by large swaths of undeveloped green spaces and/or active agricultural lands. Howard believed that this model offered a desirable mix of both urban and country life.

Boiled down to its essence, the Garden Cities model rests upon the concepts of growth management and land conservation. In terms of developed land, Howard was a proponent of planned urban and suburban cities, areas containing a mix of residences, commercial centers, and industrial areas. Surrounding these cities and suburbs were large, permanently protected greenbelts that contained natural landscapes that provided clean air, clean water, and scenic areas to city residents. Also within these greenbelts were active farmlands that could help to sustain urban areas with food and other resources. Beyond providing food to residents and providing ecosystem services, the greenbelts could serve as firm growth boundaries for the urban areas, checking their expansion and limiting the sprawl of urban uses into the countryside.

Howard's ideas were very well received by the public, and by landscape architects and the early cohort of what we would now call urban planners. Beyond these accolades, Howard's ideas helped to shape planning efforts in Great Britain for decades. Howard participated in the development of the early garden cities of Letchworth and Welwyn. Later, these ideas had a profound influence upon Britain's new town planning initiative that was pursued after World War II. In the United States, Howard's Garden Cities model shaped the development of many planned new towns, including several financed and built by the federal government. Some of these ideas also found their way into the New Urbanism movement, and many modern local and state smart growth efforts can trace their lineage back to Howard's utopian vision.

While the Garden Cities concept has had a profound impact upon urban and suburban landscapes in Britain, the United States, and many other countries, it also illustrates the fundamental importance of linking land conservation and land development. The brilliance of this model rests in part upon the understanding that successful metropolitan planning and long-term regional sustainability need to be based upon coordinated efforts to protect resource lands and to promote development in well-planned urban centers. Under the Garden Cities model there was to be a symbiotic relationship between green spaces and developed lands, with these two very different landscapes reinforcing each other.

It is this fundamental link between green landscapes and urban landscapes that lies at the heart of this book. Unfortunately, as planning has evolved as a profession, this conservation–development linkage has been hard to maintain. With the rise of subfields within planning, such as environmental planning, land use planning, and transportation planning, there has been a tendency to simplify problems and the policy responses to them. As a consequence the development of land and the conservation of land are addressed through different, often disconnected policies and overseen by different organizations. For example, in Florida, the state's land planning policies and programs and the state's land conservation policies and programs are administered by different agencies, the former by the Department of Community Affairs and the latter by the Department of Environmental Protection. Even in Florida, which is recognized for its progressive planning practices, land development and land conservation remain largely disconnected from each other. Land use planners are tasked with addressing issues of urban sprawl and declining center cities, while environmental planners are tasked with addressing problems of water supply shortages, the depletion of species habitats, and the protection of important agricultural lands.

The goal of this book is to investigate and report on current efforts in the United States to link growth management and land conservation through public land acquisition. The book's chapters elucidate the opportunities, challenges, and unintended consequences of linking these often disparate planning activities. Among the opportunities discussed are the significant human health benefits of public investments aimed at protecting sensitive lands, maintaining a viable agricultural industry, and developing a comprehensive green space system within a region. Other chapters describe the challenges of forging explicit linkages between growth management and land conservation, illustrating that this synergy is not easily achieved.

A number of chapters describe model programs and explain the mechanisms that could be employed and adapted in land acquisition efforts in other locales in the U.S. or in international settings. The quality of the programs analyzed in this volume indicate that there is a solid foundation of good policy to build upon and that there is no need to reinvent conservation practice, although some creativity and sensitivity to context will need to be employed when using these tools or replicating these programs. As documented, there are many methods that have been employed to secure lands that hold unique public benefits and can contribute to local or regional growth management goals.

Other chapters in the volume describe the role of local governments, the importance of public support, and the effectiveness of public–private partnerships in balancing growth and conservation. A lack of support for a growth management regime that incorporates land conservation could have serious consequences on the short-term gains and the long-term sustainability of linking these symbiotic efforts. Evidence from these chapters suggests that a partnership between public and private interests is required to more successfully link growth management and land conservation efforts.

Lastly, this volume also explores how both the monetary value and the aesthetic value of open space can shape and alter development patterns. Several chapters illustrate how monetized value needs to be an important consideration in the targeting and prioritizing of land identified for potential acquisition. The economic value of open space is evidenced by the premium placed on living near these oases of undeveloped and often publicly accessible spaces. These chapters raise a troubling question for proponents for public land acquisition. In creating conserved spaces through land acquisition, is the public sector actually encouraging development in areas that would otherwise not have experienced development pressure? Unforeseen by the editors and authors at the outset of this project, it is these unintended consequences of public land acquisition that proved to be a major part of this volume's story.

The Organization of the Book

The book is organized into two major sections. The first section includes chapters that provide an overview of the need to link growth management and land acquisition/conservation programs. It also includes chapters that assess efforts in Florida to forge these linkages. In Chapter 2, Tom Daniels and Mark Lapping lay the foundation for why land preservation, and not simply regulation, is essential to smart growth management practices. They illuminate the various mechanisms, such as conservation easements, used to acquire and preserve the myriad forms of public green space found in both urban and rural contexts. Chapter 3 presents an overview of the importance of farmland preservation in a growth management strategy. Tom Daniels discusses the history of farmland preservation in the U.S. and provides lessons from the state of Pennsylvania as the national leader in farmland preservation.

Chapter 4 features Andrew McLeod's account of the history, current state, and future prospects for the Florida Forever public land acquisition program. The longevity and unparalleled scope of Florida Forever situate it as a model for comprehensive land conservation efforts. In Chapter 5, Tim Chapin and Harrison Higgins present Florida's Rural Land Stewardship Areas program as uniquely situated "at the nexus of land conservation and growth management." The documentation of the state's attempts to implement rural land stewardship in Florida provides valuable lessons to those who wish to create public policies which balance land protection and development.

The second section includes a mix of chapters that illuminate the challenges and opportunities for successfully linking growth management and land acquisition by a range of state and local programs in the United States. Chapter 6 demonstrates that land conservation may actually have unintended and deleterious effects on local growth management efforts. Yan Song's analysis of the Portland, Oregon land market indicates that open space preservation and the desirability of being near preserved land can actually instigate development in proximity to these lands. Chapter 7 discusses an integral, yet often overlooked, reason for pursuing a linked policy approach. Christopher Coutts summarizes the ways that green infrastructure supports public health and uses the Florida Communities Trust land acquisition program to uncover the public health goals that may be inherent to, but not explicit in, land conservation programs.

Refocusing to the local level, Chapter 8 analyzes the role of local government in open space preservation. SeJin Lee and Richard Feiock present an analysis of the political economy for local governments as they engage in land conservation. In Chapter 9, Tim Chapin confronts the issue of public support as an essential ingredient for successful land acquisition and growth management programs. His analysis demonstrates that public support for land acquisition and growth management is based in different subgroups of the population, highlighting potential public relations challenges that planners can face when pursuing these initiatives.

Chapter 10 focuses on Maryland's progressive GreenPrint program to examine the importance of land values in the prioritization of land targeted for acquisition. Karen Palm Szobota and Lori Lynch find that incorporating parcel acquisition costs would likely alter Maryland's current scheme and potentially improve the state's system for identifying properties for acquisition. In Chapter 11, David Clutter presents a case from the state of Wisconsin to explore some potential barriers and necessary supports to accomplishing land conservation using public–private partnerships. He concludes with a number of factors that would strengthen policies aimed at guiding public–private cooperation in land conservation efforts.

In the book's conclusion the editors synthesize these chapters and highlight the major conclusions from the volume. Taken as a whole the chapters suggest that while there is great value in linking land acquisition and growth management, successfully forging this link has proven to be a challenge. In this chapter the editors discuss the prospects for linking land acquisition programs to broader smart growth planning efforts, identifying where common ground exists and highlighting the role of public policy in forging these links.

PART I
Linking Growth Management and Land Conservation

Chapter 2
Land Preservation: An Essential Ingredient in Smart Growth[1]

Tom Daniels and Mark Lapping

The term "smart growth" became popular as part of Maryland's 1997 legislation, which provided financial and planning incentives to combat sprawl and promote compact development (Daniels, T.L. 2001a). Development was to be concentrated in growth areas known as Priority Funding Areas; and hundreds of thousands of acres of rural lands were to be "preserved" as farmland and open space through the Rural Legacy Program, which authorized millions of dollars for the purchase of development rights from willing landowners. Thus, land preservation should be seen as an integral part of Maryland's—and indeed any major Smart Growth effort (Daniels, T.L. 2001a; Downs 2001).

Smart growth has been difficult to define precisely. Downs (2001) offers 14 potential elements of smart growth, from regional tax base sharing to compact, mixed-use development to preserving open space. Downs notes there is little agreement among anti-growth forces, pro-growthers, and the inner city residents about the desirability of most of the smart growth elements. Yet, the need for land preservation is one of the few issues on which the three groups agree.

A number of states and communities were undertaking growth management efforts prior to 1997 that could be considered smart growth (Porter 1997). But the name "smart growth" afforded a catchy, politically acceptable alternative to "dumb growth" and offered the promise of continued development and economic growth *coupled with* environmental improvement and greater social integration. Dumb growth can be broadly defined as sprawling, haphazard, and poorly planned development in the outer suburbs and ex-urbs which also draws the economic and social vitality out of cities and older suburbs (Libby and Bradley 2000, 260). Sprawl has been identified as America's leading land use problem, causing premature and excessive conversion of farmland, open space, and natural areas (Freilich 1999). Moreover, sprawl's dispersed land use patterns contribute to automobile dependence, consumption of imported oil, air pollution from vehicle-miles traveled, increased public service costs, and water pollution

---

1 This chapter was originally published as Daniels, Tom and Mark Lapping, "Land Preservation: An Essential Ingredient in Smart Growth," *Journal of Planning Literature*, 19(3), pp. 316–29 (February 2005). Copyright © 2005 by Sage Publications. Reprinted with permission.

from on-site septic systems and increased storm water runoff from the paving of open space with roads and parking lots (Daniels and Daniels 2003; Freedgood 2002). Equally important to limiting the outward expansion of development is creating attractive and efficient cities and suburbs to accommodate growth and development (Gratz and Mintz 1998, Langdon 1994). Much of the debate about smart growth has focused on designing pedestrian-oriented communities that have human-scaled buildings and can be served by mass transit (Calthorpe 1993, Katz 1994, Calthorpe and Fulton 2001). But parks, greenways, and open space are also crucial for making cities and suburbs attractive for residents (Schuyler 1986).

The preservation of privately-owned land should be considered a necessary part of smart growth both for controlling sprawl and for creating livable communities (Pruetz 1998; Daniels, T. 1999; Wright and Czerniak 2000). Private land preservation may involve any of the following techniques: the purchase or donation of land in fee simple, the purchase or donation of conservation easements (also known as development rights), the transfer of development rights, or limited development. The three common features of these land transactions are: 1) they are voluntary on the part of willing sellers or donors; 2) there are negotiations between buyer and seller or donor and donee; and 3) the seller or donor receives compensation in cash and/or through tax benefits (Wright and Czerniak 2000). For governments, this last feature, in particular, is crucial in avoiding a "taking" of private property without just compensation.

There are two main types of land preservation associated with smart growth: 1) the preservation of land for parks, recreation, and greenways within built-up urban and suburban areas; and 2) the preservation of rural land for the production of food and fiber, to maintain valuable natural areas—such as wildlife habitats and water supply sources—and to channel development to more appropriate locations.

Most of the preservation of privately held land has occurred only since 1980 (Gustanski and Squires 2000). A fundamental question is whether government land preservation administrators and private land trusts have a strategic vision for land preservation or whether land is being preserved at random with little effect on metropolitan development patterns and land use change (Gustanski 2000; Heimlich 2001; Hollis and Fulton 2002).

Because land use planning is largely under the jurisdiction of state and local governments, this paper focuses on land preservation programs operated by state and local governments and private nonprofit organizations, and not on federal land preservation programs. The chapter first reviews the literature on why land preservation is used in smart growth efforts rather than only land use regulations, and then evaluates the literature on the mechanics of conservation easements and land purchases. The chapter next analyzes the literature on how land preservation has performed as part of smart growth efforts, and finally suggests areas for future research.

Why Land Preservation and Not Only Land Use Regulation?

The land preservation literature persuasively explains several reasons why land preservation has gained in popularity over the past 25 years. In the 1980s, the Reagan Administration's attacks on environmental laws and cuts in federal land acquisition programs, such as the Land and Water Conservation Fund, touched off a widespread increase in the number of private nonprofit land trusts (Myers 1993a). The land trust movement has also grown as a result of frustrations with the rapid pace of growth in many communities and the ineffectiveness of local planning to protect important landscapes and natural resources. Between 1980 and 2002, the number of land trusts rose threefold from about 400 to more than 1,200, and there is at least one land trust in every state (Land Trust Alliance 2003).

Land preservation is often necessary because of impending development pressures (Richardson 2000). The landowner is ready to sell; the question is who will buy it and what will the buyer do with the land. Land markets have repeatedly failed to create satisfactory land use patterns, and instead have fostered residential and commercial sprawl that wastes land resources, provides too little public open space, and destroys wildlife habitat (Freilich 1999; Healy and Short 1981). Land markets are influenced by public infrastructure investments in roads, schools, and sewer and water facilities, and by local governments whose primary interest is often the hunt to expand the property tax base. This growth bias is inimical to the retention of open space, farmland, and natural areas, or the creation of tax-exempt public parklands. Private developers have traditionally found little incentive to create public parks, trails, or greenways. Local governments often avoid creating these public areas because they prefer private development that will expand the property tax base. But the hunt for property tax base is often misguided: most residential development pays less in property taxes than it demands in public services. The American Farmland Trust has conducted more than 80 Cost of Community Services studies that indicate that residential development demands more in public services than it generates in property taxes, whereas farmland generates more in property taxes than it demands in services (Freedgood 2002).

A chief attraction of land preservation is that it provides greater permanence in the landscape. Land use regulations are notoriously impermanent, subject to variances, re-zonings, special exceptions, and conditional uses (Whyte 1968, Langdon 1994, Daniels, T. 1999). In many parts of the United States, annexation of county land by cities has furthered sprawling development patterns. Some communities have used large lot "conservation zoning" to limit the amount of development that can occur on private land in an attempt to protect natural features. But five-acre and ten-acre lots do little to protect wildlife habitats, and larger lot sizes for conservation zones will likely face legal challenges as exclusionary (Daniels and Daniels 2003). Ineffective land use regulations are an example of "government failure." That is, government land use regulations may actually result in more sprawl and a greater loss of natural areas and working rural landscapes than if the land market had been left alone.

The threat of lawsuits against local governments over Fifth Amendment "takings" of private property value through land use regulations has deterred many local governments from adopting stronger land use regulations (Geisler and Daneker 2000, xiii; Wright and Czerniak 2000). As a result, local land use regulations alone are unlikely to produce long term sustainable land use patterns. Moreover, since 1991, 26 states have enacted so-called "takings" laws, which require governments to pay compensation to landowners if a new government regulation would devalue a landowner's property beyond a certain percentage (Jacobs 1999). Thus, for example, enacting stricter zoning to protect farmland in these states is seen as simply not legally or politically possible. In short, except in a very few cases such as Oregon, land use regulations have not been aimed at protecting a critical mass of natural areas to support biodiversity or maintain working farm and forest landscapes (Beatley 2000, Daniels and Bowers 1997). Finally, Geisler and Daneker (2000, xiv) make a compelling case that the preservation of private land results in land ownership that is a "hybrid" of both public and private ownership, better in some ways to meet social desires as well as private needs through generally local control and decentralized land management.

What Does Land Preservation Do and How Is It Done?

The literature on land preservation has focused on the mechanics of conservation easements and land purchases rather than on how land preservation can fit in the comprehensive planning process to achieve community Smart Growth goals (Brenneman and Bates 1984, Diehl and Barrett 1988; Small 1988, 1992, 2002; Wright 1994; Trust for Public Land 1995). Part of the reason for this is that in many communities land preservation efforts have preceded planning for smart growth (Brewer 2003; McQueen and McMahon 2003). Still, there have been few assessments of the effectiveness of land preservation in influencing growth and development.

Land preservation simply means restricting the uses of a property over a long time. The uses are limited when private property is acquired in a fee simple transaction by a government agency, such as land for a county park, or by a qualified nonprofit organization, such as land for a nature preserve. Whereas land owned by a government agency is almost always open to the public, land owned by a nonprofit organization is private property and may not be open to the general public. Also, it is fairly common for a non-profit organization to purchase land and then sell it subject to restrictions on use to a government agency.

Another way to restrict the use of property is when a landowner willingly sells or donates a conservation easement either to a government agency or to a qualified private organization (Diehl and Barrett 1988). As a nonprofit charitable organization that has received 501(c)(3) status from the Internal Revenue Service, a private organization—usually a land trust, conservancy, or sports group—may accept donations of land, conservation easements, and money, and donors may claim donations as income tax deductions (Small 1987, 2001).

The terms conservation easement and development rights are used interchangeably, but as a convention, conservation easements are acquired by non-profit organizations and development rights are purchased by government agencies in purchase of development rights programs or by developers in transfer of development rights programs. Development rights are often explained as one of the rights in the bundle of rights that make up the ownership of land (Geisler and Daneker 2000). A development right may be separated from the rest of the bundle and given away or sold. A conservation easement is in many ways the opposite of a right-of-way easement, which grants a neighboring landowner a right to cross another's property. A conservation easement is technically a "negative easement in gross," which spells out specific restrictions that apply to the use of an entire piece of land (Daniels, T.L. 1991). In general, all residential, commercial, industrial, and institutional uses are prohibited unless expressly allowed in the Deed of Easement. Permitted uses may include farming, timber harvesting, maintaining open space, or building a limited number of dwellings. The Deed of Easement is a legally binding document that is recorded at the county courthouse and runs with the land, so if the land is sold or transferred to heirs, the restrictions in the Deed of Easement apply to subsequent landowners. Land subject to a conservation easement is still private property, usually without any right of public access.

The donation or bargain sale (part cash, part donation) of a conservation easement is the main way that private nonprofit land trusts preserve land (Daniels and Bowers 1997). Many federal agencies have also acquired conservation easements by purchase or donation, including the National Park Service, the Fish and Wildlife Service, the Natural Resources Conservation Service, the Farm Service Agency, and the U.S. Forest Service. Several state departments of natural resources have programs to acquire conservation easements, and dozens of counties and local governments have acquired conservation easements, primarily through purchase (American Farmland Trust 2002).

A conservation easement may restrict land in perpetuity or for a certain number of years—known as a term easement. For instance, the federal Wetlands Reserve Program, the Farm and Ranchland Preservation Program, and the Grasslands Reserve Program may acquire conservation easements in perpetuity or for a 30-year term (Wiebe et al. 1996). Heimlich (2001, 6) notes that easements have proven to be durable, rarely being reversed. Daniels and Bowers (1997, 151) describe the stringent conditions under which some states allow landowners to repurchase easements. Also, land subject to a conservation easement can be condemned for a public purpose, but this has rarely occurred.

There are several potential tax benefits from donating a permanent conservation easement (Small 2001, 2002). The landowner may use the value of the easement as an income tax deduction, subject to certain limits defined in Section 170(h) of the Internal Revenue Code. There may be estate tax benefits depending on the size of the landowner's estate. A few states offer state income tax credits for people who donate a conservation easement on their land (e.g. Salkin 2002, 278). In some states, the landowner may receive a reduction in the assessed value of the property for property tax purposes. For instance, the Maryland Environmental Trust, as state agency, has the authority to grant a 15-year property tax abatement on any property on which it receives a conservation easement donation (Daniels and Bowers 1997, 214).

Estate and land transfer planning have become necessary because of the increased value of real estate, especially in metropolitan regions (Small 1988, 1992, 2002). Federal estate taxes begin at 37 percent on estates valued at more than $1 million in 2004. The personal exemption from the estate tax rises to $3.5 million by 2009. There will be no estate taxes in 2010, but in 2011 the estate tax returns at 2003 rates and exemptions (Small 2002).

One way for a landowner to reduce the value of an estate, and hence reduce estate taxes, is to donate a permanent conservation easement to a land trust or government agency (Small 2001, 2002). The value of a conservation easement is determined by a professional appraiser in a written appraisal. The value is the difference between the estimated fair market value of the property if it were sold today and the estimated value of the property subject to the restrictions of the conservation easement (Diehl and Barrett 1988).

Conservation easements have dominated the land preservation literature because they are a less costly way to preserve land than fee-simple acquisition, much more complicated than outright purchase, and do not require a government role. William H. Whyte (1959) wrote the initial major work on conservation easements, noting that conservation easements were first used in Massachusetts by the Trustees of Reservations to protect the parks that Frederick Law Olmsted designed around Boston. Coughlin and Keene (1981) produced a seminal work on farmland preservation, including conservation easement acquisition efforts by the public and private sectors, for the federally-sponsored National Agricultural Lands Study. Brenneman and Bates (1984) edited an important set of essays covering the legal aspects of conservation easements, creating a land trust, and how conservation easements work in practice.

Diehl and Barrett (1988) presented an excellent and widely-used guide to the use of conservation easements. Topics in their book include federal laws regulating the donation of conservation easements, how to draft a Deed of Easement, and the importance of monitoring easements. Attorney Stephen Small (1988, 1992, 2002) has authored short but very informative books that walk landowners through the logic and basics of preserving land using the sale and donation of conservation easements. He demonstrates how conservation easements can be an effective part of an estate plan or land transfer plan. Small also has written very helpful summaries of the federal tax laws relating to conservation easements (1987, 2001).

The Land Trust Alliance (LTA), a national organization devoted to promoting the creation and development of land trusts, serves as a clearinghouse of information about land trust practices and has published a variety of useful books and reports on land preservation (Barton and Hijikata 1997; LTA 1989–2003; LTA 1990). Numerous land trusts have produced publications on conservation easements, and the annual reports of the larger land trusts make interesting reading about land preservation strategy and impact on local land use patterns (e.g. The Conservation

Fund 2003; Montana Land Reliance 2003; The Nature Conservancy 2003; The Trust for Public Land 2002; Vermont Land Trust 2003).

Land trust organizations have been increasingly drawn into land use planning because they recognize that land preservation alone will not produce smart growth. Wright (1993) makes a persuasive case that land trusts are conducting "de facto" land use planning through their preservation of land. Daniels and Bowers (1997) make the important observation that some of the most effective land preservation programs, such as Sonoma County, CA and Lancaster County, PA, are essentially public-private partnerships where public and private land preservation efforts occur within a framework of comprehensive planning.

Statewide and national land trusts have professional staff and increasingly are using GIS systems to identify and evaluate important environmental areas and resource lands and to monitor properties they own or on which they hold conservation easements (Leavitt 2002). These large land trusts have become serious players in local and regional land use planning efforts; there are many examples of public-private easement purchases and other partnership efforts involving land trusts and government agencies (Endicott 1993). On the other hand, most land trusts are small and locally focused (Foti and Jacobs 1989; Brewer 2003). They are often are staffed by volunteers, and have generally preserved no more than a few thousand acres. The shortcomings of most land trusts are a lack of staff and financial resources, and the ability to create only "islands" of protected land, often amid encroaching development. Islands of preserved land are often insufficient to protect entire ecosystems or working landscapes (Daniels and Daniels 2003). Whittaker (1999) makes the key point that many local land trusts are established in response to a short-term land use crisis. As a result, she observes, many land trusts lack a long-term strategy for land preservation.

Financing Land Preservation

Public financing of land preservation has relied upon a variety of sources, including the federal Land and Water Conservation Fund, state and local general fund revenues, the sale of bonds by state and local governments (such as New Jersey's Green Acres Program)—often with voter approval, and earmarked sales-tax revenues (Myers 1993a, McQueen and McMahon 2003). Land purchases have protected recreation areas, parks, wildlife habitats, ands sensitive environmental lands, such as flood hazard areas. Thus, land acquisition has helped to achieve a variety of community goals. McQueen and McMahon (2003) have documented a number of these achievements as part of their excellent summary of financing options for governments and land trusts to purchase land in fee simple. Significantly, many nonprofit land trusts have been able to receive public funding to help carry out public land preservation efforts (Myers 1993b).

Orfield (2002) argues that land preservation efforts have not been able to keep pace with land development. Yet, state and local taxpayers have been remarkably willing to raise taxes to pay for land preservation (Lindsey and Knaap 1999). In the five years, 1998 to 2002, voters approved more than 500 ballot measures involving more than $20 billion (TPL 2003). As of 2002, land trusts had protected more than 6 million acres nationwide (LTA 2003). Still, the literature needs more examples of how land preservation can be made more effective by combining it with community goals and programs. For instance, McQueen and McMahon (2003) advocate green infrastructure planning in which land preservation serves to "integrate land use planning and biodiversity, or to shape and direct growth" (134).

Preserving Land in Cities and Suburbs

The land preservation literature makes strong arguments in favor of preserving three types of land within cities and suburbs: parklands, greenways, and trails. These lands are typically lumped together under the rubric of "green infrastructure." Some researchers have made persuasive arguments that the provision of green infrastructure should be equated with the provision of sewer and water lines, roads and schools (so-called "gray infrastructure") (Beatley and Manning 1997; American Planning Association 2000; McQueen and McMahon 2003). But land preservation within cities and suburbs has not been explicitly linked to overall smart growth efforts.

Parklands

The literature for preserving land for parks in cities and suburbs inevitably emphasizes Frederick Law Olmsted's design for Central Park in New York City and the increased value of private property near or adjacent to the park (Spirn 1984; Schuyler 1986; Fox 1990). Parks offer areas for both passive recreation, such as walking, and active recreation, such as baseball fields, tennis and basketball courts, volleyball, and other sports. The President's Commission on Americans Outdoors (1987) reported that the highest need for open space was in metropolitan areas, where most Americans live. The National Recreation and Parks Association suggests levels-of-service for five different kinds of parks: mini-park, neighborhood park, school park, community park, and large urban park (Mertes and Hall 1995).

Brabec (1992), Lerner and Poole (1999), Crompton (2002), Geoghegan (2002), and Tajima (2003) made important contributions to the literature by conducting and summarizing studies that document higher real estate values closer to parks, greenways, and preserved open space in urban areas. These studies indicated that land preservation can actually expand the property tax base. In the long run, land preservation can end up costing residents less than they would pay to provide public services to developed land (Crompton 2002).

Since 1972, The Trust for Public Land has been active in acquiring land in urban areas for public use, especially for parks (Poole 1993). Daniels (Daniels, T. 1999) describes how voters in greater Portland, Oregon in 1995 approved $65 million for acquiring up to 6,000 acres of parkland and open space within the region's urban growth boundary as a way to maintain and enhance the quality of life. The Project for Public Spaces (1999) carries on the pioneering work of William H. Whyte in promoting the creation of parks and small public urban spaces. Bonham et al. (2002, Ch. 8) profile how Philadelphia is attempting to manage a large inventory of vacant lands and restore them for use as gardens, parks, and open space as part of the city's revitalization efforts. Garvin (2001) profiles a number of case studies in making a strong argument for creating and maintaining parks and open space in urban redevelopment. Daniels and Daniels (2003) offer a general comment that a growing number of communities are adopting mandatory dedication standards for parks in their subdivision and land development ordinances. Developers of residential subdivisions are required to set aside land or fees in-lieu-of-land for parks. It is helpful if communities have identified desired future locations of parks, trails, and greenways in a specially adopted open space plan. Mertes and Hall (1995) in their standard and very accessible book explain how an open space plan can help facilitate the interconnection of parks with trails and greenways.

Greenways and Trails

Greenways and trails are linear open space areas through woods, fields, and along highways, rail or utility corridors, and waterways. Little (1990) wrote the first major book on the importance of greenways, which included several compelling case studies; and Flink et al. (2001) produced a useful guide to creating trails. Greenways and trails provide a variety of recreational opportunities, such as walking, running, biking, and horseback riding, and can link residential areas with schools, parks, and commercial areas to minimize the use of cars. Greenways along waterways provide important buffers to keep the impervious surfaces of developed areas at a distance from water resources, to intercept and filter stormwater runoff, and to absorb floodwaters and thus protect built-up areas. Greenways along highways help to absorb exhaust fumes, noise, and bright lights. Greenways also break up monotonous roadsides and can reduce the number of curb cuts for commercial or residential areas. Greenways can provide important wildlife habitat corridors and promote a variety of recreational pursuits, such as boating, canoeing, fishing, and bird watching (Little 1990).

Daniels and Daniels (2003) note that the creation of regional trails and greenways can be a catalyst for counties and municipalities to undertake other beneficial regional planning efforts such as water resources planning, habitat conservation, floodplain management, and recreation plans. Efforts to create trails and greenways have generally enjoyed widespread public support. Funding to buy land to create greenways have come from federal Land and Water Conservation Fund, some state programs, many communities, and several nonprofit organizations (Little 1990: Flink et al. 2001).

Platt (2000) explains how in 1990, Maryland created a Greenways Commission to foster and connect green corridors across the state. Over the next 10 years, more than 900 miles of greenways had been established, with many more miles in progress (Platt 2000, 19). In 1998, Florida took the lead among states in the creation of a statewide greenway system including recreational trails. The system will connect natural areas and landscapes to support the "ability of these ecosystems to function as dynamic systems" (Florida Dept. of Environmental Protection 1998, 11). At the local level, Greater Chattanooga, Tennessee, which has been recognized as one of the nation's leading environmentally-conscious cities, is creating a 75 to 100 mile riverside greenway and trail system (Beatley and Manning 1997).

Many communities have taken advantage of established rights-of-way along utility corridors to create trail networks. Waterways make especially attractive locations for trails because of their scenic and recreational qualities and because most other types of development are not permitted within flood plains. Abandoned railroad corridors make excellent rails-to-trails projects because of the established rights-of-way and linkages among neighboring communities. At least 700 rails-to-trails projects have been developed nationwide, according to Daniels (1999). Platt (2000) notes that the Transportation Equity Act of 1998 (TEA-21) required ten percent of its surface transportation funds to be set aside for transportation enhancements such as greenways and trails.

Since the early 1980s, Boulder, Colorado has spent millions of dollars to buy up a 27,000-acre greenbelt that separates the city and Boulder County as well as preserves city land above the 5,750 foot mark (Pollock 1998). The greenbelt has helped to limit urban expansion and complements restrictive zoning in the countryside. Correll et al. (1978) reported that the average value of properties adjacent to Boulder's greenbelt were 32 percent higher than those just over half a mile away.

Preserving Land in the Countryside

Land preservation in the countryside has focused on three types of land: natural areas, farmland, and forestland. As in the case of parks, greenways, and trails, the question arises whether rural land preservation is taking place as part of a Smart Growth strategy or simply as a general effort to protect unique environmental features and some productive farms and forests lands (McQueen and McMahon 2003; Brewer 2003).

Natural Areas

Morisette (2001) makes a strong case for the role of land preservation in maintaining environmental quality and wildlife habitat on private lands. Johnston and Madison (1997) have produced the leading article on the use of transferable development rights (TDRs) to preserve natural areas of critical state concern, particularly in the New Jersey Pinelands and the Lake Tahoe region between California and Nevada. The Pinelands covers more than 900,000 acres in southern

New Jersey, overlying one of the largest aquifers along the East Coast. In 1979, the State of New Jersey established the Pinelands Commission which then drafted a comprehensive plan designating most of the Pinelands as a "preservation" area with only very limited development. The plan also included a "protection" area where more development could occur. A crucial part of this plan was a transfer of development rights program, established in 1983, to compensate landowners in the preservation area and to move potential development into the protection area (Pizor 1986; Gottsegen 1992; Mason 2004). As of 2000, more than 19,000 acres of land had been preserved through the transfer of development rights program (Brennan et al. 2000).

The Lake Tahoe Regional Planning Agency was jointly established in 1969 by California and Nevada. A prime concern of the Agency is regulating development so that runoff from septic systems and roads does not pollute Lake Tahoe, which is also a major tourist attraction. In the 1980s, the Agency evaluated all lands within the 207,000-acre basin and set categories for how much impervious surface would be allowed to cover a property. The Agency also established a quota of about 300 new dwellings per year (Twiss 2004).

Pruetz (1997) has written the leading book on transfer of development rights (TDRs) and describes how, in 1987, the Tahoe Regional Planning Agency created a TDR program to allow the transfer of underused impervious surface from one property to another. Also, the TDR can be used to enable property owners to remove existing structures. The Agency's TDR program was unsuccessfully challenged as a taking under the 5th Amendment in 1997 (Pruetz 1997, 12–13; Twiss 2004).

The Nature Conservancy has been the leading non-profit preserver of natural areas, with more than 12 million acres preserved in the United States alone (TNC 2003). The organization's Last Great Places campaign is targeting special ecosystems for preservation, but not necessarily in concert with state or local smart growth strategies.

Daniels and Daniels (2003) note that since the late 1980s, many states, often with voter approval, have substantially increased expenditures for buying environmentally significant open space, parklands, easements on farmland, buffers for drinking water sources, and natural areas. In 1988, California voters approved $776 million in bonds to protect natural areas, farmland, and Pacific coastline. Twelve years later, California voters approved more than $4 billion in state bonding for purchasing land for parks to protect watersheds, drinking water supplies, and coastal areas. In 1990, the Florida legislature earmarked $3 billion for the Preservation 2000 Initiative, which resulted in the purchase of about 900,000 acres of environmentally sensitive lands and riparian areas. In 1999, the legislature repeated itself by passing the $3 billion Florida Forever measure for natural land purchases over the next ten years (Beatley 2000, 13). In 2001, the Maryland legislature approved a $35 million GreenPrint program to create an integrated system of greenways especially along stream corridors (Daniels, T.L. 2001a).

Farmland Preservation

The preservation of privately-held farm and ranchland was not considered a serious land use issue before 1980. In 1981, Coughlin and Keene authored the landmark publication on farmland protection techniques as part of the National Agricultural Lands Study. Lapping (1982) emphasized the importance of protecting a critical mass of farms and farmland in order to keep the agricultural support businesses in operation. Lapping et al. (1989) pointed out the fundamental split between federal farm income support programs and local control of land use planning decisions about the protection of farmland. But most of the emphasis in the 1980s was still on the regulation of farmland, especially through zoning (Toner 1984).

Since the early 1990s, the leading source of current information on farmland preservation has been provided by *Farmland Preservation Report*, a monthly newsletter (Bowers 1990–2004). The newsletter tracks farmland preserved by counties and states, as well as the latest preservation legislation. Farmland Information Library (Farmland Information Library 2003) has provided a useful on-line source of information about farmland preservation research. American Farmland Trust (2002) has created useful technical reports on land preservation techniques, such as the purchase and transfer of development rights, but data in the reports about the acreage preserved by state and local governments is not reliable.

Daniels (Daniels, T.L. 1991) provided a major overview of the purchase of development rights to preserve farmland, including the pros and cons of the technique, and why it was growing in popularity. He cites the main benefit as greater long term protection of land; yet he recognizes the potential high cost of purchasing development rights, the possibility of landowner hold-outs who leaves holes of unpreserved land, and the fact that landowners and local governments may be closing off future options by preserving land. Freedgood (1991) lists the purposes of purchasing development rights as: 1) keeping farmland affordable by limiting the development potential; 2) providing working capital for farms; and 3) overcoming estate planning problems that could result in the conversion of farmland. Daniels (Daniels, T.L. 2001b) contends that the purchase of conservation easements is basically paying landowners for the "unearned increment" in land value—that portion of land value caused by public investment in infrastructure. He observes that Henry George advocated taxing away the unearned increment in his famous "Single Tax." Daniels suggests using the Single Tax within growth boundaries to encourage development and the purchase of development rights to preserve lands outside the boundaries. The Single Tax on land forces landowners to develop open land or build more intensively, and thus can help to concentrate development in urban areas; purchasing development rights removes development potential and thus can curb sprawl in the countryside.

Daniels and Bowers (1997) and American Farmland Trust (1997) have produced the leading guidebooks on farmland protection and preservation. Bick and Haney's guide to conservation easements (2001), distributed by the American

Farm Bureau Federation, is an extremely cautious description of what landowners need to watch out for in preserving their land.

Daniels (Daniels, T. 1997) warned that cluster development was not a form of farmland preservation, but rather a suburban type of development aimed at allowing residential development while protecting some open space and "rural character." By contrast, Arendt (1994) has advocated clustering as a farmland preservation technique. Yet clustering has not been used in the leading agricultural areas, but rather in suburbanizing communities (Daniels 1997). Corser (2003) describes the use of limited development with land preservation in Routt County, Colorado, noting that developers, rather than ranchers, have been the ones to negotiate bonus lots in return for land preservation.

In one of the few analyses of a farmland preservation program, Conaway (1987) provides a frank assessment of the Carroll County, Maryland program and suggests improvements. Lyons (1989) profiles a case study of Suffolk County, New York—the eastern end of Long Island—where the purchase of development rights to farmland was pioneered, starting in the mid-1970s. Lyons calls the program a success, even though relatively few acres had been preserved and at a fairly high cost. American Farmland Trust (1996) discusses the process of getting a purchase of development rights program started in Peninsula Township, Michigan. Nickerson and Lynch (2001) unexpectedly found no significant difference in the prices of preserved and unpreserved farmland in Maryland.

Daniels (Daniels, T.L. 2000a, 2000b) evaluates the farmland preservation effort in Lancaster County, PA where in recent years more farmland has been preserved than developed and where farmland preservation complements the widespread use of agricultural zoning and urban growth boundaries. Hollis and Fulton (2002) fail to understand how the purchase of development rights to farmland can help to create permanent parts of growth boundaries and channel development toward areas with adequate infrastructure as demonstrated in Daniels and Bowers (1997) and Daniels (Daniels, T.L. 2000b). It is somewhat ironic that the success of Calthorpe and Fulton's approach to smart growth in *The Regional City* (2001) to create livable cities and suburbs is predicated on growth boundaries and limits on development in the hinterlands, yet they do not recognize that this can perhaps be done more effectively with a combination of land preservation and regulation than simply Oregon-style regulation.

Identifying which land to preserve is an important part of farmland preservation. Daniels (Daniels, T.L. 1994) discusses the use of a modified Land Evaluation and Site Assessment (LESA) system to prioritize applications for easement sale. Tulloch et al. (2003) present a case study of using a parcel-specific GIS system to rank farmlands in importance for preservation.

An integral part of Maryland's 1997 Smart Growth legislation is the Rural Legacy Program which has resulted in the purchase of conservation easements on more than 39,000 acres at a cost of roughly $100 million (Bowers 2003a). Rural Legacy areas are designated by county governments with the goal of preserving as much of these areas as possible. The lands typically include a mix of farmland, forestlands, and natural areas. The Rural Legacy Program complements the state farmland preservation program which has preserved more than 200,000 acres (American Farmland Trust 2002).

Public funding for farmland preservation has been strong. For instance, in 1998, New Jersey voters approved spending $1 billion over the next ten years to preserve an anticipated one million acres of farmland, recreation land, and open space (The Conservation Fund 1999). In 2002, Congress approved $985 million in grants to state and local governments and land trusts to preserve farmland (Daniels and Daniels 2003). As of 2002, about 850,000 acres of farmland had been preserved through public programs at a cost of about $1.2 billion (Bowers 2002).

Heimlich and Anderson (2001) estimate that it would cost $130 billion to preserve the 94.7 million acres of cropland under the pressure of urbanization. Heimlich (2001) argues that "we are not going to solve the farmland protection problem by purchasing easements" (1). Jacobs (2000, 425) echoes this sentiment by contending that land preservation should be seen as a supplement to and not a replacement for public-sector land use planning.

Tustian (1983) and Banach and Canavan (1989) boast the success of Montgomery County, Maryland's transfer of development rights program. As of 2003, Bowers (2003b) notes that Montgomery County had preserved more farmland (59,415 acres) than any other county in the United States. Brabec and Smith (2002) try to make the case that transfer of development rights is superior to purchase of development rights, but their comparison between Montgomery County, Maryland and two towns in Suffolk County, New York is too narrow, and not convincing. Daniels and Bowers (1997) and Machemer and Kaplowitz (2000) contend that transfer of development rights is far more difficult to put into practice than a purchase of development rights program. Indeed, no other county has come anywhere close to preserving as much farmland with transferable development rights as Montgomery County (Johnston and Madison 1997, Bowers 2003b).

Preservation of Forestland

The preservation of working forestland has not been high on the land preservation agendas of most states or land trusts, and has been addressed only sparsely in the land preservation literature. But as with the preservation of farmland, it is also necessary to secure a critical mass of forestland in order for the industry to survive. Rural residential sprawl fragments forestlands into smaller tracts that may not be large enough or sufficiently contiguous to support commercial forestry. As nonforesters purchase forestlands, they drive up the price of land and reduce active forest management (Mansius 2002). This increases the potential for forest fires as well as diseases that affect trees, animals, and humans (Society of American Foresters 2003). A study in the South concluded that "urbanization will have the most direct, immediate and permanent effects on the extent, condition and health of forests" in the region (U.S. Forest Service 2002, 91). Many forests are prime water re-charge areas and are important for long term water quality and supplies.

Several studies indicate the negative impacts of land-fragmenting sprawl on wildlife habitats (DeGraaf and Healy 1988). Taken together, these issues suggest that there is justification for preserving forestlands in areas experiencing sprawl.

The federal government spurred interest in forestland preservation when Congress enacted the Forest Legacy Program in 1990. The Program allows the U.S. Forest Service to purchase permanent conservation easements on forest land, purchase forest land, or make grants to states for acquisitions of forest land or easements. First, a state forester must draft an assessment of need—identifying forestlands with important commercial timber or riparian or ecological values that are threatened by development—for approval by the U.S. Forest Service. A state must provide at least 25 percent of project costs. As of 2001, the Forest Legacy Program had resulted in the purchase of conservation easements on more than 200,000 acres in 15 states (Daniels, T.L. 2001c). The 2002 Farm Bill authorized another $60 million for the program (Daniels and Daniels 2003).

Daniels (Daniels, T.L. 2001c) reported that a few land trusts have preserved large amounts of forestland. The Society for the Protection of New Hampshire Forests has helped to protect over one million acres of New Hampshire forestlands through the purchase and donation of conservation easements and outright land purchases. The Vermont Land Trust holds conservation easements on more than 100,000 acres of forestland, and has often joined with the state agencies, private foundations, and other conservation groups to preserve large tracts of forest lands in northern Vermont. The Pacific Forest Trust in Boonville, California has preserved more than 25,000 acres through conservation easements in California, Oregon, and Washington and has consulted on conservation practices on more than 750,000 acres (Pacific Forest Trust 1999, 2001).

Wayburn (1994) wrote a particularly helpful article on how land trusts can craft conservation easements to protect forest lands, and Lind (2002) has written a very useful and practical guide to using conservation easements to manage productive forestlands, yet protect wildlife habitat, wetlands, and streams.

Future Research Needs and Directions

Most of the literature on land preservation has been generated by land preservation practitioners, rather than by planners or academics. Land preservationists have focused on acquiring land and conservation easements, rather than on how land preservation is influencing growth patterns (Diehl and Barrett 1998; Small 1987, 2001). Thus, practitioners have not determined whether land preservation has been a reactionary ad-hoc effort or an effective part of a comprehensive planning process and smart growth strategy. For instance, in his history of land trusts, Brewer (2003) calls for more planning to help guide land preservation but does not explain how to do this. On the other hand, planners have been slow to recognize the power of land preservation as a planning tool, and planning academics have generally avoided the topic (Danielsen et al. 1999; Szold and Carbonell 2002).

There several shortcomings in both the land preservation and smart growth literature. First, research needs to analyze of the effectiveness of smart growth programs and the role land preservation plays. For instance, the smart growth movement would benefit from several case studies of the successful uses of green space within urban and suburban areas to revive and improve these places (Spirn 1984; Bonham et al. 2002). Second, there is a dearth of evaluations of land preservation programs in metropolitan areas, especially over long periods of time (Hollis and Fulton 2002; McQueen and McMahon 2003). The prime question is whether a critical mass of land can be preserved to enable wildlife, farming, or forestry to survive and thrive (Daniels, T. 1999). Longitudinal studies are sparse, in part because most programs are young, and attempts to evaluate some preservation programs have been premature (Maynard et al. 1998). Third, private foundations are emerging as a significant source of funding for land preservation (Greene 1999). The impact and effectiveness of this funding source for land trusts has not been explored in depth (McQueen and McMahon 2003). Fourth, a valid criticism of private land preservation is that it is voluntary and thus somewhat random, happening one parcel at a time, rather than encompassing large landscapes in one comprehensive program (McQueen and McMahon 2003). To refute this criticism, research would need to demonstrate timely and cost-effective ways to preserve large landscapes and how this preservation fits in smart growth programs. Fifth, how well are government agencies and land trusts meeting their obligations to manage the lands they own as well as monitor and enforce conservation easements? (Gustanski and Squires 2000). Land trusts and government agencies are discovering that preserved lands are changing hands and new owners need to be educated and advised about the restrictions on the land they own. These efforts will demand increasing attention and expense on the part of government agencies and land trusts. Legal challenges to conservation easements are a particular concern as to the durability of land preservation. Finally, a debate has arisen whether land preservation techniques are being taught in academic planning programs (Wright and Czerniak 2000; Jacobs 2000). A survey of planning programs could be undertaken to discern the breadth and depth of land preservation techniques in planning curricula.

Conclusion

Planning in America has traditionally meant "planning for development." But residents in hundreds of communities have recognized that it is also necessary to plan for the preservation of recreational land, natural environments, and working farm and forest landscapes. Striking a balance among the natural environment, working landscapes, and the built environment is one of the biggest challenges that local governments face. This means that planning for smart growth is at least twice as challenging as planning for growth alone—a reality that the smart growth literature has not recognized (see Downs 2001; Szold and Carbonell (2002). On the one hand, the smart growth literature needs to show how smart growth efforts can benefit from land preservation. On the other, land preservation, as McQueen and McMahon (2003) point out, will have to become more proactive and less reactive. That is, land preservation must take place within the comprehensive planning process to work toward smart growth goals.

Smart growth ideally combines regulations, design guidelines, and financial incentives into a region-wide package (Daniels, T.L. 2001a). Planners have long preferred to use regulation and design guidelines to influence growth and development. But the preservation of land through cash inducements and/or tax benefits are not only here to stay, they are becoming increasingly popular in an era where land use regulations have been on the defensive both legally and politically.

Planners and academics, together with land preservationists, need to present more studies on how the acquisition of land and conservation easements can help to clarify where development should or should not go, and how land preservation can help to achieve the smart growth goals of curbing sprawl and reviving cities and suburbs. Because public and private dollars for land preservation are limited, government agencies and land trusts will need to be strategic about the land they decide to preserve (McQueen and McMahon 2003). A key objective is the formation of large blocks of preserved land to maintain core habitats and migration corridors, and to enable farm and forestry operations to continue with a minimum of complaints from neighbors. But just as important are the preservation of urban and suburban parks, greenways, and trails that enhance the built environment, encourage alternative modes of transportation, and provide an attractive alternative to sprawling low density development.

Finally, an issue prevalent in much of the land preservation literature is a sense of urgency to preserve land (Brewer 2003; McQueen and McMahon 2003). Daniels and Daniels (2003) offer the opinion that many parts of the United States are in a race against time to protect important lands from development; and given current rates of population growth, development, and land protection, the race in many communities will be largely won or lost within the next 20 years.

References

American Farmland Trust. 2002. *Purchase of Development Rights*, and *Transferable Development Rights*. Washington, D.C.: American Farmland Trust.

American Farmland Trust. 1997. *Saving America's Farmland: What Works?* Washington, D.C.: American Farmland Trust.

American Farmland Trust. 1996. *Forging New Protection: Purchasing Development Rights to Save Farmland.* Washington, D.C.: American Farmland Trust.

American Planning Association. 2000. Green infrastructure: A strategic approach to land conservation. Planning Advisory Service Memo, October, 2000. Chicago: American Planning Association.

Arendt, Randall. 1994. *Rural by Design*. Chicago: American Planning Association.
Banach, Melissa and Denis Canavan. 1989. Montgomery County, Maryland: A transfer of development rights success story, in *Plowing the Urban Fringe: An Assessment of Alternative Approaches to Farmland Preservation*, H. Hiemstra and N. Bushwick (eds), Fort Lauderdale, FL: Florida Atlantic University, Joint Center for Environmental and Urban Problems.
Barton, Katherine and Judith Hijikata (eds) 1997. *Standards and Practices Guidebook: An Operating Manual for Land Trusts*. Washington, D.C.: Land Trust Alliance.
Beatley, Timothy. 2000. Preserving biodiversity: Challenges for planners, *Journal of the American Planning Association* 66(1), 5–20.
Beatley, Timothy and Katherine Manning. 1997. *The Ecology of Place: Planning for Environment, Economy, and Community*. Washington, D.C.: Island Press.
Bick Steven and Harry L. Haney. 2001. *The Landowner's Guide to Conservation Easements*. Dubuque, IA: Kendall Hunt Publications Company.
Bonham, J. Blaine, Jr., Darl Rastorfer, and Gerri Spilka. 2002. Old cities/green cities. Planning Advisory Service Report 506/507. Chicago: American Planning Association.
Bowers, Deborah. 2003a. Farmland preservation in Maryland. Paper presented at the American Farmland Trust Conference, Monterey, CA, 17 March, 2003.
Bowers, Deborah. 2003b. *Farmland Preservation Report*, 13(9), 1. Street, MD: Bowers Publishing.
Bowers, Deborah. 2002. *Farmland Preservation Report*, 12(7), 1. Street, MD: Bowers Publishing.
Bowers, Deborah. 1990–2004. *Farmland Preservation Report*. Street, MD: Bowers Publishing.
Brabec, Elizabeth and Chip Smith. 2002. Agricultural land fragmentation: The spatial effects of three land protection strategies in the eastern United States. *Landscape and Urban Planning* 58, 2–4: 255–68.
Brabec, Elizabeth. 1992. On the value of open spaces. *Scenic America Technical Information Series* 1, 2. Washington, D.C.: Scenic America.
Brennan, Margaret F., Donn A. Derr, and Mark J. Reggimenti. 2000. Lessons learned: An examination of transfer of development rights programs. Paper presented at the American Farmland Trust Conference, West Windsor, New Jersey, 10 April.
Brenneman, Russell L. and Sarah H. Bates 1984. *Land-saving Action*. Covelo, CA: Island Press.
Brewer, Richard. 2003. *Conservancy: The Land Trust Movement in America*. Hanover, NH: University Press of New England.
Calthorpe, Peter. 1993. *The Next American metropolis: Ecology, Community, and the American Dream*. Princeton, NJ: Princeton Architectural Press.
Calthorpe, Peter and William Fulton. 2001. *The Regional City: Planning for the End of Sprawl*. Washington, D.C.: Island Press.

Conaway, K. Marlene. 1987. The Carroll county, Maryland, agricultural land preservation program. In *Sustaining Agriculture Near Cities*, W. Lockeretz (ed.), Ankeny, IA: Soil and Water Conservation Society.

Correll, M.R., J.H. Lillydahl, and L.D. Singell. 1978. The Effects of Greenbelts on Residential Property Values: Some Findings on the Political Economy of Open Space. *Land Economics* 54: 207–17.

Corser, Susan Ernst. 2003. From ranchland to conservation community. *Planning* 69, 26–31.

Coughlin, Robert E. and John C. Keene (eds), 1981. *National Agricultural Lands Study, The Protection of Farmland: A Reference Book for State and Local Governments*. Washington, D.C.: USGPO.

Crompton, John L. 2002. Parks and economic development. Planning Advisory Service Report #502. Chicago: American Planning Association.

Daniels, Thomas L. 2001a. Smart growth: A new American approach to regional planning. *Planning Practice and Research*, 3–4: 271–81.

Daniels, Thomas L. 2001b. Coordinating opposite approaches to managing urban growth and curbing sprawl: A synthesis. *American Journal of Economics and Sociology*, 60, 1: 229–43.

Daniels, Thomas L. 2001c. State and local efforts in conserving privately-owned working landscapes. Paper for the National Governors' Association. Washington, D.C.: National Governors' Association.

Daniels, Thomas L. 2000a. Farm follows function. *Planning*, 66(1), 14–17.

Daniels, Thomas L. 2000b. Integrated working landscape protection: The case of Lancaster county, Pennsylvania. *Society and Natural Resources*, 13(3), 261–71.

Daniels, Thomas L. 1994. Using lesa in a purchase of development rights program: The Lancaster county, Pennsylvania Case. In F. Steiner, J. Pease, and R. Coughlin (eds), *A Decade with Lesa: The Evolution of Land Evaluation and Site Assessment*. Ankeny, IA: Soil and Water Conservation Society.

Daniels, Thomas L. 1991. The purchase of development rights: Preserving agricultural land and open space. *Journal of the American Planning Association*, 57(4), 421–31.

Daniels, Tom. 2001. Critical mass and farmland preservation. Paper presented at the American Farmland Trust National Conference, St. Charles, IL, 12 November, 2001.

Daniels, Tom. 1999. *When City and Country Collide: Managing Growth in the Metropolitan Fringe*. Washington, D.C.: Island Press.

Daniels, Tom. 1997. Where does cluster development fit in farmland preservation? *Journal of the American Planning Association*, 63(1), 129–37.

Daniels, Tom and Katherine Daniels. 2003. *The Environmental Planning Handbook for Sustainable Communities and Regions*. Chicago: APA Planners Press.

Daniels, Tom and Deborah Bowers. 1997. *Holding our Ground: Protecting America's Farms and Farmlands*. Washington, D.C.: Island Press.

Danielsen, Karen A., Robert E. Lang, and William Fulton. 1999. Retracting suburbia: Smart growth and the future of housing. *Housing Policy Debate* 10(3), 513–40.

DeGraaf, Richard and William H. Healy (eds), 1988. *Is Forest Fragmentation a Management Issue in the Northeast?* Radnor, PA: Northeast Forest Experiment Station, U.S. Forest Service, General Technical Report NE-140.

Diehl, Janet and Thomas Barrett. 1988. *The Conservation Easement Handbook.* San Francisco: The Trust for Public Land and Alexandria, VA: The Land Trust Exchange.

Downs, Anthony. 2001. What does 'smart growth' really mean? *Planning* 66(4), 20–5.

Endicott, Eve (ed.), 1993. *Land Conservation through Public-Private Partnerships*. Washington, D.C.: Island Press.

Farmland Information Library. 2003. Farmland Information Library website. www.farmlandinfo.org., accessed 20 September, 2003.

Flink, Charles A., Kristine Olka, and Robert M. Searns. 2001. *Trails for the 21st Century* (2nd ed.) Washington, D.C.: Island Press.

Florida Department of Environmental Protection. 1998. Plan for a statewide system of greenways: Five-year Florida greenways system implementation. Tallahassee: Florida Department of Environmental Protection.

Foti, Pamela E. and Harvey M. Jacobs. 1989. Private public-interest land use planning: Land trusts in the upper mid-west. *Journal of Soil and Water Conservation* 44(4), 317–19.

Fox, Tom. 1990. *Urban Open Space: An Investment that Pays*. New York: The Neighborhood Open Space Coalition.

Freedgood, Julia. 2002. *The Cost of Community Services Studies: Making the Case for Conservation.* Washington, D.C.: American Farmland Trust.

Freedgood, Julia. 1991. PDR programs take root in the northeast, *Journal of Soil and Water Conservation* 46(5), 329–31.

Freilich, Robert H. 1999. *From Sprawl to Smart Growth: Successful Legal, Planning, and Environmental Systems*. Chicago: Section of State and Local Government Law, American Bar Association.

Garvin, Alexander. 2001. Parks, recreation and open space. Planning Advisory Service Report 497/498. Chicago: American Planning Association.

Geisler, Charles and Gail Daneker 2000. Introduction, in C. Geisler and G. Daneker (eds), *Property and Values: Alternatives to Public and Private Ownership*. Washington, D.C.: Island Press.

Geoghegan, Jacqueline. 2002. The value of open spaces in residential land use. *Land Use Policy* 19, 91–8.

Gottsegen, Amanda Jones. 1992. *Planning for Transfer of Development Rights: A Handbook for New Jersey*. Mt. Holly, NJ: Burlington County Planning Commission.

Gratz, Roberta Brandes and Norman Mintz. 1998. *Cities Back from the Edge: New Life for Downtown*. New York: John Wiley & Sons.

Greene, Stephen. 1999. Preserving open space for the ages. *The Chronicle of Philanthropy*, 29 July, 1999, pp. 1–2.

Gustanski, Julie Ann. 2000. Land trusts and conservation decision making: The integrated land conservation decision-support model. In J.A. Gustanski and R. Squires (eds), *Protecting the Land: Conservation Easements Past, Present, and Future*. Washington, D.C.: Island Press, 453–85.

Gustanski, Julie Ann and Roderick Squires (eds), 2000. *Protecting the Land: Conservation Easements Past, Present, and Future*. Washington, D.C.: Island Press.

Healy, Robert G. and James Short. 1981. *The Market for Rural Land: Trends, Issues, Policies*. Washington, D.C.: The Conservation Foundation.

Heimlich, Ralph E. 2001. Farmland protection programs: How would we know they worked? Paper presented at the Conference on Protecting Farmland at the Fringe: Do Regulations Work? Strengthening the Research Agenda. 5–7 September, 2001, Baltimore, MD.

Heimlich, Ralph E. and William D. Anderson. 2001. Development at the urban fringe and beyond: Impacts on agricultural and rural land. Washington, D.C.: US Department of Agriculture, Economic Research Service, AER-803.

Hollis, Linda E. and William Fulton. 2002. Discussion paper, Open space protection: Conservation meets growth management. Washington, D.C.: The Brookings Institution.

Jacobs, Harvey M. 2000. The ambiguous role of private voluntary methods in public land use policy: A comment. *Journal of Planning Education and Research* 19(4), 424–6.

Jacobs, Harvey M. 1999. *State Property Rights Laws: The Impacts of those Laws on My Land*. Cambridge, MA: Lincoln Institute.

Johnston, Robert A. and Mary E. Madison. 1997. From landmarks to landscapes: A review of current practices in the transfer of development rights. *Journal of the American Planning Association* 63(3), 365–78.

Katz, Peter. 1994. *New Urbanism: Toward an Architecture of Community*. New York: McGraw-Hill.

Land Trust Alliance. 2003. *2002 Annual Report*. Washington, D.C.: Land Trust Alliance.

Land Trust Alliance 1989–2003. *Exchange: The Journal for Land Conservation*. Washington, D.C.: Land Trust Alliance.

Land Trust Alliance. 1990. *Appraising Easements: Guidelines for Valuation of Historic Preservation and Land Conservation Easements*. Arlington, VA: Land Trust Alliance.

Langdon, Philip. 1994. *A Better Way to Live: Reshaping the American Suburb*. Amherst, MA: University of Massachusetts Press.

Lapping, Mark B. 1982. Toward a working rural landscape. In C. Reidel (ed.), *New England Prospects*. Hanover, NH: University Press of New England.

Lapping, Mark B., Thomas L. Daniels, and John W. Keller. 1989. *Rural Planning and Development in the United States*. New York: Guilford Publications.

Leavitt, James (ed.), 2002. *Conservation in an Internet Age: Threats and Opportunities*. Washington, D.C.: Island Press.

Lerner, Steve and William Poole. 1999. The economic benefits of parks and open space. Trust for Public Land website, www.tpl.org/newsroom, accessed 30 August, 2003.

Libby, James M., Jr. and Darby Bradley. 2000. Vermont housing and conservation board: A conspiracy of good will among land trusts and housing trusts, in C. Geisler and G. Daneker (eds), *Property and Values: Alternatives to Public and Private Ownership*. Washington, D.C.: Island Press, pp. 259–81.

Lind, Brenda. 2002. *Working Forest Conservation Easements*. Washington, D.C.: Land Trust Alliance.

Lindsey, Greg and Gerrit Knaap. 1999. Willingness to pay for urban greenway projects. *Journal of the American Planning Association*, 65(3), 297–313.

Little, Charles. 1990. *Greenways for America*. Baltimore: Johns Hopkins University Press.

Lyons, William. 1989. Suffolk county, New York: Pioneering the purchase of development rights method to protect farmland. In H. Hiemstra and N. Bushwick (eds), *Plowing the Urban Fringe: An Assessment of Alternative Approaches to Farmland Preservation*. Fort Lauderdale, FL: Florida Atlantic University, Joint Center for Environmental and Urban Problems.

Machemer, Patricia and Michael D. Kaplowitz. Transferable development rights: A market-based land use control. 2000. In M. Kaplowitz (ed.), *Property Rights, Economics, and the Environment.* Stamford, CT: JAI Press Inc., 143–73.

Mansius, Donald. 2002. The Maine forest service perspective. In Urban Forestry Center (ed.), *Forest Fragmentation and Urban Sprawl: Effects on Forests*. Portsmouth, NH: Urban Forestry Center, U.S. Forest Service.

Mason, Robert. 2004. The pine barrens. In *Big Places, Big Plans: Large-scale Regional Planning in North America*, M. Lapping and O. Furuseth (eds), Aldershot: Ashgate.

Maynard, Leigh J., Timothy W. Kelsey, Stanford M. Lembeck, and John C. Becker. 1998. Early experience with Pennsylvania's agricultural conservation easement program. *Journal of Soil and Water Conservation* 53(2), 106–12.

McQueen, Mike and Ed McMahon. 2003. *Land Conservation Financing*. Washington, D.C.: Island Press.

Meck, Stuart (ed.). 2002. *Growing Smart Legislative Guidebook: Model Statutes for Planning and the Management of Change*. Chicago: American Planning Association, 2002.

Mertes, James D. and James R. Hall. 1995. *Park, Recreation, Open Space and Greenway Guidelines*. Alexandria, VA: National Recreation and Park Association.

Montana Land Reliance. 2003. *2002 Annual Report*. Helena, MT: Montana Land Reliance.

Morisette, Peter M. 2001. Conservation easements and the public good: Preserving the environment on private lands. *Natural Resources Journal* 41(2), 373–426.

Myers, Phyllis. 1993a. Financing open space and landscape protection: A Sampler of state and local techniques. In E. Endicott (ed.), *Land Conservation through Public-Private Partnerships.* Washington, D.C.: Island Press.

Myers, Phyllis. 1993b. Direct funding of nonprofit land protection: A new genre of state land conservation programs. In E. Endicott (ed.), *Land Conservation through Public-Private Partnerships.* Washington, D.C.: Island Press.

The Nature Conservancy. 2003. *2002 Annual Report*. Arlington, VA: The Nature Conservancy.

Nickerson, Cindy and Lori Lynch. 2001. The effect of farmland preservation programs on farmland prices. *American Journal of Agricultural Economics* 83(2), 341–51.

Orfield, Myron. 2002. *American Metropolitics: The New Suburban Reality*. Washington, D.C.: The Brookings Institution.

Pacific Forest Trust. 2000. Press Release, Energy company buys carbon credits in conserved California redwood forest, 9 November 2000. Reprinted in *Pacific Forests*, Spring 2001. Boonville, CA: Pacific Forest Trust.

Pacific Forest Trust. 1999. *Annual Report, 1998*. Boonville, CA.

Pizor, Peter. 1986. Making tdr work: A study of program implementation. *Journal of the American Planning Association*, 52(2), 203–11.

Platt, Kalvin. 2000. Going green. *Planning*, 66, 8: 17–20.

Pollock, Peter. 1998. Controlling sprawl in Boulder: Benefits and pitfalls. *Land Lines* 10(1), 1–3.

Poole, William. 1993. Preserving urban and suburban gardens and parks: The trust for public land and its partners. In E. Endicott (ed.), *Land Conservation through Public-Private Partnerships*. Washington, D.C.: Island Press.

Porter, Douglas R. 1997. *Managing Growth in America's Communities*. Washington, D.C.: Island Press.

The President's Commission on Americans Outdoors. 1987. *Americans Outdoors: The Legacy, the Challenge*. Washington, D.C.: Island Press.

Preutz, Rick. 1998. Viewpoint. *Planning*, 64(1), 46.

Preutz, Rick. 1997. *Saved by Development: Preserving Environmental Areas, Farmland and Historic Landmarks with Transfer of Development Rights*. Burbank, CA: Arje Press.

Project for Public Spaces. 1999. *Public Parks, Private Partners*. New York: Project for Public Spaces.

Richardson, Sharon E. 2000. Applicability of South Carolina's conservation legislation to implementation of landscape conservation in the ace basin. In J.A. Gustanski and R. Squires (eds), *Protecting the Land: Conservation Easements Past, Present, and Future.* Washington, D.C.: Island Press.

Salkin, Patricia. 2002. The smart growth agenda: A snapshot of state activity at the turn of the century. *Saint Louis University Public Law Review*, 21(2) 271–312.

Schuyler, David. 1986. *The New Urban Landscape: The Re-definition of City Form in Nineteenth-century America*. Baltimore: Johns Hopkins University Press.

Small, Stephen J. 2002. *Preserving Family Lands, III*. Boston, MA: Landowner Planning Center.

Small, Stephen J. 2001. *Third Supplement to the Federal Tax Law of Conservation Easements*. Washington, D.C.: Land Trust Alliance.

Small, Stephen J. 1992. *Preserving Family Lands* (2nd ed.). Boston, MA: Landowner Planning Center.

Small, Stephen J. 1988. *Preserving Family Lands*. Boston, MA: Landowner Planning Center.

Small, Stephen J. 1987. *The Federal Tax Law of Conservation Easements*. Washington, D.C.: Land Trust Alliance.

Society of American Foresters. 2003. Forest fragmentation increases lyme disease risk. *Forestry Source*, 4, 14.

Spirn, Anne Whiston. 1984. *The Granite Garden: Urban Nature and Human Design*. New York: Basic Books.

Szold, Terry S. and Armando Carbonell (eds), 2002. *Smart Growth: Form and Consequences*. Cambridge, MA: Lincoln Institute of Land Policy.

Tajima, Kayo. 2003. New estimates of the demand for urban green space: Implications for valuing the environmental benefits of Boston's Big Dig project. *Journal of Urban Affairs*, 25, 641–55.

The Conservation Fund. 2003. *2002 Annual Report*. Arlington, VA: The Conservation Fund.

The Conservation Fund. 1999. *Common Ground* 10, 2. Arlington, VA: The Conservation Fund.

The Trust for Public Land. 2003. *Land Vote 2002 Report*. San Francisco: Trust for Public Land.

The Trust for Public Land. 2002. *2002 Annual Report*. San Francisco: Trust for Public Land.

The Trust for Public Land, 1995. *Doing Deals: A Guide to Buying Land for Conservation*. Washington, D.C.: Land Trust Alliance and The Trust for Public Land.

Toner, William. 1984. Ag zoning gets serious. *Planning* 50(12), 19–24.

Tulloch, David L., James R. Myers, John E. Hasse, Peter J. Parks, and Richard G. Lathrop. 2003. Integrating gis into farmland preservation policy and decision making. *Landscape and Urban Planning* 63(1), 33–48.

Tustian, Richard E. 1983. Preserving farmland through transferable development rights: A case study of Montgomery county, Maryland, *American Land Forum* 4(3), 63–76.

Twiss, Robert. 2004. Planning and land regulation at Lake Tahoe: Five decades of experience. In M. Lapping and O. Furuseth (eds), *Big Places, Big Plans: Large-scale Regional Planning in North America.* Aldershot: Ashgate.

U.S. Forest Service. 2002. The southern forest resources assessment summary report. Washington, D.C.: U.S. Forest Service.

Vermont Land Trust. 2003. *Annual Report 2002*. Montpelier, VT: Vermont Land Trust.

Wayburn, Laurie A. 1994. Saving the forest for the trees, and other values. *The Back Forty: A Newsletter of Land Conservation.* San Francisco: The Hyperion Society/Hastings College of the Law.

Whittaker, Marci. 1999. Preserving open space on the rural-urban fringe: The role of land trusts. In O. Furuseth and M. Lapping (eds), *Contested Countryside: The Rural-Urban Fringe in North America.* Aldershot: Ashgate, pp. 263–87.

Whyte, William H. 1968. *The Last Landscape.* Garden City, NY: Doubleday.

Whyte, William H. 1959. Securing open space for urban America: Conservation easements. Technical Bulletin 36. Washington, D.C.: Urban Land Institute.

Wiebe, Keith, Abebayehu Tegene, and Betsy Kuhn. 1996. *Partial Interests in Land: Policy Tools for Resource Use and Conservation.* Washington, D.C.: U.S. Department of Agriculture, Economic Research Service Report Number 744.

Wright, John B. 1994. Designing and applying conservation easements. *Journal of the American Planning Association* 60(3), 380–8.

Wright, John B. 1993. Conservation easements: An analysis of donated development rights. *Journal of the American Planning Association* 59(4), 487–93.

Wright, John B. and Robert J. Czerniak. 2000. The rising importance of voluntary methods of land use control in planning. *Journal of Planning Education and Research* 19(4), 419–23.

Chapter 3
Farmland Preservation as a Growth Management Strategy: Lessons for State and Local Governments

Tom Daniels

Farmland preservation in the United States features the willing sale of development rights (also known as conservation easements) by a landowner to a government agency or private land trust (NGO) to restrict the use of land to farming and open space in return for a cash payment and/or tax benefits. The right to develop land is part of the bundle of rights that come with owning land in America, and can be separated from the rest of the bundle and sold or given away. In the process, the land remains private property, usually with no right of public access (see "A Note on Property Rights and Farmland Preservation" below).

This chapter describes and analyzes how America's state and county governments and private non-profit land trusts are using farmland preservation programs to manage growth and development. The first section presents an overview of farmland preservation efforts in the United States. This is followed by an analysis of the strengths and weaknesses of the leading state and local farmland preservation programs in managing growth. A final section summarizes the lessons learned in the use of state and local farmland preservation programs for managing growth and development.

Growth management involves the application of land use regulations, financial incentives (such as farmland preservation), design standards, and infrastructure spending to influence the rate, timing, location, and style of private and public development. In addition, growth management programs seek to affect the environmental, social, and fiscal costs and benefits of development by influencing the real estate market to perform in socially desirable ways. There are three primary justifications for state and local growth management programs: 1) to maintain and enhance economic competitiveness with other regions in a global economy; 2) to achieve development that is environmentally, socially, and economically sustainable; and 3) to create metropolitan planning efforts to address regional economic, social, and environmental problems to which the federal government is not responding (Wallis 2002).

Growth management is expected to take on added importance over the next 40 years as America's population increases by more than 130 million, from 306 million in 2008 to a projected 439 million in 2050 (U.S. Bureau of the Census

2008). Population growth and farmland are on a collision course because farmers and ranchers own most of the privately held land in America, and Americans have shown a preference for spread out development. The nation's 800 metropolitan counties, where four-fifths of Americans live, are expected to absorb most of the nation's additional residents by 2050. But these counties produce about one-quarter of the food supply, including most of America's fruits, vegetables, and milk (Daniels 2009).

Much of the development in the United States since World War II can be characterized as sprawl: discontinuous, leapfrog patterns of urban and suburban growth, commercial strip development along highways, and scattered residential development in the countryside. Compared to compact development patterns, sprawling development creates a need for new infrastructure, greater dependence on cars and imported oil, more air and water pollution, and the loss of farmland to other uses (Burchell et al. 2005, Daniels and Daniels 2003). It is not an economically or environmentally sustainable form of development.

Which pattern of growth—sprawling or compact—that metropolitan counties and expanding non-metropolitan counties choose over the next 40 years will have major consequences for the environment, regional economic competitiveness, and farm operations. Farmland preservation can play a role in curbing sprawl and promoting more compact, sustainable development as well as maintaining local sources of food, which will become increasingly important if energy prices and transportation costs rise significantly.

Farmland Preservation Efforts in the United States

Agriculture is one of America's most important economic activities. In 2007, farmers and ranchers produced $300 billion in food and fiber, of which $89.9 billion were exported and exceeded imports of food and fiber by $18 billion (U.S. Bureau of the Census 2009, U.S. Department of Agriculture [USDA] 2009). Farmland almost always generates more in local property taxes than it demands in services, creating a net revenue gain (Daniels and Bowers 1997) In addition, farm and ranchland provide a variety of environmental services, such as water re-charge, wildlife habitat, scenic vistas, and carbon storage. Finally, farmland can help contain suburban expansion and limit opportunities for low density rural residential sprawl. But farmland, with a gentle slope and deep well-drained soil, is usually the easiest land to develop for non-farm uses. Moreover, in virtually every metropolitan region in the United States, farmland is more highly valued as a potential building site for houses and commercial development than as an area for raising crops and livestock. Left to market forces, more farmland would be developed than Americans would want. Therefore, 28 states, hundreds of local governments, the federal government, and more than 300 private land trusts have created purchase of development rights programs to maintain farmland for the future.

Land is fundamental to agriculture, and there has been keen interest in the changes in the amount of farmland. The Agricultural Census of the U.S. Department of Agriculture indicates that, from a national perspective, the loss of farmland, while substantial and a problem deserving of attention, is not yet at the level of a national crisis. As of 2007, the United States had 922 million acres of farm and ranchland, of which 309 million acres were cropland (USDA 2009). By comparison, in 1987 there were 964 million acres of agricultural land, and 282 million acres of cropland. These figures suggest that farmland has been converted to other uses at a rate of about two million acres a year; and the amount of cropland has increased by more than one million acres a year.

Although the evidence indicates that conversion of farmland to other uses is not a nationwide threat, it is a very real problem in many metropolitan counties and states. For instance, between 1987 and 2007, the amount of farmland in Chittenden County, Vermont, declined by almost 15,000 acres or 15 percent of the farmland base. Over the same 20 years, Wisconsin (America's Dairyland) saw more than 1.4 million acres of farmland, or 8.5 percent of the state's total, converted to other uses (US Bureau of the Census 1994, USDA 2009). Florida experienced a decline of nearly two million acres in agricultural land, or 17.5 percent of its agricultural land base, between 1987 and 2007. This rate of decrease made Florida one of the leading states in the conversion of farmland to other land uses.

The 2007 Agricultural Census reported 2.2 million farms in America, but about two-thirds of those farms produce less than $10,000 a year in the sale of crops and livestock and account for about three percent of the nation's agricultural production. Farms with more than $10,000 a year in gross sales can be considered commercial farming operations. The top 125,000 farms accounted for 75 percent of the nation's agricultural production (USDA 2009). The recent trend in U.S. farming is toward more small farms with less than $10,000 a year in gross sales and more large farms with sales of more than $250,000 a year, but a shrinking number of medium-size farms with sales between $100,000 and $250,000 a year.

Farmers make up less than two percent of the U.S. population. Yet they receive about $20 billion a year in crop payments from the federal government, especially for corn, soybeans, wheat, rice, cotton, peanuts, and sugar (USDA 2009). These payments are based on the volume of production and favor large farmers. One might ask why, if farmers are receiving handsome payments from the federal government, should state and local governments be willing to pay farmers not to develop their land?

Why Farmland Preservation?

Farmland preservation through the sale of development rights has enjoyed widespread popularity because it helps farmers address three challenges. First, farmers face two choices in their operations: to be a large, low-cost producer of a bulk commodity, such as milk or grain, or to specialize in a niche product, such as organic vegetables. Most U.S. farms are family operations and are undercapitalized.

They do not have the funds either to expand to become more efficient in producing a bulk commodity or to make a transition to a niche product. Second, farmers face the choice of whether to sell the farm or pass it to the next generation. The average age of U.S. farmers is 57 years old (USDA 2009). This means that in the next 20 years, tens of millions of acres of land will change hands. Complications occur in farm families when no children want to take over the farm or when one of the children wants to farm but the others, with equal ownership claims, do not. Because land is a farmer's store of wealth, it is common for the land to be sold to the highest bidder when the farmer retires. And third, especially in metropolitan counties, farmers face the temptation to sell land for development rather than to continue farming.

A farmer who sells development rights receives a cash payment that can be reinvested in the farm operation to improve efficiency and profitability, enabling the farmer to stay in business. Alternatively, the farmer can sell development rights and then sell the farm to one of the children (or someone else who wants to farm) at a reduced agricultural price. This way the farm is transferred to the next generation. The sale of development rights and the subsequent sale of the farm (restricted to farming and open space uses by the conservation easement) offer the farmer a valid financial alternative to selling land for development.

From a state and local government perspective, farmland preservation is attractive for several reasons. First, farmland preservation can give a local government better control over the pace and location of growth, such as promoting more compact development and limiting sprawl. Second, preserved farmland is still private property and the owner continues to pay local property taxes, unlike land owned by the government or a private non-profit land trust which is exempt from local property taxes. Third, the preservation of farmland raises the value of non-farm properties, especially those near preserved farmland: a view of preserved farmland is a highly desirable amenity. Fourth, farmland preservation reduces the amount of developable land in the community, which means fewer public services such as schools, police, and fire protection have to be provided. Thus, farmland preservation slows the increase in cost of community services and keeps down the rise in local property taxes.

Finally, it is important to note that farmland preservation programs began and have been most active in the northeast region of the United States. Here, farmers qualify for few federal farm subsidies. The region contains only two percent of the nation's farmland and has 60 million residents. Thus, development pressures are fairly intense.

Farmland preservation through the purchase of development rights began in the mid-1970s in Suffolk County, New York, on the eastern end of Long Island. In 1977, Maryland became the first state to implement a statewide farmland preservation program. Since then, 27 more states have adopted farmland preservation programs, as have a few hundred county and township governments and land trusts (Bowers 2009a, Farmland Information Center 2009).

In 1996, Congress passed the Farm and Ranchland Protection Act to make grants to state and local governments and land trusts to purchase development rights to agricultural land. In 2002, Congress authorized $985 million over five years for farmland preservation and another $734 million in its 2008 farm bill. Private, non-profit land trusts and conservation easements first emerged in 1891 as a way to preserve important land (Brewer 2003). Today, more than 300 private, non-profit land trusts list farmland preservation as one of their main goals. To date, landowners have sold or donated conservation easements on more than two million acres of farmland and 1.3 million acres of ranchland (Daniels 2009). The focus of farmland preservation has been on maintaining commercial farming operations that contribute significantly to the local and regional farm economy.

Farmland Preservation Strategies and Obstacles for Managing Growth

The success of a farmland preservation program in managing growth will depend in large part on where the farmland is preserved, the cost of preserving the farmland, and supporting land use controls, such as low-density agricultural zoning, urban growth boundaries to limit the extension of sewer and water lines into the countryside, preferential property taxation for farmland, and right-to-farm laws which protect farmers who follow "normal" farming practices (Daniels and Bowers 1997).

A key strategy in farmland preservation is the acquisition of large contiguous blocks of land. Large blocks keep development pressures at a distance and minimize conflicts between farmers and non-farm neighbors. As a result, farmers can operate their farms without fear of lawsuits from neighbors complaining about noise, dust, and odors. A second key decision is whether to preserve farmland close to development or at a distance from development. Preserving farmland near development is more expensive because purchasing development rights is based on the development potential of land, which tends to be higher the closer it is to sewer and water lines. On the other hand, purchasing development rights close to development can block its further expansion. By comparison, preserving farmland far from development is less expensive and less likely to have conflicting non-farm development nearby, but provides little growth management benefit.

Local governments and land trusts face several obstacles in creating effective farmland preservation programs. Money is always a problem. In general, if the average per-acre cost of preserving farmland exceeds $10,000, a local government or land trust will be hard pressed to find the funds to preserve large contiguous blocks of farmland or to preserve farmland close to development. Instead, they may be able to preserve only "islands" of farmland which, especially when not located in areas with agricultural zoning, can act like a magnet for developers who buy the neighboring land and then build houses with a "preserved view." Such residential development can conflict with farming operations and does not manage overall growth, thus defeating the purposes of preserving the land. Further, if costs are so high that little land can be preserved, local government officials and the public at-large may become reluctant to approve additional funding for farmland preservation in the future.

The shortage of funds also guarantees that there are many more farmers interested in selling their development rights than there are funds available, particularly in tough economic times. This means spending decisions must be made wisely. Unfortunately, many local governments and land trusts lack a clear, proactive strategy of what farmland to preserve and they may mistakenly choose to preserve the farmland of any owner who is willing to sell or donate the development rights. Alternatively, they may confuse farmland preservation with open space preservation, preserving small properties of less than 50 acres for their aesthetic benefits while neglecting the larger commercial farming operations that can maintain agriculture as a local industry and provide open space and growth management benefits.

Summary

Farmland preservation through the purchase of development rights has the potential to be an effective growth management technique in the United States, but there are several obstacles that can undermine its usefulness. In the next section, we assess the performance of the leading state and county farmland preservation programs, and examine how to best use farmland preservation as a tool for managing growth. However, before discussing the leading farmland preservation programs, it is important to note the important role property rights play in shaping the protection of agricultural lands.

In America, a landowner's property rights are often described as a bundle of rights that include air rights, water rights, mineral rights, the right to lease, the right to sell, the right to pass the property on to heirs, the right to use, and the right to develop the property. Any one of these rights can be severed from the bundle and separately sold or given away. There are three main ways that farmland can be "preserved" through voluntary transactions of willing buyers and sellers. The first is through fee simple acquisition. The buyer purchases all of the rights to a property and takes ownership from the seller. When a government agency or a private, non-profit land trust purchases land in fee simple, generally that land will be held in its current land use and hence "preserved." But fee simple acquisitions of farmland are rare because of the high cost of buying land.

Second, a landowner may sell or donate the right to develop the property to a government agency or land trust. The value of the development rights is determined by an appraisal, based on the difference between the fair market value of the property and the value of the property restricted to farming and open space uses. In selling or donating the development rights, the landowner receives cash and/or tax benefits, and the government agency or land trust accepts the responsibility to monitor the property and enforce the terms of the easement. The landowner and the government agency or land trust sign a "deed of easement" which is recorded at the county courthouse and runs with the land. When the land is sold or passed on to heirs, the restrictions in the deed of easement apply to future landowners. The deed of easement is technically known as a negative easement in gross, and more commonly as a conservation easement (Daniels 1991). In agricultural conservation easements, the permitted uses typically include traditional crop and animal raising and the construction of agricultural buildings, but no residential, industrial, institutional, or commercial uses are allowed unless stated in the easement.

The terms purchase of agricultural conservation easement (PACE) and purchase of development rights (PDR) are used interchangeably among farmland preservationists, though by convention the latter usually refers to a land trust program while PDR refers to a government program. Most sales or donations of development rights are in perpetuity, although some term easement programs exist, such as the 30-year easements of the federal Wetland Reserve Program. Under the sale or donation of a conservation easement (or development rights), the land remains private property. The land trust or government agency only holds the right to enforce the deed of easement and in fact the land trust or government agency must monitor the property and enforce the easement against violations in order to maintain the validity of the deed of easement.

Third, a local government may create a transfer of development rights (TDR) program to move development potential from rural lands to designated growth areas. In a TDR program, the local government gives landowners in "sending areas" a certain number of TDRs, usually based on acreage, such as one TDR per five acres owned. The government then requires developers who want to build at a higher density in designated growth areas (also known as "receiving areas") to purchase TDRs from the landowners in the sending areas. For instance, a developer could be allowed to build an additional dwelling unit on an acre for each TDR purchased. When a TDR is purchased, the local government must keep track of how many TDRs remain on a property in the sending area. Some local governments use a TDR bank to purchase TDRs from landowners and then re-sell them to developers. When all of a landowner's TDRs have been sold, a conservation easement is placed on the land and held by the local government.

State and County Farmland Preservation Programs

This section examines the structure, funding, and performance of the leading state and local government farmland preservation programs and evaluates their strengths and weaknesses in managing growth.

Twenty-eight states have enacted statewide farmland preservation programs. The primary purpose of these programs is to provide a funding mechanism for farmland preservation. In large states, the state program makes grants to county governments to preserve farmland, ensures that the county programs are operating according to certain standards, but allows the counties to select the farms for preservation and manage the details of preserving the farms. In small states, such as Vermont and Massachusetts, the state program works directly with the landowners. Funding for state farmland preservation programs has varied considerably across

Table 3.1 Leading state farmland preservation programs, 2008

State	Year Program Created	Acres Preserved	Number of Easements	Funds Spent
Pennsylvania	1988	407,647	3,701	$675,897,230
Colorado	1992	387,756	246	$117,699,880
Maryland	1977	336,110	2,413	$552,488,057
New Jersey	1983	173,346	1,776	$757,576,867
Vermont	1987	126,755	490	$54,212,000
Delaware	1991	89,619	496	$111,674,389
Massachusetts	1977	61,936	728	$172,032,674
California	1995	40,784	126	$61,511,000
Connecticut	1978	34,500	254	$108,525,800
Ohio	1999	33,250	174	$19,754,679
Total		**1,691,703**	**10,404**	**$2,631,372,576**

Source: Farmland Information Center 2009.

the states. For example, New Jersey has spent more than $750 million, while Florida and Texas have not yet authorized funding for their programs (Farmland Information Center 2009, Ingram et al. 2009).

Farmland preservation has been particularly popular in the northeastern United States of Pennsylvania, Maryland, New Jersey, Vermont, Delaware, Massachusetts, and Connecticut (see Table 3.1). The states in this region have relatively little public land compared to the western states (such as Colorado and California) where the federal government owns and controls much of the land. Also, farmers in the Northeast receive relatively little financial help in federal farm support payments, especially compared to farmers in the Great Plains and Midwestern states. The Northeast contains only two percent of the nation's farmland, but is home to more than 60 million people, creating substantial development pressure on the farmland base.

California is the nation's leading agricultural state with nearly $34 billion in farm output in 2007. Yet California has preserved only 40,784 acres through its state program (Farmland Information Center 2009). Moreover, California is the only state among the top 10 states in agricultural output that has a statewide farmland preservation program.

The ten states in Table 3.1 have invested a total of $2.6 billion in farmland preservation, and to date five of them have preserved at least 100,000 acres. The future of these and other state farmland preservation programs will depend on the overall health of the economy, nationally and in specific states, and the willingness of voters and politicians to authorize funding.

Pennsylvania: The Nation's Leading State-Level Farmland Preservation Program

Pennsylvania has the leading state-level farmland preservation program in the nation, both in terms of the number of acres and the number of farms preserved (Pennsylvania Department of Agriculture 2009a). Pennsylvania's farmland preservation program can be evaluated according to: 1) the structure of the program, including site selection, county program certification, and funding from the state to the counties; 2) funding mechanisms; 3) the cost of the program; and 4) acres preserved. The strengths and weaknesses of the Pennsylvania farmland preservation program, particularly as a growth management tool, will also be identified and discussed.

Pennsylvania Program Structure Pennsylvania created its farmland preservation program in 1988 following passage of a statewide referendum. This affirmative vote authorized the state to sell $100 million in bonds and use the proceeds to make grants to counties for the purchase of development rights to farmland. In order to implement the farmland preservation program, a Farmland Preservation Board and a Bureau of Farmland Protection were created within the Pennsylvania Department of Agriculture. Next, counties that wanted to participate in the program had to appoint a farmland preservation board and adopt program guidelines which the state board would review and approve. All counties participating in the farmland preservation program have hired full-time or part-time staff.

Landowners who wish to sell their development rights to a county must first enrol their farmland in an agricultural district, called an agricultural security area. There are currently more than 3.7 million acres enrolled in these agricultural districts throughout Pennsylvania, accounting for 44 percent of all Pennsylvania farmland (Pennsylvania Department of Agriculture 2009a). Minimum eligible farm size for the sale of development rights is 50 acres.

As of early 2009, Pennsylvania's Bureau of Farmland Protection had eight employees. This staff size has enabled Pennsylvania to process more farmland preservation projects than any other state in recent years and to operate a streamlined program. Bowers (2000) noted that "In Pennsylvania, a farmer who submits an application to sell an easement will wait from eight months to one year before sitting down to the settlement table."

Through the Bureau of Farmland Protection, Pennsylvania provides funding to counties to purchase development rights and to conduct appraisals, title searches, boundary surveys, and easement settlements. Counties are not required to put up matching funds, but those that do receive additional state funds. The state funds are distributed according to a complicated formula based on property transfer revenues and amount of matching funds provided by a county compared to the other counties. This formula has put more money into counties under heavy development pressure and with greater matching fund contributions. Even so, 57 of the state's 67 counties are receiving farmland preservation funding from the state (Pennsylvania Department of Agriculture 2009a).

Pennsylvania is also encouraging private land trusts to preserve farmland. The state provides up to $500,000 a year in reimbursement grants to cover land trust expenses involved in acquiring conservation easements on agricultural land. The Pennsylvania Department of Agriculture (2009a) has reimbursed land trusts for $950,150 in expenses for preserving 15,798 acres of farmland.

Funding Sources The Pennsylvania farmland preservation program has received a steady stream of funding, which assures farmers that money will be there if they decide to sell their development rights. Since 2002, the program has been authorized in the state budget at a minimum dedicated level of $20.5 million per year (Pennsylvania Department of Agriculture 2009a). The state has raised these funds from general obligation bonds, a dedicated two-cent a pack tax on cigarettes, and the sale of state-owned agricultural lands. The program also receives federal funding through the Farm and Ranchland Protection Program, as well as county matching funds which have exceeded $300 million over the life of the program.

Program Costs Since 1989, the state and local governments have spent slightly more than $1 billion on farmland preservation. On average, then, over the 20 years of the program more than $50 million a year has been spent on farmland preservation. A total of 418,880 acres have been preserved at an average cost of about $2,400 per acre.

Acres Preserved Pennsylvania's farmland preservation program preserved 418,880 acres from 1989 to mid-2009, or an average of more than 20,000 acres a year (Pennsylvania Department of Agriculture 2009b). But acres preserved alone are not an accurate measure of the success of a farmland preservation program. The location of the preserved land relative to developed areas and the creation of large contiguous blocks of preserved farmland are key to maintaining a critical mass of farms and farmland that will enable the farm support businesses to continue as well as keep potential land use conflicts at a minimum. A few counties, in particular Lancaster and Berks, have created large contiguous blocks of preserved farmland that are further supported by agricultural zoning that allows only one house per 25 acres, 40 acres, or 50 acres, depending on the local township. But only a handful of Pennsylvania counties have townships with strong agricultural zoning.

Strengths and Weaknesses The strengths of the Pennsylvania program are:

1. Funding for farmland preservation is steady and dedicated. Farmers have confidence that if they apply to sell their development rights, money will be available at some time in the future.
2. The counties provide matching funds. Counties have contributed more than $300 million for farmland preservation and thus have "bought into" farmland preservation. The farmland preservation program is perceived as

a grass roots program, not a "top down" state program, because the farmers apply to the counties to sell their development rights.

3. The counties also do the appraisals, title searches, and easement settlements. This has saved a lot of time as opposed to having the state do these tasks.
4. County farmland preservation boards rank and select applications. This creates a tie to local land use planning which identifies where to preserve farmland and where development should go.
5. Farmland preservation can be a powerful growth management tool when combined with agricultural zoning and urban growth boundaries, as in Lancaster County (see discussion of county farmland preservation programs below). Since 1996, more farmland has been preserved than developed in that county, which simultaneously has added population at twice the rate of the state. Thus, farmland preservation can encourage more compact development.

Despite being the leader in farmland acres preserved, the Pennsylvania program has some serious flaws that are retarding its ability to preserve more acres, and in a cost-effective way.

1. In 2001, the state lifted its $10,000 an acre cap on easement purchases. This makes it difficult to purchase sufficient acreage for the preservation of critical masses of farmland. For instance, with a cap of $10,000 per acre, 100 acres can be preserved at a cost of $1 million. But in 2005, with no cap, preserving a 56-acre farm cost the state, along with Montgomery County (outside of Philadelphia), $3 million—or almost $54,000 per acre (Bowers 2005). Farmland preservation should not be competing head-to-head with land zoned for development.
2. The state criteria that guide county rankings of applications give preference to farms under considerable development pressure, which are also the farms with the highest easement prices. Instead, preference should go to farms that are adjacent to farms that are already preserved. The goal is to create large contiguous blocks of permanently preserved farmland that enables the farm support businesses to continue to operate. If the farm support businesses fail, then the remaining farmers will face greater costs in finding farm services.
3. The requirement that land eligible to sell development rights be in an agricultural security area has slowed preservation. This requirement should be removed, as is being done in Maryland's program, for instance. Determining whether farmland qualifies for preferential property tax assessment is a simpler way to identify its eligibility for a purchase of development rights program.
4. Pennsylvania's farmland preservation program is not part of a state-level growth management effort. Rather, responsibility for growth management planning and initiatives is shared among local governments, a situation

> which is correlated with sprawling development (Rusk 1999). Pennsylvania has almost 3,000 units of local government with cities, boroughs (villages), townships, and counties. The cities, townships, and boroughs exercise land use controls; the counties may draft comprehensive plans, although these plans are only advisory. Thus, in Pennsylvania development can happen almost anywhere, especially on open land in the countryside. By contrast, the state of Maryland has included farmland preservation as part of its Smart Growth planning efforts (Daniels 2001).

Pennsylvania has been growing slowly in population, at a rate of just 3.4 percent in the 1990s, but development has been occurring in a sprawling pattern. According to a report by the Brookings Institution (2003), 72 percent of the new housing in Pennsylvania in the 1990s was built in the second class (or more rural) townships. Overall, the state's farmland preservation program has not been able to overcome the permissive rural zoning that allows houses on one- and two-acre minimum lot sizes in most of the countryside. Lancaster County, for instance, is the only county that requires a farm to be located in an agricultural zone that allows no more than one house per 20 acres, before the county will purchase the development rights on that farm. This should be the practice for farmland preservation across Pennsylvania.

Growth Management in the Twelve Leading Counties in Farmland Preservation

Counties in the United States may employ one or more techniques to manage growth. Three common techniques are: urban growth boundaries, low density agricultural zoning, and the purchase of development rights to preserve farmland (Daniels 2010). More than 100 local governments in the United States have adopted growth boundaries or urban service areas (Avin and Bayer 2003). A growth boundary is a line on a map within which there is enough buildable land to accommodate growth and development over a 20 year period. The boundary can be expanded over time but urban services, particularly sewer and water lines, will not be extended beyond the boundary. The idea is to create more compact development that is cheaper and easier to service and minimizes sprawling development patterns. Some counties use a single growth boundary while others use several growth boundaries around a number of cities and towns. In 1958, Fayette County and the City of Lexington, Kentucky, created the nation's first urban service area (growth boundary). But growth boundaries gained national attention after the State of Oregon mandated growth boundaries for all of its cities as part of the 1973 State Land Use Act.

Almost 700 local governments were employing agricultural zoning as of 1995, the last time a national survey of agricultural zoning was conducted (American Farmland Trust 1997). Effective agricultural zoning allows development densities that range from one house per 20 acres in the East to as low as one house per 640 acres in the West, and designates agriculture as the preferred land use.

Table 3.2 Leading counties in farmland acres preserved, 2009

County	Farmland acres preserved	Total acres in Farms*	Percent of farmland preserved	Market value of farm output (millions of $)*
Lancaster, PA	82,118	425,336	19.3	1,072.1
Montgomery, MD	71,469	67,613	100.0	33.2
Berks, PA	65,126	222,119	29.3	367.8
Chester, PA	56,711	166,891	34.0	553.3
Carroll, MD	54,858	141,934	38.7	87.4
Burlington, NJ	50,954	85,790	59.4	86.3
Baltimore, MD	49,377	78,282	63.1	68.4
Harford, MD	44,926	75,166	59.8	42.8
York, PA	43,936	292,507	15.0	212.6
Frederick, MD	43,653	202,087	21.6	127.0
Marin, CA	43,642	133,275	32.7	57.8
Sonoma, CA	43,128	503,895	8.6	647.6
Total	**649,898**	**2,394,895**	**27.1**	**3,356.3**

Sources: Bowers 2009b, USDA 2009; *2007.

The growth management benefit of agricultural zoning is that it limits the intrusion of non-farm residences into farming areas; this is especially the case where agricultural zoning is combined with urban growth boundaries. When non-farm residences enter farming areas, complaints and conflicts between neighbors ensue, land prices are bid up beyond what a farmer can afford, farmland is converted to non-farm uses, and farmers are tempted to sell out rather than continue to farm. Also, from a public perspective, agricultural zoning holds down the cost of purchasing development rights (Daniels and Bowers 1997).

The purchase of development rights was first adopted by a county government in New York in the 1970s, and since then dozens of counties have created purchase of development rights programs to preserve farmland. In many cases, farmland preservation has been used because of a fear of a political backlash or lawsuits if the county tried to impose lower density agricultural zoning. For example, of the twelve leading counties in farmland preservation (see Table 3.2), only Baltimore, Lancaster, Marin, Montgomery, and Sonoma have agricultural zoning. But in those counties without agricultural zoning the cost of preserving farmland is generally higher, rural residential sprawl is a greater problem, and population growth is occurring at a faster rate (see Table 3.3).

All twelve counties are considered metropolitan because of their population size. Altogether these counties have preserved more than 640,000 acres or 1,000 square miles, or more than one-quarter of their farmland (see Table 3.2). This is an impressive achievement, but it does not indicate whether the preserved land is scattered or in large contiguous blocks.

Table 3.3 Population and farmland change in 12 leading farmland preservation counties

County	2008 Population	Percent population increase, 1990–2008	Percent farmland change, 1987–2007
Lancaster, PA	490,562	18.8	+5.3
Montgomery, MD	927,583	22.5	-34.5
Berks, PA	403,595	19.9	-8.7
Chester, PA	491,489	30.5	-12.1
Carroll, MD	169,353	37.2	-14.9
Burlington, NJ	445,475	12.7	-16.9
Baltimore, MD	785,618	13.5	-15.6
Harford, MD	240,351	32.0	-24.8
York, PA	424,583	25.0	+30.7
Frederick, MD	225,721	50.2	-14.5
Marin, CA	246,960	8.1	-20.5
Sonoma, CA	466,477	20.2	-8.3
U.S.	304,059,724	22.2	-4.4

Sources: U.S. Bureau of the Census 2006a, 2008, USDA 2009.

Program Structure All of the twelve county farmland preservation programs, except that in Marin County, are public programs and all have full-time staff and advisory boards. The Maryland and Pennsylvania counties along with Burlington County, New Jersey, have long received an annual allocation from their state programs. The counties have primary responsibility for managing the process of preserving the farmland—from ordering appraisals to conducting settlements.

Since 1980, Marin County has relied on a private land trust, the Marin Agricultural Land Trust, to preserve farmland. Lancaster County has two farmland preservation programs, a county government program, and a private land trust focused on farmland. Baltimore County has preserved farmland through a county program bolstered by state funding as well as the donation of easements to a state agency, the Maryland Environmental Trust. Sonoma County has preserved land through its county government, mainly with funds raised from a local sales tax of 0.25 percent; there is also a private land trust. Montgomery County has created perhaps the most successful transfer of development rights program in the nation to preserve farmland. The county has preserved more than 40,000 acres in over 6,000 transfers. In addition, Montgomery County has raised funds to purchase development rights on about 30,000 acres, and has attracted some state preservation funds.

The purchase of development rights involves several steps, which a county or land trust manages:

- Application. The landowner applies to the county or land trust to sell development rights.
- Appraisal. The value of the development rights is determined by a professional appraiser hired by the county or land trust. The value is the difference between the fair market value of the property and value restricted to farming and open space.
- Offer. The county or land trust makes the landowner an offer to purchase the development rights, based on the appraised value. The county may offer less than the appraised value, but cannot offer more.
- Title search. When the landowner accepts the offer for the development rights, the county or land trust then orders a title search which shows the owner(s) of the property and any mortgage holders, who will need either to be paid off or to subordinate the mortgage to the deed of easement (so that if the holder forecloses on the mortgage, the deed of easement will not be removed).
- Signing and recording of deed of easement. The landowner receives payment for the development rights and the county or land trust records the deed of easement at the county courthouse.
- Monitoring. The county or land trust has the obligation to monitor the farmland at least once a year for compliance with the terms of the deed of easement.

Funding Sources A key issue is the availability of funding to purchase development rights. Most often, counties have sold bonds to raise the money. The bonds are paid off over time from increases in local property taxes. Some counties have simply appropriated funds on a pay-as-you-go basis, which again means increases in the local property tax. A few counties have used real estate transfer taxes and others have used the local sales tax. State programs have provided major funding for counties in Maryland and Pennsylvania. And since 2002, the federal government through its Farm and Ranchland Protection Program has made hundreds of millions of dollars in matching grants to counties. Private land trusts have worked with several public county programs, thus adding another source of funding. Land trusts have raised funds from private foundations, companies, members, and major donors.

Program Costs The goal in purchasing development rights is to strike a balance between a price that the landowner will accept and a cost the county or land trust can afford. The average price for development rights has been under $10,000 an acre in all twelve counties, and less than $5,000 an acre in most counties. Berks and Lancaster Counties, for instance, use a per acre cap—$2,500 an acre in Berks and $4,000 an acre in Lancaster—as a way to hold down program costs and to stretch their dollars to preserve more farmland.

Lancaster and Sonoma Counties have spent more than $100 million to preserve farmland; Baltimore and Marin have spent more than $50 million; and

Table 3.4 Growth boundaries in four metro counties

County	Number of Growth Boundaries	Dates Implemented
Baltimore, MD	1	1967
Lancaster, PA	26	1993–2000
Marin, CA	1	1997
Sonoma, CA	8	1996–2000

Source: Daniels 2010.

Table 3.5 Agricultural zoning in five metro counties

County	Agricultural Zoning Standards	Area Zoned in Agriculture (in acres)	% of County Zoned for Agriculture
Baltimore, MD	1 house per 50 acres; Large minimum lot size	100,000	26.1
Lancaster, PA	1 house per 20, 25, or 50 acres; Fixed area ratio	350,000	57.7
Marin, CA	1 house per 60 acres; Large minimum lot size	200,000	60.0
Montgomery, MD	1 house per 25 acres; Fixed area ratio	93,000	29.3
Sonoma, CA	Varies from 1 house per 10 acres to 1 house per 160 acres; Large minimum lot size	700,000	69.4

Sources: Bowers 2006, Daniels 2010, Daniels and Bowers 1997, Hart 1991, USDA 2009.

Montgomery County's transfer of development rights program has attracted more than $111 million from private developers (Bowers 2009a, Daniels 2010).

Acres Preserved The leading twelve counties in farmland preservation have preserved about one-quarter of all farmland preserved so far in the United States. Berks, Chester, Lancaster, and York Counties in Pennsylvania and Baltimore, Carroll, Frederick, and Harford Counties in Maryland form a contiguous region. This eight-county region has more than 500,000 acres of preserved farmland, has preserved nearly one-third of its farmland base, and produced more than $2.5 billion in farm output in 2007—which, if it were a state, would rank it 34th among all states (USDA 2009).

Strengths and Weaknesses The strengths of the county programs are:

1. The large amount of farmland preserved so far indicates a willingness on the part of many farmland owners to sell their development rights. This support from the farming community is essential for a successful farmland preservation program. The twelve leading counties have preserved just over one-fourth of their farmland base (see Table 3.2). Montgomery County is noteworthy for having preserved virtually all of its farmland. Six counties have preserved 32 percent or more of their farmland, with Baltimore and Harford Counties and Burlington County having preserved more than half of their farmland.
2. Reflecting widespread support from elected officials and the public-at-large, there has been continued funding over the long run from primarily public sources. Farmers who apply to sell their development rights know that the money will be available at some point in time. The funding strengthens the purchase of development rights as an alternative for farmers to selling their land for development.
3. Farmland preservation through acquisition of development rights can be used with other techniques to manage growth in metropolitan counties. For instance, Lancaster County and Sonoma County have targeted the preservation of farmland along urban growth boundaries to in effect make parts of these boundaries permanent (see Table 3.4). Lancaster has also been able to create nine contiguous blocks of more than 1,000 acres of preserved farmland.
4. Marin County was the first of the twelve counties to adopt strict agricultural zoning (see Table 3.5). In 1972, Marin's County Commissioners approved agricultural zoning based on a minimum lot size of one house per 60 acres (Hart 1991). That standard has held ever since. Baltimore County has the strictest agricultural zoning in the Northeast at one house per 50 acres (Daniels and Bowers 1997: 145). This standard is also found in five townships within Lancaster County, although most townships allow only one house per 25 acres. Sonoma County has a very diverse agriculture, from intensive grape production for its famous wines to cattle grazing on large acres, and thus has a wide range of densities in its agricultural zones.
5. Program costs are reasonable. As stated earlier, the price for development rights averages under $10,000 per acre in all twelve counties and under $5,000 in most of them. The reasonable program costs have been important for continued public funding.
6. Farm preservation programs can promote local agriculture and lead to increased farm output. In turn, a strong and expanding agricultural industry bodes well for keeping farmland in production and minimizing its loss to sprawling development. Of the twelve counties, Berks, Chester, Frederick, Lancaster, Sonoma, and York each had agricultural output exceeding $100 million in 2007 (see Table 3.2). This was an increase of $80 million, on

average, since 2002. With farm output of $1 billion in 2007 (a $200 million increase over five years), Lancaster stands out in particular and is, in fact, one of the top 20 agricultural counties in the U.S. Among five of the remaining counties (Baltimore, Burlington, Carroll, Harford, and Marin), output was smaller and rose more modestly over the 2002–2007 time period, and Montgomery County saw a decrease in farm output over the same time.

7. Farmland preservation bolsters rather than detracts from the local economy. Of the five counties that adopted agricultural zoning along with preservation programs, Baltimore, Lancaster, and Montgomery have achieved the highest credit rating (AAA), Marin is close behind at AA+, and Sonoma has a solid AA rating. In short, the fiscal condition of these counties is strong. This suggests that growth management and farmland preservation bolster rather than detract from a county's fiscal health.

Despite several positive achievements, these county programs have some shortcomings in managing growth:

1. Eight of the counties do not have urban growth boundaries, and seven do not have widespread effective agricultural zoning. For instance, Berks and Chester have effective agricultural zoning only on certain parts of their agricultural land base. The lack of these techniques makes these counties vulnerable to urban and suburban expansion through the extension of sewer and water lines into the countryside and rural residential development in agricultural areas. Both of these types of development undermine farming. Furthermore, counties without agricultural zoning and growth boundaries may be relying too heavily (and unrealistically) on farmland preservation to manage growth.
2. The data on population growth are mixed (see again Table 3.3). Several of the twelve counties had rates of population growth that exceeded the national average, and a minority of the counties grew at a rate below the national average. Farmland preservation is not a no-growth technique, but population increases pose the greatest challenge to growth management programs. Again, those counties with agricultural zoning generally had lower rates of population growth.
3. Housing affordability is a common problem with growth management programs (Daniels 2010). The median household income and median single family house prices were used to create an affordability index for five of the twelve leading counties. The lower the index number, the more affordable a single family home is in relation to household income. Between 1990 and 2005, housing affordability declined in all five counties as well as the entire United States. In short, household incomes did not keep pace with the rise in the prices for single family homes. Only in Lancaster and Baltimore Counties were single family homes more affordable than for the United States as a whole in 2005. In Montgomery County housing was significantly less

affordable than for the nation as a whole in 2005 and in Marin and Sonoma counties it was more than twice as unaffordable as housing nationwide.

4. As indicated earlier, land preservation programs can be expensive to implement. Lancaster and Sonoma have spent more than $100 million, Baltimore and Marin have spent more than $50 million, and Montgomery County's purchase of development rights program has required more than $111 million from private developers (Bowers 2009c).

Summary

Farmland preservation has significant potential to be an effective growth management technique at the state and county levels. States should consider the example of Maryland and make farmland preservation part of a state growth management program, thereby linking land development and agricultural protection goals and objectives. Moreover, farmland preservation can be very expensive and should target commercial farming operations in areas zoned for agriculture, not rural residential development. The Maryland and Pennsylvania programs demonstrate that long term funding is needed to preserve large amounts of farmland. Pennsylvania's farmland preservation program has provided funds to the counties which they have matched with major appropriations. This combination of state and local funding increases the overall financial resources for farmland preservation and enhances the credibility of the program with the farming community and the public-at-large.

The county farmland preservation programs that combine purchase of development rights with agricultural zoning and urban growth boundaries appear to be the most successful in managing growth, both in terms of moderating population growth and promoting agriculture as an industry. Counties should try to preserve farmland in large contiguous blocks, as Lancaster has been able to do, and even along growth boundaries to discourage the spread of development into the countryside (see Figure 3.1). This will channel development away from farming areas and promote more compact development. Farmland preservation appears to be correlated with the solid fiscal health of county governments, suggesting that farmland preservation does not overly burden the taxpayers. Indeed, in a number of counties, private land trusts play a significant role in preserving farmland. Unfortunately, though, farmland preservation does not seem to address affordable housing shortages and, in fact, could exacerbate this problem.

Suggestions for State, Regional, and Local Farmland Preservation Programs

This section emphasizes the lessons learned from using farmland preservation as a way to manage growth. These lessons are transferable, not just within the United States but across countries as well.

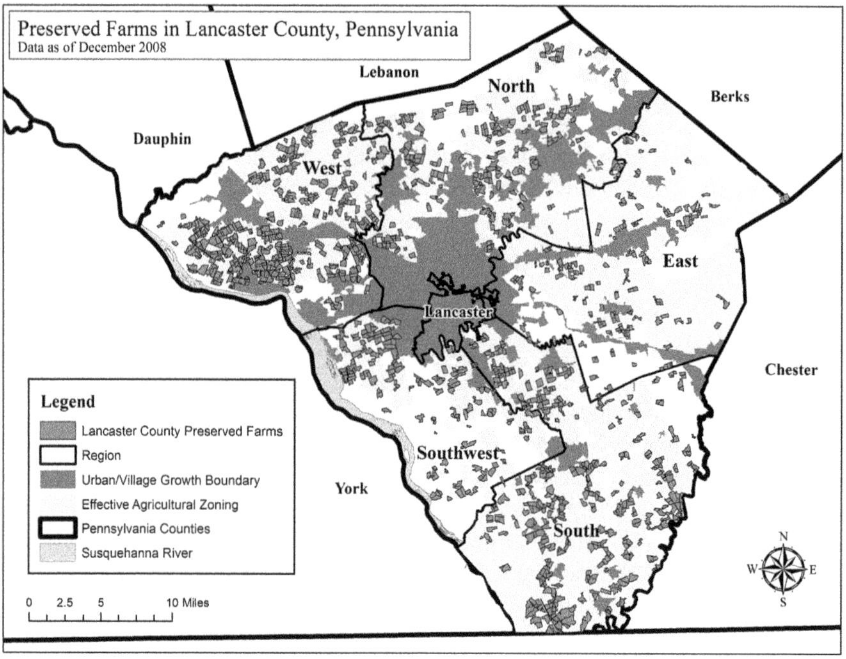

Figure 3.1 Preserved farmland, agricultural zoning, and urban growth areas in Lancaster County, PA, 2008

Perhaps the most valuable lesson from the twelve counties and the state of Pennsylvania is that farmland preservation works best as a public-private partnership. The public programs have the advantage of greater funding, along with land use planning and regulatory powers. Private land trusts, however, are usually able to move more quickly in preserving land and often are more trusted by private landowners. Private land trusts have been able to glean significant dollars from private foundations, companies, trust members, and major donors. A combination of public and private efforts can boost overall funding for farmland preservation and enable the preservation of land that neither a public agency nor a private interest could accomplish alone. Furthermore, the general public likes to see the public and private sectors working together.

Support for farmland preservation must come from the local level and from the farm community. Farmers need to see a future in farming and the local governments and land trusts have to be willing to spend money to preserve farmland. State and federal funding alone will not be sufficient. Rather, state and federal funding can be a catalyst to encourage counties and land trusts to preserve farmland.

The twelve counties profiled above have achieved an impressive record of land preservation. But farmland preservation is only one technique and cannot address all of their growth management challenges. Among the twelve counties, rates of population growth are mixed, but those counties with agricultural zoning have generally grown more slowly than the national average. On the other hand, housing affordability remains a problem in most of the counties. Still, these twelve counties are some of the most desirable places to live in the United States.

The four counties that use growth boundaries, agricultural zoning, and land preservation in a coordinated growth management package appear to have had better results than the counties without growth boundaries or widespread agricultural zoning. In other words, more than just farmland preservation is needed to produce compact development; but farmland preservation can work well with growth boundaries and agricultural zoning to promote compact development. Growth boundaries can limit the extension of sewer and water lines that would support intense urban and suburban development in the countryside, and agricultural zoning can minimize rural residential development that tends to drive up land prices, cause conflicts with farming neighbors, and ultimately squeeze out farm operations.

But ultimately, local governments, states, and the United States as a whole must effectively manage population growth. If the United States adds another 130 million residents by 2050 as projected, it will be difficult to avoid the conversion of millions of acres of high quality farmland and to maintain compact communities, especially in metropolitan areas.

References

American Farmland Trust. 1997. *Saving American Farmland: What Works.* Northampton, MA: American Farmland Trust.

Avin, U. and Bayer, M. 2003. Rightsizing urban growth boundaries. *Planning*, 69(2), 22–6.

Bowers, D. 2000. *Farmland Preservation Report*, 11(2), 1.

Bowers. D. 2005. *Farmland Preservation Report*, 15(3), 4.

Bowers, D. 2006. *Farmland Preservation Report*, 16(10), 3.

Bowers, D. 2009a. New Wisconsin program first since 2005. *Farmland Preservation Report*, 19(9), 1–2.

Bowers, D. 2009b. Nation's top 12 locally operated farmland preservation programs, 2009. *Farmland Preservation Report*, 19(10), 3.

Bowers, D. 2009c. Personal communication, 18 January, 2009.

Brewer, R. 2003. *Conservancy: The Land Trust Movement in America*. Lebanon, NH: University Press of New England.

Brookings Institution. 2003. *Back to Prosperity: A Competitive Agenda for Renewing Pennsylvania*. Washington, D.C.: Author.

Burchell, R., Downs, A., Mukherji, S., and McCann, B. 2005. *Sprawl Costs: Economic Impacts of Unchecked Development*. Washington, D.C.: Island Press.

Daniels, T. 1991. The purchase of development rights: Preserving agricultural land and open space. *Journal of the American Planning Association*, 57(4), 421–31.

Daniels, T. 2001. Smart growth: A new American approach to regional planning. *Planning Practice and Research*, 3&4: 271–81.

Daniels, T. 2009. Saving farms and farmland: Ag land preservation has reached maturity. *Planning*, 75(8), 38–43.

Daniels, T. 2010. The use of green belts to control sprawl in the United States. *Planning Practice and Research* (in press).

Daniels, T. and Bowers, D. 1997. *Holding Our Ground: Protecting America's Farms and Farmland*. Washington, D.C.: Island Press.

Daniels, T. and Daniels, K. 2003. *The Environmental Planning Handbook for Sustainable Communities and Regions*. Chicago: American Planning Association.

Farmland Information Center. 2009. *Fact Sheet: Status of State Pace Programs*. Northampton, MA: American Farmland Trust.

Hart, J. 1991. *Farming on the Edge: Saving Family Farms in Marin County, California*. Berkeley, CA: University of California Press.

Ingram, G.K., Carbonell, A., Hong, Y., and Flint, A. 2009. *Smart Growth Policies: An Evaluation of Programs and Outcomes*. Cambridge, MA: Lincoln Institute of Land Policy.

Pennsylvania Department of Agriculture. 2009a. *2008 Farmland Preservation Annual Report*. Harrisburg, PA: Author.

Pennsylvania Department of Agriculture. 2009b. *Preservation Board Safeguards Additional Farmland for Future Agriculture Production*. Press Release, 11 June 2009. Harrisburg, PA: Author.

Rusk, D. 1999. *Inside Game/Outside Game: Winning Strategies for Saving Urban America*. Washington, D.C.: The Brookings Institution.

U.S. Bureau of the Census. 1994. *Census of Agriculture, 1992*. Washington, D.C.: Author.

U.S. Bureau of the Census. 2006a. *Population Estimates*. Washington, D.C: U.S. Bureau of the Census.

U.S. Bureau of the Census. 2006b. *Nation's Population to Reach 300 Million on October 17*. Press Release, 12 October 2006. Washington, D.C: U.S. Bureau of the Census.

U.S. Bureau of the Census. 2008. An Older and More Diverse Nation by Midcentury. Press Release, 14 August. Washington, D.C.: Author.

U.S. Bureau of the Census. 2009. *Statistical Abstract of the United States, 2009*. Washington, D.C.: Author.

U.S. Department of Agriculture. 2009. *Census of Agriculture, 2007*. Washington, D.C.: Author.

Wallis, A. 2002. *The New Regionalism*. Available at: http://www.munimall.net/eos/2002/wallis_regionalism.nclk [accessed: 9 January 2007].

Chapter 4
Florida Forever: Conserving Land and Guiding Growth in the Sunshine State

Andrew H. McLeod

In recent years Florida has earned a reputation for the effective use of land acquisition as a tool to protect its unique and beautiful places. Since 1990, Florida has protected parkland, rare forests, wandering rivers, cold springs, trails, historic sites, and spectacular beaches totaling the equivalent of 3,797 square miles. This conservation legacy is the result of Florida Forever, a $300 million annual State investment in an array of preservation projects. A complex, multi-faceted program, Florida Forever and its predecessor, Preservation 2000, have succeeded by constantly responding and adapting to environmental needs in a large, dynamic, and highly diverse state.

Yet, State-backed land protection in Florida faces an uncertain future. In the face of unprecedented economic and fiscal adversities, the State in 2009 made no annual appropriation to Florida Forever. In 2010, with still greater political pressures resulting from a weak economy and another large budget deficit, Florida Forever received only 5 percent of its historical annual funding. These stunning funding reversals came on the heels of a unanimous, ten-year reauthorization of the program by the very same Legislature in 2008.

This chapter will explore the features, history, and achievements of Florida Forever and of Preservation 2000 before it. It will also explore the program's role in influencing development and land use in the Sunshine State. Finally, this narrative will describe the substantial challenges ahead for Florida Forever in a heterogeneous, ever-changing southern state of 18 million people.

Program Hallmarks

Several elements have been fundamental to the long success of Florida Forever and of Preservation 2000 before it. These include:

- Strong, bipartisan backing. Florida's booming post-war growth created a broad consensus in support of land protection as a means to prevent the despoliation of the state's magnificent natural resources. The majority of Floridians and leaders from both major political parties agreed that permanent land protection, funded aggressively by the State, was the best way to temper the worst effects of rampant growth.

- Diversity of conservation purposes. Originally intended to protect primarily ecologically important areas, Florida Forever has responded to the needs of a changing Florida, its scope has broadened, and it has become a large umbrella program for conservation activities in rural, suburban, and urban Florida.
- Willing sellers and buyers. Only landowners who wish to sell their property, or a protective interest on their land, participate in Florida Forever transactions. Projects funded by Florida Forever are not imposed or required by any government or regulatory agency.
- Reliable, appropriate financing. The documentary stamp tax possesses a direct, visible connection between land conversion and publicly funded, mitigative land conservation. Steadily increasing for most of Florida Forever's history, the documentary stamp tax only failed the program when the state's economy, built on growth and tourism, collapsed beginning in 2006–07.
- Borrowing to protect land now. Florida Forever uses the documentary stamp tax revenue to pay off long-term bonds, spreading the cost of today's conservation projects into the future. The money raised through the sale of revenue bonds make possible the protection of irreplaceable natural gems before they are destroyed or developed. This bargain has long made sense to far-sighted Floridians.

Florida's Land Protection Tradition

A Legacy of Belated Conservation

The early history of Florida was dominated by the proposed commercial use of the state's land base. Vast peninsular Florida was an overwhelmingly rural, remote, and sparsely populated state well into the 20th century. Through most of this time the prevailing instinct toward Florida's endless, saturated acreage was to drain it, fill it, and sell it. In 1850, the State owned as much as 21 million of the approximately 30 million acres within its borders. Thirty years later, Governor William Bloxham sold four million acres of the Everglades to a private buyer who then drained 50,000 acres of it. In 1905, Governor Napoleon Bonaparte Broward championed the draining of the Everglades anew, an effort that proceeded off and on for the next half century. All told, Florida lost as much as half of its 20 million acres of wetlands during the 20th century. (Davis and Arsenault 2005, p. 125)

Following 1950, a period that historian Gary Mormino calls "Florida's Big Bang," the state's population grew from 2.7 million people (the least populated in the South) to approximately 16 million in 2000. "Wordsmiths coined new terms to understand the paradigm and the firestorm of change," Mormino (2005, p. 6) wrote, "jet age, space age, climate control, growth management, retirement community, theme

Table 4.1 Milestones in state land conservation

Year	Milestone
1964	$20 million bond for outdoor recreation land
1972	$40 million bond for outdoor recreation land; Environmental Land and Water Management Act; State Comprehensive Planning Act
1979	Conservation and Recreation Lands (CARL) program
1981	Save Our Coast and Save Our Rivers programs
1985	Growth Management Act
1990	Preservation 2000 program
2000	Florida Forever program established
2008	Florida Forever reauthorized for 10 years
2009	No Florida Forever appropriation for FY 2009–10

park, the I-4 corridor, impact fee, edge city, boomburb, time-share condominiums, suburban sprawl, shopping mall, Snowbird, white flight, Sunbelt, Interstate, and Internet."

While serving as an economic engine of Florida, the clearing of land for growth and development also provided the impetus for new environmental sensitivity. (For background on Florida development and struggles over the environment, see Davis, J.E. and Arsenault, R. and Pittman, C. and Waite, M.) Republican Governor Claude Kirk (1967–71), and most notably Democratic Governors Reubin Askew (1971–79) and Bob Graham (1979–87), undertook a series of important environmental protection measures to get a handle on voracious development. Among these were the creation of water management districts to protect and direct water supply, and a landmark Florida growth management law (see Table 4.1). Governor Askew laid down the environmental gauntlet in a 1973 speech:

> As the nation's fastest growing large-population state, Florida is forever facing choices between trees or towers, creeks or canals, marshes or marinas, water or waste, beaches or barriers, sunshine or smog, men or machines, and green lands or ghettos. How we make those decisions in the years ahead could very easily determine for us the most important decision of all—that of life or death for our state as we know her. (Jon Nordheimer, "Florida seeks to curb runaway growth," *The New York Times*, November 19, 1973, p. 17)

The State undertook a series of land acquisition initiatives to set aside parks and recreation areas. Funding came variously from sales taxes on items such as bathing suits and outdoor equipment, the proceeds of the existing documentary stamp tax on real estate, and excise taxes on the extractions of phosphate, oil, gas, and other solid minerals. Purchases were made only from owners of property willing to sell to the State. Eminent domain or regulatory requirements were not elements

Table 4.2 Preservation 2000 funding allocations, 1990–99

Purpose/Agency	Percent Allocation
Conservation and recreation land (DEP)	50.0%
Water resource protection (WMDs)	30.0%
Local comprehensive plan implementation	10.0%
Wildlife management areas additions (FFWCC)	2.9%
State forest additions (DOF)	2.9%
State park additions (DEP)	2.9%
Greenways and trails (DEP)	1.3%

of Florida Forever acquisitions. From 1979 to 1990, the State's first permanent land-buying initiative, the Conservation and Recreation Lands (CARL) program, was responsible for the protection of 181,000 acres of conservation and recreation lands.

Preservation 2000

In 1989, Republican Governor Bob Martinez (1987–91) appointed a Commission on the Future of Florida's Environment to examine threats to Florida's environmental health and suggest potential solutions. The chairman was noted conservationist Nathaniel P. Reed, a prominent Republican and a founder of the growth-management watchdog group, 1000 Friends of Florida. The Commission determined that, despite the success of the CARL program and earlier efforts, the pace of land acquisition was not keeping up with rapid development. Without additional safeguards, the Commission warned, the state would lose three million acres of wetlands and forests by 2020.

Determining that Florida had an unmet conservation land acquisition need of more than $5 billion and that land prices were escalating faster than the rate of inflation, the Commission recommended that Florida sell long-term bonds to fund land purchases. The Commission concluded that "the single most effective way to accomplish large scale gains in our environmental well-being is to substantially increase the level of funding for the state's land acquisition programs" and that there was "strong, statewide public support for an expanded land acquisition program" (Report of the Commission on the Future of Florida's Environment, Commission on the Future of Florida's Environment, 1989, p. 7).

Governor Martinez proposed a $3 billion land preservation fund, based upon $300 million in yearly bonded funds over ten years. With bipartisan backing and the active support of Florida nonprofit groups led by The Nature Conservancy, Audubon of Florida, and the Trust for Public Land, Preservation 2000 was enacted by the Legislature in 1990. The successor to the CARL program and predecessor to Florida Forever, Preservation 2000 elevated the conservation of land in Florida to new heights (see Table 4.2).

The Act provided for a 17-cent increase in the documentary stamp tax, a successful compromise with the state's powerful real estate and housing interests. The new program also permitted $3 billion in general obligation bonding for land protection over ten years, but did not mandate that $300 million be spent each year. While the increased documentary stamp tax was not legally dedicated to land buying, the explicit expectation was that Preservation 2000 debt service would be covered by the increased revenue. This expectation was fully met with the exponential growth that occurred over the next fifteen years, as documentary stamp collections saw an increase of more than 800 percent from 1990 to 2004.

Consistent with the recommendation of Governor Martinez's Commission, supporters of Preservation 2000 advocated that the full $300 million be expended each year, and from the first year of the program this was done. This tradition of $300 million annually continued throughout the length of Preservation 2000 and Florida Forever until 2009.

Between 1990 and 2000, Preservation 2000 protected an impressive 1.8 million acres of wide-ranging conservation land throughout Florida. The individual projects included:

- 10,000 acres on the ecologically important Lake Wales Ridge in Highlands, Lake, Osceola, and Polk Counties;
- 10,000 acres of wildlife-rich lands around Charlotte Harbor and the Myakka River in southwest Florida;
- the 9,000-acre Belle Meade property of old-growth flatwoods in Collier County;
- more than 1,000 acres of first magnitude springs, some of Florida's most unique resources, in Hernando, Jackson, Leon, and Washington Counties
- 1,000 acres of the Archie Carr State Reserve for loggerhead turtle nesting on the coasts of Brevard and Indian River Counties; and
- Walton County's Topsail Hill, a spectacular stretch of pristine beachfront that includes the highest dunes in Florida.

Preservation 2000 supporters sought to build on the overwhelming backing for the program by securing a permanent connection to the stamp tax. Reorganized as the "Green Space for People Coalition," the proponents pushed legislation in 1994 and successive legislative sessions, but each time unsuccessfully. Ultimately they became convinced that the issue must be taken back to the people on the 1998 election ballot.

Amendment 5 and the Florida Forever Act

The state's Constitution Revision Commission, which meets once every 20 years to review and perhaps revise the state's charter, was the focus of the new initiative. The Nature Conservancy, Trust for Public Land, Audubon of Florida, Sierra Club, Defenders of Wildlife, and the Rails-to-Trails Conservancy succeeded in

Table 4.3 Florida Forever funding allocations, 2001–08

Purpose/Agency	Percent Allocation
Conservation and recreation land (DEP)	35.0%
Water Resources (WMDs)	35.0%
Florida Communities Trust (DCA)	22.0%
Grants for local recreational facilities (DEP)	2.0%
Wildlife management areas additions (FFWCC)	1.5%
State forest additions (DOF)	1.5%
State park additions (DEP)	1.5%
Greenways and trails (DEP)	1.5%

convincing the Commission to forward a Constitutional amendment to the voters for possible adoption.

The measure, Amendment 5, proposed making permanent the State's authority to borrow for environmental land conservation (under Preservation 2000, this authority had been permitted for only for ten years). Amendment 5 combined the conservation bonding provision with a package of other environmental issues, including creation of a new wildlife agency. Amendment 5 also expanded the policy to protect natural resources by requiring the State to make "adequate provision" for their conservation and protection. Additionally, it made more difficult the State's selling off of conservation land, requiring a two-thirds vote of the agency holding title to the land and a finding that the land was no longer required for conservation purposes.

Republican Jeb Bush, then a gubernatorial candidate, endorsed Amendment 5. In the November 1998 election, an overwhelming 72 percent of Florida's voters approved Amendment 5, and 55 percent made Bush Florida's new Governor. Building on the momentum, Amendment 5 supporters and Governor Bush (1999–2007) pushed a measure to utilize the new bonding authority in the 1999 legislative session, Bush's first as Governor. The Florida Forever Act—authorizing the annual sale of up to $300 million in bonds for a second ten years—passed easily, again with the support of a coalition of Republicans and Democrats.

The Florida Forever Act altered Preservation 2000's conservation priorities and funding allocations (see Table 4.3). The new law gave greater emphasis to projects that protected water resources and water supply. The Act directed state land-buyers to focus on acquiring urban and community parks, with almost a quarter of annual funding going to the Florida Communities Trust, a program dedicated to helping local governments and eligible nonprofit organizations acquire and/or develop parks, open space, and greenways. The Act also put a priority on buying properties that could be protected by conservation easements.

Also unlike Preservation 2000, Florida Forever allowed bond funds to be used for facilities development, land management, species inventories, ecological restoration, and invasive/exotic plant removal. Finally, the Florida Forever Act improved upon Preservation 2000 by establishing new goals and performance measures for State land-buying decisions.

An Evolving Conservation Tool for a Dynamic State

The salutary impacts of Florida Forever, evident in every corner of the state and in each of its 67 counties, are attributable to the program's ability to adapt to the changing conservation needs of a complex, heterogeneous, and growing state. Florida Forever is, in fact, a bundle of varied land conservation programs gathered under one name. The individual component programs both complement, and, at times, rival each other. It is composed of three large constituent programs and seven smaller ones, in a total of eight state agencies. Taken together, the program's parts serve to preserve priority ecological land, protect watersheds and drinking water supplies, create community parks, combat urban sprawl, preserve working farm and forest land, and increase sites for hunting and fishing. To achieve this, the program employs a strategic two-pronged funding scheme, plays a key role in guiding growth prudently, and complements local government land conservation efforts.

Department of Environmental Protection's "Florida Forever" Program

The land acquisition activities undertaken by the Florida Department of Environmental Protection (DEP) are, and always have been, the most visible component of Florida Forever today. Indeed, the acquisitions undertaken by the Department are still widely referred to as "Forever Forever" in and of itself or as the "CARL program" dating from 1979.

Under Preservation 2000, the DEP received more than half of all program funding. Under Florida Forever that amount was decreased to about 40 percent. This is composed of the 35 percent allocated to the Department overall, 1.5 percent for greenways and trails inholdings and additions, 1.5 percent for state park inholdings and additions, and 2 percent for park development grants. Each individual program sets its own priorities and forwards them to the Department for approval.

From the early days of Florida statehood, final authority for buying, selling, and managing most State land has resided with the Board of Trustees of the Internal Improvement Trust Fund, an anachronistic-sounding body that is nonetheless very relevant in the 21st century. Known simply as the Board of Trustees, it is composed of the Governor and the three, statewide-elected members of the Cabinet: the Attorney General, the Chief Financial Officer, and the Commissioner of Agriculture and Consumer Services. These four officials collectively possess the authority to expend the DEP's 40 percent share of Florida Forever funds. As frequently as every two weeks, the Board meets in public, debates project priorities and details, and casts votes onprojects. Involving the State's top state officials regularly and visibly in this manner has served Preservation 2000 and Florida Forever well, increasing the programs' accountability and popularity.

Since the days of the CARL program, the DEP has utilized a ranking system to prioritize projects for acquisition. Today the DEP uses ten sets of natural resource data and criteria provided by several agencies and partnering organizations and coordinated by the Florida Natural Areas Inventory (FNAI) to evaluate the natural resources value of proposed and current Florida Forever projects. These non-exclusive, overlapping categories are:

- Rare species habitat.
- Natural communities (strategic habitats).
- Watersheds (surface water).
- Wetlands, sustainable forestry.
- Landscapes and ecological greenways.
- Trails, aquifer recharge.
- Archaeological and historic resources.

All candidate and existing projects are judged in each of these categories as very high, high, medium, medium-low, or low. The DEP also classifies projects as fee purchase, less-than-fee purchase, and near completion or not. Furthermore, the DEP employs two rankings—the A and B Lists—to prioritize projects based on their merits. Projects on the A List are those considered most important for acquisition by the DEP. B List projects are a lower priority and may be pursued only if the State pays no more than 50 percent of appraised value. In 2008, the DEP created administratively "Super 21" category of the A List projects deserving of greatest priority.

When reauthorizing Florida Forever in 2008, the Legislature went further, creating new ranking criteria. When this provision is fully implemented in 2010, projects will be grouped in five revised categories:

- Climate change.
- Critical natural quality.
- Less-than-fee.
- Partnerships.
- 85 percent complete.

Projects may involve many, individual acquisitions from numerous landowners. All projects involve landowners known to be willing sellers. Some projects remain on the Florida Forever list for years.

The Acquisition and Restoration Council, a technical advisory group composed of agency heads and gubernatorial appointees and housed at the DEP, determines how projects are listed. Semi-annual revisions of the Priority List are forwarded to the Governor and Cabinet, which approve or reject the entire list or remove or re-classify projects.

After placement on the Florida Forever list, a project is pursued for acquisition contingent on a variety of factors, including: continued willingness of the seller, availability of funding, cost, adjacent land uses and conservation opportunities, management needs, parcel configuration, and the threat of conversion. Once a project is successfully negotiated with a landowner and terms with the State agreed to, the transaction must achieve formal approval from the Governor and Cabinet. Most projects are approved, but require more explanation or renegotiation before approved in granted by the Governor and Cabinet. Closings of these purchases is completed following these approvals and based on all terms dictated by the Governor and Cabinet.

Water Management Districts

Created in 1973, the State's five regional water management districts exist to protect the quality and quantity of drinking water for Floridians. They do so with a wide array of powers, including water withdrawal permitting and enforcement; wetlands permitting, monitoring, and restoration; public education and outreach; and land acquisition and management.

The districts—South Florida, Southwest Florida, St. Johns River, Suwannee River, and Northwest Florida—are independent agencies of the State governed by gubernatorially appointed boards of directors. They have received varying levels of funding over the years. Originally 30 percent under Preservation 2000, the districts' share was increased to 35 percent under the Florida Forever Act and then retuned to 30 percent when the program was reauthorized in 2008. The districts also have the unusual authority to raise additional revenue themselves through ad valorem taxes in their jurisdictions. Both sources of funding are used to purchase land needed by the districts to fulfill their water supply and protection duties.

All properties purchased or conservation easements acquired by a water management district are owned by that district, rather than the DEP. More than 30 percent of all district transactions are conservation easement purchases. In these cases, the fee title is owned by a private entity and only the easement is owned by the district, thus lowering for the public the acquisition and long-term management costs.

Florida Communities Trust

The Florida Communities Trust (FCT) is unlike other Florida Forever component programs. Housed in the Department of Community Affairs (DCA), the FCT exists to facilitate purchases that support the State's Growth Management Act and to advance, through local comprehensive plans, the

> conservation, use, and protection of natural resources in the area, including air, water, water recharge areas, wetlands, waterwells, estuarine marshes, soils, beaches, shores, floodplains, rivers, bays, lakes, harbors, forest, fisheries

> and wildlife, marine habitat, minerals and other natural and environmental resources, including factors that affect energy conservation. (Florida Statutes, 163.3177(5)(b))

The FCT awards competitive grants to local governments and nonprofit groups to make land purchases in accord with their local comprehensive plans. The grant recipients purchase the properties, take full title, and bear all long-term management costs. Grant applications are currently ranked using a numerical scoring system that evaluates the quality of the natural resources on the project sites and the extent that the projects satisfy requirements of the comprehensive plans. A board made up of the secretaries of the DCA and DEP, as well as four members appointed by the Governor, makes the final grant decisions.

Established in 1989, the FCT was allocated 10 percent of the funding available through Preservation 2000. The parks and recreational projects financed with this money created substantial popular support for the program. Municipalities also strongly supported this unique funding partnership with the State. As a result, the portion of funding to the FCT was boosted to 22 percent under the Florida Forever Act (while the CARL program's share was reduced by a similar amount). This shift reflected the political strength of the urban and suburban regions of the state and the increasingly diverse range of conservation needs receiving widespread support.

FCT grants have been used to acquire a wide range of public lands for varied public uses. For example, the FCT has enabled local grant recipients to protect

- The Sun 'n' Lakes Preserve in Highlands County, an additional portion of a 13-mile greenway in western Highlands County adjacent to Hardee County;
- The Myakkahatchee Creek Environmental Park;
- A 1,600-acre expansion of an existing greenway by the City of North Port in Charlotte County;
- Blackwater Creek Preserve, 1,799 acres in urban Hillsborough County;
- Native American shell middens at the Paleo Hammock Preserve in southeast Florida's St. Lucie County; and
- Sugden Regional Park, 120 acres for public use in Collier County.

Guiding Growth with Land Protection

While the Florida Communities Trust exists by statute to advance the goals of growth management by aiding local comprehensive plan implementation, all of Florida Forever's constituent programs taken together have had a profound impact on the manner in which Florida grows. This reflects the substantial challenges of implementing effective growth management regulation in Florida—and the practical, site-specific impacts of Florida Forever.

Since the passage of the Growth Management Act in 1985, a complex, often-altered regime of statewide growth and land use control has evolved. A central objective has been to prevent development on land that is environmentally sensitive. Accordingly, the State and localities have adopted and enforced plans and regulations that limit land conversion and development to the capacity of the land necessary in terms of water supply, coastal hazard, and sensitivity of habitats.

Florida Forever complements this tenet of growth management in a major way. Preservation 2000 and Florida Forever have long identified and assessed the essential ecological regions and corridors in Florida and made the permanent protection of these areas a goal. Examples of the large landscapes prioritized under Florida Forever are:

- Major river systems, including the St. John's, Suwannee, St. Mary's, Apalachicola, Caloosahatchee, Kissimmee, Withlacoochee, and others;
- Greater Everglades ecosystem;
- Northwest Florida Greenway extending across half a dozen counties in the Panhandle;
- A large landscape anchored by the Osceola and the Ocala National Forests;
- The east-west corridor from Charlotte Harbor to Lake Okeechobee across the peninsular Florida; and
- The Wekiva-Ocala complex, Green Swamp, and five other natural resource jewels of the metropolitan Orlando region.
- Florida Forever acquisitions facilitate prudent growth management in other ways as well. Under the Water Management Act of 1972, the State allowed for the designation of "Areas of Critical State Concern" deserving special protection and management. The five areas subsequently selected of this designation—the Big Cypress region of southern Florida (later a national preserve), the Green Swamp of Lake and Polk Counties, the Florida Keys, Apalachicola Bay in Franklin County, and the City of Key West—all receive special priority in the utilization of Florida Forever funds. For instance, between 2003 and 2008, $98 million was spent to protect over 11,100 acres of the Florida Keys, a rare subtropical upland and coral reef environment under heavy pressure from development.

The pursuit of control growth by encouraging compact growth, urban infill and redevelopment, and adequate public infrastructure has proven exceedingly difficult to implement over the past 30 years of growth management laws and regulations. For instance, a requirement of "transportation concurrency" (mandating that new developments construct and dedicate public improvements, such as roads and utilities) has been ineffective, often unintentionally driving development into suburban and rural areas where existing roads exist.[1]

Furthermore, political support for growth management has been inconsistent over the years. When the economy is booming and development is occurring widely, as it was from the 1990s until about 2007, there is often strong sentiment to limit suburban sprawl and offset the adverse effects of development. Alternatively, as Florida's economy has deteriorated since 2007, efforts to roll back environmental laws and regulations have increased. For instance, capitalizing on a desire for jobs through development, the 2009 Legislature passed and Governor Crist signed legislation (SB 360) to weaken transportation concurrency. At the same time, popular dissatisfaction with uncoordinated, uncontrolled growth enabled a group of Floridians to gather enough signatures to place on the November 2010 statewide ballot a measure called Hometown Democracy. A proposed amendment to the State Constitution, this measure would slow growth by requiring that all local comprehensive plan changes be subject to a local referendum. Opponents call the measure draconian, overly burdensome, and harmful to economic activity.

Battles over growth management—and swings in popular opinion about growth controls are common. Surprising is the recent equivocation over Florida Forever. By denying its funding in 2009 and 2010, the State Legislature has undermined the most popular and effective means by which to conserve Florida's "green infrastructure" and guide growth.

Florida Forever's Two-Pronged Funding Design

Dating to the 1930s, the State documentary stamp tax is an excise tax on deeds, liens, mortgages, or other documents that transfer an interest in real estate. In essence, the documentary stamp is a tax on development and land transactions. Beginning in 1967, proceeds from the documentary stamp tax, which had previously gone to the state's general revenue fund, began to fund land purchases. This continued through Preservation 2000.

In 1999, the Florida Forever Act authorized that a portion of documentary stamp tax proceeds be used for Florida Forever debt service, as well as for infrastructure and affordable housing debt. When documentary stamp tax revenue is used to guarantee long-term Florida Forever revenue bonds, the state in effect advances money for its immediate need: the purchasing of properties that otherwise won't be available for protection in the future because they will have been developed. Future taxpayers share the cost for paying future debt service, because they will also benefit from the availability of parks and other protected lands. Under Florida Forever, this bonding expenditure has become traditional.

---

1 More effective has been the State's so-called "Rule 9J-5" to prevent sprawl by establishing minimum criteria for the content of local comprehensive plans and plan amendments.

The authority to bond documentary stamp tax revenue stream for Florida Forever does not obviate the need for the Legislature to appropriate program funding each year. Documentary stamp tax revenue ensures that future funding will be available to pay the Florida Forever bond debt, but an appropriation for the program is still necessary each and every year. Accordingly, the Florida Forever agencies lobby the Governor and the Legislature to request their share of funding, $300 million, be included in the State budget. This occurred, almost routinely, each year from 1990 through 2008.

However, as a political issue and matter of State budgeting, funding is never guaranteed. During the 1990s and early 2000s, revenues were flush and documentary stamp tax revenue boomed along with Florida's real estate cycle. The downside of conservation funding being tied to the stamp tax, however, has been painfully evident in recent years as real estate transactions and the amount of money available for Florida Forever diminished.

(Only twice, in 2004 and 2006, has the State paid for Florida Forever without bonding. Because Florida's economy was so strong and documentary stamp income so great, the state used available general revenue—"cash"—for Florida Forever, opting to not add to the its indebtedness.)

Local Government Acquisition Programs

The impact of Florida Forever is complemented and furthered by other public land protection efforts. In fact, local governments have an impressive track record in funding and negotiating land acquisitions. The DEP, water management districts, and Florida Communities Trust especially have leveraged Florida Forever dollars on many occasions by partnering with local governments.

Since 1972, 30 of the state's 67 counties, and eight cities, have established their own local land acquisition programs. Since 1996, voters have passed more than 50 local ballot measures for preservation, generating about $2 billion in government funds and buying 375,000 acres of conservation and recreation land.

Florida's Land Conservation "Mega-projects"

The State has undertaken several large land acquisitions that, because of their size or unusual nature, were conducted outside of Florida Forever. These include the Babcock Ranch and the U.S. Sugar/River of Grass projects.

Located in Charlotte and Lee Counties in southwest Florida, the 91,356-acre Babcock Ranch was one of the largest single ownerships in Florida. Habitat for the Florida panther and other species of importance, the ranch serves as a link to a complex of old-growth forests and wet flatwoods.

In 2002, Governor Bush and the Cabinet added the ranch to the Florida Forever List as a Group A project. After unsuccessful State attempts to buy the property, it was sold to a private concern in 2005, and the DEP immediately bought almost 74,000 acres (more than 80 percent of the original ranch) from the new owner.

The total cost was $350 million in phased payments over four years. Lee County contributed $40 million of the total. The State's $310 million share came in the form of a special (non-Florida Forever) appropriation.

The conservation outcome—achievement of a tract of continuous conservation land from Lake Okeechobee to the Gulf of Mexico—was strongly endorsed by the backers of Florida Forever and surrounding communities.

The U.S. Sugar transaction, dubbed the "River of Grass" by its supporters, seeks to advance Everglades protection by buttressing the Comprehensive Everglades Restoration Plan (CERP), a multi-year, multi-billion dollar project to restore the Everglades ecosystem and its historic flow ways. Begun in 2001, CERP would restore and protect Lake Okeechobee and the St. Lucie and Caloosahatchee Rivers and their estuaries, as well as provide for drinking water supplies and fisheries in South Florida (Comprehensive Everglades Restoration Plan, 2009).

In June 2008, Governor Crist proposed that the South Florida Water Management District (SFWMD) buy 187,000 acres of agricultural land located in Palm Beach and Hendry Counties and owned by U.S. Sugar, for $1.75 billion. In November 2008, in the face of a declining economy, Crist agreed to limit the purchase to 180,000 acres for $1.34 billion. In April 2009, the deal was pared back a second time to 72,500 acres for $536 million, with a ten-year option for the SFWMD to purchase the remaining 107,000 acres. The SFWMD approved the terms the following month.

One of the largest conservation land acquisitions in Florida history, the U.S. Sugar transaction was conceived and executed outside of the Florida Forever program. All of the funding comes from SFWMD ad valorem taxes used to launch certificates of participation. (The ad valorem revenue is collected by the SFWMD in all or parts of the 16 counties in its region, including Miami, Broward, and Palm Beach, over 30 years.)

Nonetheless, like Babcock Ranch, the U.S. Sugar transaction—dubbed by its proponents the "River of Grass" project—has major conservation benefits that complement Florida Forever.

Florida Forever Extended

In 2004–2005, Florida's growth economy continued to boom. Local governments issued more than 250,000 permits for new houses, condos, and apartments in 2004—more than in any other state and the equivalent of one out of every seven new housing units nationally. Population continued to surge, reaching a high of approximately 1,100 new residents per day by 2006. The nonprofit 1,000 Friends of Florida reported that, at this rate of growth, Florida's population would increase to more than 36 million by 2060, requiring an additional seven million acres be developed to house new residents, (Zwick and Carr, 2006, p. 7)

Florida Forever's supporters came to believe that the program was being outpaced by the rate of development. The program's $300 million annual investment in conservation was decreasing in real value and realizing less and less impact in a booming real estate market. The Florida Forever Priority List was estimated to contain $17 billion worth of high priority projects alone.

Loosely organized since the passage of Amendment 5 and the Florida Forever Act in 1998–99, the most visible backers of Florida Forever, including The Nature Conservancy, Audubon of Florida, Florida Wildlife Federation, Trust for Public Land, 1000 Friends of Florida, Defenders of Wildlife, and Florida Recreation and Park Association, reorganized anew as the Florida Forever Coalition. The Coalition, embodying a variety of environmental and recreational concerns, including ecology, species protection, hunting and fishing, local public parks, and growth control, demonstrated the breadth and appeal of the Florida Forever program. Soon dozens more organizations from across the state joined the Coalition.

In late 2007, the Coalition announced support for major legislation to extend and expand Florida Forever. It called for an increase in funding, starting at $600 million per year and increasing to $900 million annually in 2013, when all Preservation 2000 debt would be retired. This could be done, the Coalition argued, with a combination of bonding backed by the document stamp tax and General Revenue over a ten-year period.

As the 2008 General Session of the Florida Legislature began, the Coalition surpassed more than 100 member organizations. Thirty-eight of 67 counties passed formal resolutions in support of Florida Forever, accounting for more than 92 percent of Florida's residents.

Led by Governor Crist and Republican State Senate President Ken Pruitt, the Legislature took the historic step of reauthorizing Florida Forever for another ten years. Regrettably, the new program was to be undertaken at precisely the same level of annual spending—$300 million.

The reauthorized Florida Forever program created two new allocations, $10.5 million for the purchase of conservation easements on working farm and ranchland and $7.5 million to protect historic and economically viable commercial waterfronts, by taking money away primarily from the water management districts (see Table 4.4). The new law also increased funding for land management, created a new focus on climate change mitigation in Florida Forever projects, and revised and improved the project ranking process.

Economic Crisis and a Funding Reduction

No sooner had the Florida Legislature extended Florida Forever in 2008 than the economic downturn became a severe recession. The flow of new residents to Florida declined to near zero within two years. The weakening in the housing market led to a torrent of foreclosures. As housing prices fell, documentary stamp revenue plummeted and the outlook for Florida Forever funding became precarious.

Meeting in a special session to address a gaping $2 billion deficit, the Legislature in early 2009 cut two-thirds of Florida Forever's spending for the DEP and water management districts for the remaining five months of the fiscal year. This saving

Table 4.4 Florida Forever funding allocations, 2009

Purpose/Agency	Percent Allocation
Conservation and recreation lands (DEP)	35.0%
Water resource protection (WMDs)	30.0%
Florida Communities Trust	21.0%
Rural and family lands (DOF)	3.5%
Working waterfronts (FCT)	2.5%
Grants for local recreational facilities (DEP)	2.0%
Wildlife management areas additions (FFWCC)	1.5%
State forest additions (DOF)	1.5%
State park additions (DEP)	1.5%
Greenways and trails (DEP)	1.5%

of about $4 million in the budget would eliminate less than $100 million in Florida Forever long-term bonding. Governor Crist objected and vetoed the cut.

However, the fiscal crisis was only more severe by the time that the regular session of the Legislature convened two months later. Documentary stamp revenues were projected to be $1 billion annually, down from $4 billion just two years prior.

In order to strengthen the case for funding, The Nature Conservancy (2009) reported that billions of dollars in economic benefits derive from ecotourism, hunting and fishing, military base buffering, and other activities made possible by Florida Forever. Additionally, the Conservancy and the Trust for Public Land documented that, even in a very adverse economic climate, fully 81 percent of residents surveyed indicated a positive impression of Florida Forever, and 67 percent backed full funding.

Governor Crist proposed the current year funding necessary to support $300 million in bonding and worked with the Senate to make technical adjustments, ensuring that all previously authorized bonds would be covered by dwindling documentary stamp receipts. The Senate also proposed an appropriation for new bonding.

However, opposition to Florida Forever funding in the Florida House was too strong. The lower house refused to approve any new bonding for land protection. For the first time in two decades, when the Governor finally signed into law the State budget for FY 2009–2010, it contained no new bonding funding for the nation's premier conservation program.

In 2010, reeling from "zero funding" the prior year, Forever Florida's backers made a renewed, stronger push for funding. The Florida Forever Coalition undertook more grassroots advocacy and added important new voices to its ranks. The Florida Chamber of Commerce and some of Florida's largest ranching interests endorsed restored funding, as did the three announced candidates for Governor (two Republican, one Democrat) and former Governors Askew, Graham, Martinez, and Bush (two Democrats, two Republicans).

Acknowledging the continuing economic recession, lack of documentary stamp tax revenue, and growing state budget deficit, the Coalition Florida Forever lowered its legislative proposal to $15 million, which would generate $50 million in revenue bonds—one-sixth of the traditional annual funding.

With continued support from the Governor and the Senate, the budget ultimately passed contained a total appropriation of $15 million for Florida Forever—just 5 percent of the traditional $300 million. This financial "life support" kept Florida Forever operating, but a level that is sufficient for none of it component programs, let along the entirety of Florida Forever.

Continuing Challenges

With the elimination of its annual funding in 2009 and the allocation of only $15 million in 2010, Florida Forever finds itself at a crossroads.

Defining Success

The sufficiency of Florida's land conservation activities is, in many respects, in the eye of the observer. A program as multi-faceted, complex, and long-standing as Florida Forever can be assessed from many perspectives and by many measures.

What natural land, and in what composition, is necessary to protect the watersheds and aquifers, species and habitat? How much park and recreational land is adequate, in cities and suburbs, for tourism, in the wild? What acreage is necessarily owned by the public, and what instead, can be protected with easements and managed for conservation? How and when do regulations, growth management policies, or economic incentives achieve conservation outcomes that complement or obviate the need for conservation achieved through acquisition?

Florida Forever projects undertaken in the past decade have yielded substantial, multiple benefits (Table 4.5). Florida Forever has increased the land under protected public ownership or management for conservation from 25 percent of the state's total in 2001 to approximately 28 percent. The diversity of protected lands is great (Table 4.6). The State's more than 5.2 million conserved acres include 3.4 million acres of public hunting lands, 702,000 acres of State Parks, and 158,700 acres in working agriculture. Federal protected holdings total more than 4 million acres and include three National Forests, three National Parks, 2.3 million acres for hunting, and 530,000 acres of military bases that are managed for conservation.

Despite these achievements on the ground, the Florida Forever Priority List still contained more than 100 projects totaling more than two million acres. Compared to the 2.4 million acres already protected under Preservation 2000 and Florida Forever, this suggests there remains a large, vital mission for Florida Forever for years to come.

Table 4.5 Types of Florida Forever purchases, 2001–08

Type	Acres
Watershed Protection	645,350
Aquifer Recharge	625,700
Ecological Greenway	638,450
Rare Species Habitat	426,290
Species Habitat Priorities	259,330
Sustainable Forestry	202,130

Table 4.6 Florida managed conservation lands, 2008

Type	Acres
State	5,300,000
Federal	4,000,000
Local	409,000
Private	176,000

The current "Super 21" projects, the top priority subset of the Group A projects, total more than 870,000 acres. These foremost Florida Forever projects include:

- St. Joe Timberlands (extending over 11 Panhandle counties).
- Northeast Florida Timberland and Watershed Reserve (Nassau, Duval, and Clay counties).
- Wekiva-Ocala Greenway (Lake, Orange, Volusia, and Seminole).
- Corkscrew Regional Ecosystem Watershed (Collier and Lee).
- Lake Wales Ridge (Highlands, Polk, Lake, and Osceola).

Below the "Super 21" projects in priority are another 45 Group A projects comprising 530,000 acres and 43 Group B projects of a total of 642,000 acres. Two of these remaining projects encompass 200,000 acres or more individually, four cover 100,000 acres or more, and the remaining 82 range in size from 1 to 100,000 acres.

Assessments of continuing Florida Forever needs have also been made by private partners. In 2006, The Nature Conservancy determined that one-third of Florida's land resources should be in core conservation holdings and another third should remain in productive agriculture. Given the state's current 28 percent of protected land, the report declared 2.3 million additional acres—1.7 million acres of projects on the Florida Forever Priority List and 615,000 landscape acres not yet listed—are necessary to ensure the state's ecological integrity. Assuming the continued rapid real estate market at the time, the Conservancy had estimated this would require 10 to 12 years of active and consistent land acquisition efforts. The report concluded:

> Protecting over 2 million acres within the areas outlined on the map developed for this report by fee simple acquisition from willing sellers, at a cost, in today's market of nearly $5,000 per acre, would require more than $10 billion. The use of alternative protection techniques, such as an increased focus on less-than-fee approaches like conservation easements, together with other innovative techniques that work with landowners to achieve meaningful, long-term protection at a lower cost than outright acquisition, clearly should be pursued in order to reach the goal. ("Protecting Wild Florida: Preserving the Best and Last Wilderness of Florida, Forever," the Florida Chapter of The Nature Conservancy, 2006, p. 2)

In 2007, the Trust for Public Land partnered with the Florida Recreation and Park Association, Florida League of Cities, and Florida Association of Counties to consider other conservation purposes of the Florida Forever program. According to their report, county and city governments have determined that a total of 120,000 acres are necessary for them to meet the level of recreational and outdoors services identified in their locally adopted comprehensive plans. This acreage amount is largely distinct from the two million acres identified for its natural resource values by The Nature Conservancy the year before. The local governments calculated the cost of acquiring these 120,000 acres would be an estimated $4.36 billion, reflecting local real estate markets. Separately, the report also documented needs of $2.29 billion for renovations and restorations to existing local park facilities, and $3.86 billion needed to design and build new park amenities.

Managing Acquired Land

Perhaps the largest unappreciated element of Florida's decades-long land conservation undertaking is the essential role of proper management of the properties conserved by the public. The Florida Forever Act, and Preservation 2000 before it, mandated that lands acquired through these programs be managed to provide the greatest benefit to the public and to achieve the purposes for which they were acquired.

The range of management responsibilities is broad. For instance, State Parks must facilitate public access and provide and maintain a variety of visitor amenities; the Fish and Wildlife Conservation Commission manages public land for the health and perpetuation of fish and wildlife; and the State Division of Forestry manages state forests for multiple purposes, including wildlife habitat, outdoor recreation, and timber harvesting.

Far and away the largest management obligations for state conservation lands are those that relate to the environmental well-being of the natural resource itself. The DEP, water management districts, Fish and Wildlife Conservation

Commission, and other agencies share huge responsibilities in the control of numerous exotic species, wide utilization of prescribed burning to maintain the health and diversity of upland ecosystems, and hydrological restoration in wetlands. The expanding amount of public land being acquired, growing pressure for recreational use, the spread of exotic plant species, encroaching urban development, and tight budgets have made conservation and land management an increasingly ambitious task.

With the increase in State land purchases under Preservation 2000 and Florida Forever, the State land management obligations—which were modest prior to 1990—have grown substantially. The Florida Forever Act provided that up to 1.5 percent of the funds expended on acquisitions may be made available for the purposes of management, maintenance, and capital improvements for land. The 2008 Florida Forever reauthorization improved upon this, making 1.5 percent the minimum amount to be expended, rather than the maximum.

Acquisitions that occur through the purchase of conservation easements decrease land management costs to the public. Under Florida Forever, 32 percent of the water management districts' acquisitions entailed easements. Only 16 percent of DEP projects involve easements, but this percentage is expected to grow. For instance, the Rural Family Lands Protection Program, created in 2001 but funded for the first time only in 2008, will increase the DEP's easement purchases.

Nonetheless, the fall in documentary stamp revenues beginning in 2007 undermined land management just as it did land acquisition. In the search to fund all of State government, the Legislature took away funds set aside in trust funds for land management. By all estimates, the lack of financial resources has adversely affected the quantity and quality of resource management and restoration of public conservation lands. There is estimated to be as much as a one-half billion dollar backlog in management funding needs.

Future Financing

The structure of Florida Forever funding for the past two decades—revenue bonds backed by the documentary stamp tax—has been instrumental to its success, but also an element of its decline in recent years. Questions remain as to whether the documentary stamp tax revenue is sufficiently large or predictable to support Florida Forever in the future.

A funding source tied to growth is effective when development occurs widely, but economic stagnation means revenues decline. The danger from instability in revenues was made dramatically evident in 2007–2010 with the deepening of the recession and severe decreases in documentary stamp tax revenue. From its $4 billion high in 2005, documentary stamp revenues fell by 75 percent in 2008, to approximately $1 billion. This created the possibility that the State might possess too little revenue to back existing bonds or issue new bonds.

In addition, the $300 million dedicated to Florida Forever annually had lost substantial real buying power since 1990 due to inflation. Furthermore, even when documentary stamp tax revenues were growing, other (non-environmental) programs sought and obtained from the Legislature their own allocation from these revenues, keeping the share devoted to Florida Forever unchanged.

Are there viable options to the documentary stamp tax? What source of revenue could back Florida Forever bonds more reliably in the future? Is there a viable supplementary source of funding?

Some of the possible alternative or supplemental sources of funding suggested for Florida Forever are:

- Sales taxes. Florida's sales tax is the single largest source of operating revenue for the State, representing about half of all general revenue each year since 2000. (Florida is one of only six states without a personal income tax.) At 6 percent for over 20 years, Florida's sales tax rate is higher than a majority of other states' and is popular with Florida citizens because so much of the cost falls on out-of-state visitors. A meaningful increase or dedication of the sales tax for conservation is unlikely.
- Property tax. Cities and counties in Florida depend on their local ad valorem taxes to fund a large proportion of their services. Imposition of property taxes is a local prerogative. While some individual Florida counties and cities will likely continue to pass local referenda for land protection, it is very improbable that any appreciable amount of local property tax could be directed to State conservation land buying.
- Oil and gas extraction. In the waning days of the 2009 Legislative Session, the Florida House passed a measure to make more likely oil and gas drilling in near-shore State waters and to direct some of the resulting revenue to Florida Forever. The Florida Forever Coalition opposed this proposal, however, because oil and gas leases would not generate revenue for years and would likely be an unpredictable source of funding. The Deepwater Horizon oil spill in the Gulf of Mexico in April 2010 ended any consideration of this option.
- Bottled water. In early 2009, Governor Crist proposed a severance tax on the extraction of water by commercial bottlers, seeking to raise $60 million for the state's budget. However, the beverage industry strongly opposed the idea. If ever enacted, the amounts of revenue that could be raised would likely be small, and bottlers could potentially alter their manufacturing processes to avoid such a tax.

Conclusion

Florida Forever has made possible a multitude of benefits for the residents of and visitors to Florida. Whether it will produce more environmental, recreational, and quality-of-life enhancements depends on whether this landmark program overcomes the dramatic funding shortfalls of 2009 and 2010.

Will the non-regulatory, permanent conservation afforded by Florida Forever retain its political allure as the state's economy recovers? Will an ever more urban and suburban Florida demand clean water and public parks as before, or more? With an economy less dependent on land development, will Florida Forever's reliance on revenue bonds backed by documentary stamp tax revenues be viable?

Or, rather, has a "golden age" of State land conservation in Florida passed? Have transient Floridians and their term-limited legislators lost eagerness for buying conservation land? Will stricter growth controls, such as Hometown Democracy, be approved and supplant land protection?

One thing remains certain: Florida Forever's ability to adapt to changing times and needs is one of the hallmarks of its success. If this agility remains, Florida Forever will continue shaping the landscape of Florida for the better for some time to come.

References

Crist, Charlie. 2007. *State of the State Address* [Online: Executive Office of the Governor] Available at: http://www.flgov.com/2007_sos

Davis, J.E. and Arsenault, R. (eds). 2005. *Paradise Lost? The Environmental History of Florida*. Gainesville: University Press of Florida.

Farr, J.A. and Brock, O.G. 2006. Florida's landmark programs for conservation and recreation land acquisition. *Sustain*, 14 (Spring/Summer), Kentucky Institute for the Environment and Sustainable Development at the University of Louisville

Florida Constitution and Statutes. Available at: http://www.leg.state.fl.us/Statutes/index.cfm?Mode=Constitution&Submenu=3&Tab=statutes.

Florida Department of Environmental Protection. 2009. *State Lands FAQ [Online: The Department]. Available at:* http://www.dep.state.fl.us/lands/faq.htm

Florida Department of Environmental Protection. 2009a. *Florida Forever*. [Online: The Department]. Available at: http://www.dep.state.fl.us/lands/fl_forever.htm [accessed: 4 February 2010].

Florida Department of Environmental Protection. 2009b. *State Lands History*. [Online: The Department]. Available at: http://www.dep.state.fl.us/lands/history.htm [accessed: 4 February 2010].

Florida Department of Environmental Protection. 2009d. *Water Management Districts*. [Online: The Department]. Available at: http://www.dep.state.fl.us/secretary/watman/ [accessed: 4 February 2010].

Florida Natural Areas Inventory. 2008. *Florida Forever Benchmarks, Fall 2008, A Progress Report Prepared for the Florida Department of Environmental Protection*. [Online: The Inventory]. Available at: http://www.fnai.org/PDF/FF_Benchmarks_Fall2008.pdf [accessed: 4 February 2010].

Florida Senate, Committee on Environmental Preservation and Conservation. 2008. *Land Acquisition in Florida*, Report No. 2008–123. Tallahassee: The Senate.

Mormino, Gary R. 2005. *Land of Sunshine, State of Dreams: A Social History of Modern Florida*. Gainesville: University Press of Florida.

Nature Conservancy. 2009. *Economic Benefits of Land Conservation: A Case for Florida Forever*. [Online: The Conservancy.] Available at: http://www.nature.org/wherewework/northamerica/states/florida/files/economic_benefits_of_land_conservation.pdf [accessed: 4 February 2010].

Nature Conservancy, Florida Chapter. 2006. *Protecting Wild Florida: Preserving the Best and Last Wilderness of Florida, Forever*. [Online: The Conservancy.] Available at: http://www.nature.org/wherewework/northamerica/states/florida/files/florida_forever_report.pdf [accessed: 4 February 2010].

Nordheimer, Jon. 1973. "Florida seeks to curb runaway growth." *The New York Times*, 19 November, 1973, p. 17.

Peltier, Michael. 2009. *Crist Restores $365 Million in Program Cuts*. [Online: The News Service of Florida] Available at: http://www.newsserviceflorida.com/cgi/as_web.exe?rev2009+D+633269

Pittman, C. and Waite, M. 2009. *Paving Paradise: Florida's Vanishing Wetlands and the Failure of No Net Loss*. Gainesville: University Press of Florida.

Trust for Public Land, Florida Recreation and Park Association, Florida League of Cities, and Florida Association of Counties. 2007. *Florida Parks in the 21st Century: A Sound Investment for a Growing State, 2008*. [Online: The Trust]. Available at: http://www.tpl.org/content_documents/TPL-FRPA-FAC-FLC%20PARKS%20REPORT%202008.FINAL.pdf [accessed: 4 February 2010].

Zwick, P.D. and Carr, M.H. 2006. *Florida 2060: A Population Distribution Scenario for the State of Florida*. [Online: 1000 Friends of Florida]. Available at: http://www.1000friendsofflorida.org/PUBS/2060/Florida-2060-Report-Final.pdf [accessed: 4 February 2010].

Chapter 5

Balancing Land Conservation and Land Development: The Rise and Fall of Florida's Rural Land Stewardship Areas Program

Timothy S. Chapin and Harrison Higgins

The state of Florida has a long history of public policies and public investments aimed at land conservation and the control of development, combining to promote what are now called smart growth outcomes (McLeod, this volume; Chapin, Connerly, and Higgins, 2007; Higgins and Paradise, 2007). While these efforts have not always yielded the desired outcomes, the state has a track record of commitment to both conservation and growth management (Pelham, 2007). Further, Florida has been a national leader and true innovator in these areas, designing and implementing a range of policies and programs that planners and environmental advocates from other states look at with envy. For example, along with Oregon and Hawaii, Florida was an early adopter of statewide growth management in the 1970s, requiring local governments to develop comprehensive plans and trying to link these plans to development outcomes. In the area of land conservation, Florida established the nation's largest publicly-funded land acquisition program, Preservation 2000 and subsequently Florida Forever, allocating to date over $6 billion in state revenues to purchase environmentally or culturally important landscapes and preserve them from urbanization.

Florida's Rural Land Stewardship Area (RLSA) program is another in a long line of planning and policy innovations that have been pursued in Florida. What is particularly noteworthy about the RLSA program is that it is aimed squarely at the nexus of land conservation and growth management, offering a long-term vision for yet-to-be urbanized areas of a fast-growing state. At its core, the RLSA program is intended to lead to long-term, conceptual blueprints for large swaths of rural areas in Florida that had become subject to development pressure as a result of ongoing population growth. Development pressure also resulted from challenges to Florida's agricultural economy, particular during the 1980s, as the spread of citrus blight and competition from citrus growers in NAFTA-participating countries dealt devastating blows to the thriving citrus growing industry in Florida. This loss of agricultural productivity led many citrus growers to exit the industry and seek other potential uses for their land resources.

The RLSA program was designed to yield a plan that balances the desire to spur economic development in often struggling rural areas with the need to protect and preserve environmentally important or economically productive agricultural lands. This was to be achieved by employing a relatively simple concept, the transfer of development rights (TDR), but through a potentially complex calculation that captured the local ecological, agricultural, and development values inherent in the landscape. Under the RLSA approach, land with substantial ecological resources or agricultural utility was to be valued more highly, and land with fewer resources or little utility was to be allowed to develop, but only under very strict conditions that reflected the state's desire to promote compact, dense, mixed-use development. In short, in a somewhat perverse twist, Florida's RLSA program effectively took the view that the best means of protecting yet-to-be urbanized, high quality areas of the state was to allow portions of those areas to be developed. In other words, rural development—in the form of urbanization—needed to be allowed in order to save these same rural areas from the low density, single-use form that was increasingly prevalent across the state, and that was in fact already entitled on these lands.

In many ways Florida's Rural Land Stewardship Areas program represents one of the more progressive attempts to link the goals of land conservation and growth management in the United States. Rather than treat land development and land conservation as separate processes that should be addressed by different agencies and different portions of local comprehensive plans, the RLSA program attempts to simultaneously solve for conservation and development within selected rural areas of the state. The program is ambitious, internally contradictory, and frustratingly simple in concept, yet complicated in implementation. For these reasons the RLSA program has not experienced much success; indeed regulators, landowners, and developers have all criticized it, although for different reasons in each case.

In this chapter we review Florida's experience with the RLSA program, documenting the intent behind its creation and some of the details in its design. We also report on the experiences of the two counties in Florida that have pursued this innovative, yet problematic program. Ultimately, we find that the RLSA program failed for a variety of reasons, including an overly complex TDR (or stewardship credit) methodology and an inability of planners and landowners to simultaneously tackle issues of land conservation and land development.

The Genesis of Florida's RLSA Program

Florida's Rural Land Stewardship Areas program resulted from two different initiatives, one in response to a local planning problem and the other in response to a perceived need to rethink the state's growth management and land conservation policies. The first initiative arose due to a thorny land development and conservation problem in Collier County, a fast-growing coastal county in southwest Florida. It was in Collier County that a land stewardship program was initially developed. As the Collier County stewardship program was being developed, the state undertook an evaluation of its growth management policies at the urging of then newly elected Governor Jeb Bush. Combined, these two initiatives ultimately yielded the state's RLSA program.

Collier County adopted its Rural Lands Stewardship Area overlay in October 2002. However, the origins of their program go back several years to1997 when the state's Department of Community Affairs (DCA) rejected the county's proposed comprehensive plan amendments as "not in compliance" with state law. DCA's objections rested on a range of concerns, including concerns about the inadequate protection of environmentally sensitive lands (including important groundwater recharge areas) and the plan's violation of the state's urban sprawl policies through the continued permitting of low density, single-use development in rural areas of the county. Local governments cannot amend comprehensive plans found "not in compliance", a prohibition that largely stymies developers seeking accommodation to a robust and quickly changing real estate market.

An administrative challenge followed DCA's decision in which the Florida Wildlife Federation and Collier County Audubon Society supported DCA. The Florida Administrative Law judge who presided over the case ruled the county needed to make significant changes to its comprehensive plan, determining that the county had failed to implement its existing policies for protection of natural resources. Collier County had been fighting a state-established deadline for implementing a stronger environmental and habitat protection program, but the judge held that the county must pursue this course of action to see its plan found in compliance and to enable development to proceed in the county. In response, Collier County proposed to downzone all of its rural lands, thereby reducing their developable density. In order to protect threatened natural resources, the county proposed to downzone agricultural land from a density of one dwelling unit per five acres to a density of one dwelling unit per twenty acres, and environmentally sensitive lands to a density of one dwelling unit per forty acres.

While the downzoning proposal was well-received by DCA, local agricultural landowners believed that it would be an excessive limitation of their property rights and that they might be entitled to compensation under the Bert Harris Act. Enacted in 1995, the Bert Harris Private Property Rights Protection Act requires governments in Florida to compensate landowners if their actions "inordinately burden" their property and reduce their land values. Although there have been few claims since the passage of the Act, the specter of Bert Harris has kept many local governments from enacting regulations or pursuing land use and environmental policies. After Collier County issued its downzoning proposal, six landowners formed the Eastern Collier Property Owners group. These landowners held approximately 168,000 acres in the county, encompassing nearly all of the land in what would eventually become the RLSA overlay.

Given the prospects of a messy and expensive legal fight, all parties agreed to withhold litigation in order to search for an acceptable solution and the property owners agreed to a development moratorium while a compromise was sought. With support from DCA, the Florida Administration Commission agreed to this cooling off period and set the parties to work in negotiating an agreement acceptable to all. To work towards a solution a Rural Lands Assessment Area Oversight Committee was formed in December, 1999. This 15-member committee represented a cross-section of stakeholders including experts in banking, housing, planning, development, environmental policy, and agriculture.

As the Committee recognized that an in-depth planning effort could not be undertaken without a detailed understanding of the lands under study, the first step in the planning process was the collection and analysis of information on the non-urbanized portions of eastern Collier County. By early 2001, a set of thematic maps describing the existing land use and land cover conditions in the study area were generated, showing the natural vegetation, soils, land use, agricultural activities, water resources, and data on listed species. These would later become the basis for a complex steward credit scheme.

During these early stages of the planning process the Committee also reached consensus that the use of TDRs to support a stewardship program was the preferred solution to the impasse between the state and the county. Consequently the Committee reviewed and evaluated three alternative rural land stewardship models, ultimately choosing a model that based credits in part upon the ecological value of the land. In choosing this approach, the Committee made a key distinction between a traditional TDR program and the proposed stewardship credit program. While TDR programs allocate the same number of credits for each unit within a sending area, the stewardship program provided for consideration of factors other than development potential, such as the ecological value of the sending areas. While credits were still to be generated in some areas and then transferred to other areas, as in a typical TDR approach, the calculation of credits under the proposed stewardship credit model was to be linked to the specific attributes of sub-areas within the study area. Furthermore, unlike most TDR schemes where sending and receiving areas are located at some distance from each other, under the RLSA approach both the sending and receiving areas are located within the same area.

In April 2002 the Committee issued its final report, which included proposed comprehensive plan language describing a "Rural Lands Stewardship Area" program for the county and a stewardship credit worksheet. The County Commission subsequently reviewed the proposal and voted unanimously to transmit the plan amendments to DCA for review. Environmental groups, such as Audubon and the Conservancy of Southwest Florida, and development interests, notably the Eastern Collier Property Owners, voiced their support for the adoption of the amendments. Upon receiving approval from DCA for the program, in October 2002 the county approved the comprehensive plan amendments establishing this new rural land stewardship program. Collier County's program has been in place since then.

The second factor behind the establishment of the RLSA program was the work of the Growth Management Study Commission (GMSC) appointed in 2000 by Governor Bush, who had been elected in 1999 with promises to evaluate and rethink the state's policies on development and the environment. The Commission was tasked with reviewing Florida's existing growth management legislation "in order to assure that the system meets the needs of a diverse and growing state and to make adjustments as necessary" (Florida's Growth Management Study Commission, 2001, p. 11). The GMSC's Final Report was issued in February 2001, and offered a total of eighty-nine recommendations for changes to existing state policy or the creation of new policy, including eight recommendations in the area of rural development and planning. These recommendations were in keeping with statutory provisions that encourage the use of innovative approaches to promoting and managing development. Several of the recommendations of the GMSC were ultimately pursued, including changes to rules regarding public participation in planning processes (which are still in play), a requirement for the financial feasibility of capital improvements programs (also still on the books), and the creation of a fiscal impact analysis model for use by local governments in the state (which was developed and promulgated but has largely been unused).

As laid out in the report, the GMSC's rural policy recommendations were aimed at the development of "an incentive-based state rural policy which restores rural land values and protects private property rights, including dedication of additional revenue for public purchase of conservation and agricultural easements and a special overlay of transferable density allocations for rural property to be used for the implementation of cluster development in appropriate locations" (Florida's Growth Management Study Commission, 2001, p. 9). Included in the GMSC's eight recommendations were specific proposals for promoting rural economic development, protecting the state's agricultural industry, and prioritizing land for conservation based upon compelling state interests. For example, there were calls for "a special overlay of transferable density allocations for rural property to be used for the implementation of clustered development" and a program that allows for "the transfer of [development] rights from lands intended to remain in agriculture in the long term (Florida's Growth Management Study Commission, 2001, p. 44).

From these concurrent planning processes emerged a new, innovative (and ultimately doomed) rural development policy that posited urbanization of rural areas and land conservation as intertwined and inseparable. Rather than treating growth management concerns and rural/agricultural/environmental issues as distinct and requiring different policy responses, Collier County's Rural Lands Assessment Area Oversight Committee and the state's Growth Management Study Commission envisioned a large scale, long-term rural planning process that would protect important environmental and agricultural lands and allow for the development to occur in rural areas of the state. In effect, the state's RLSA program was intended to satisfy all of the key players: farmers could continue to farm their lands because they would receive dollars in exchange for their development rights, environmentalists would see sensitive lands protected, developers would have opportunities to develop lands in rural areas, rural counties would experience economic development, and smart growth advocates would see benefits in all of the these outcomes.

Florida's RLSA Legislation

The work by Collier County on its stewardship program and the recommendations of the GMSC came together to shape state legislation that was passed during the 2001 session. It is worth noting that proponents of the Collier County RLSA worked closely with the GMSC as they developed their recommendations, and also lobbied on behalf of the legislation that ultimately was passed. Section 163.3177(11)(d) of the Florida Statutes created the state's Rural Land Stewardship Areas program.

As described by DCA, RLSA is an "incentive based planning process for conserving agricultural and environmentally sensitive lands." (Florida Department of Community Affairs (FDCA), 2007, p. 1) Participation by counties in the RLSA program is voluntary, as is the participation of local landowners once an RLSA is established. The original legislation also established RLSA as a pilot program in five counties, to be implemented in areas of a minimum size of 50,000 acres.

As laid out in the statute, the six goals of the established program were ((F.S. 163.3177(11)(d)(2)):

1. Restoration and maintenance of the economic value of rural land.
2. Control of urban sprawl.
3. Identification and protection of ecosystems, habitats, and natural resources.
4. Promotion of rural economic activity.
5. Maintenance of the viability of Florida's agricultural economy; and
6. Protection of the character of rural areas of Florida.

It is within these stated goals that some of the later problems with the RLSA model have their roots. To begin with, a number of the goals are potentially contradictory, including promoting rural economic development, controlling of urban sprawl, and protecting agricultural lands and environmentally sensitive lands. As will be detailed in later sections, the tensions between these disparate goals proved to be a significant factor in limiting the spread and implementation of the RLSA program.

In addition to establishing the primary goals of the program, the legislation enabled counties to designate rural land stewardship areas within their boundaries, and within these stewardship areas to create an overlay plan that designates the future use of these lands as agricultural, rural, open space, or developed. Within the stewardship areas incentives could also be employed to encourage the use of innovative and flexible development strategies that meet the goals of the RLSA program.

The RLSA legislation laid out the primary method for achieving these goals: the creation of county-level stewardship credit transfer programs. Borrowing from the transfer of development rights concept, county-level RLSA programs are to establish stewardship sending areas (SSAs), lands identified as having attributes worth protecting, and stewardship receiving areas (SRAs), lands more suitable for development. Once established, development rights are to be transferred from SSAs to SRAs, allowing more development within the receiving areas and severing development rights in the sending areas. As in Collier County's program, the legislation establishes that stewardship credits are to be based upon the specific attributes of the landscape within the stewardship area, including environmental attributes (e.g. sensitive lands, habitat lands), and/or agricultural attributes (e.g. active croplands or ranchlands). As such, the statute provides for a greater or lesser number of credits to be allocated according to the natural resource or other beneficial use characteristics of the land, although it leaves the specifics of the design of the credit allocation system to the local government. Once stewardship credits are transferred out of a stewardship sending area, these lands are to be protected from future development by way of permanent easements.

The final results of a fully implemented RLSA should be that a county creates a rural land stewardship area overlay containing specified sending and receiving areas. Further, the county should have established a clear process for the creation and consumption of stewardship credits, including specifics on the calculation for generating credits within SRAs and the mechanics for transferring these credits to SSAs. Lastly, the county is required to set goals, objectives, and policies for the RLSA overlay that address the six stated goals of the program. All of these items are then reviewed by DCA for compliance with the statute and, once approved by DCA and the affected local governments, the RLSA becomes a part of a county's comprehensive plan.

In 2004 RLSA's pilot status was removed and a cap on the number of programs statewide was rescinded (FDCA, 2007). The 2004 changes also allowed for the creation of multi-county RLSAs and reduced the minimum acreage requirements for establishing an RLSA from 50,000 to 10,000. In 2005, projects within RLSAs were also exempted from the state's development of regional impact (DRI) process in. There have been other minor changes to the legislation over the years, but these have largely revolved around the administration and oversight of the program by DCA.

As noted above, Florida's RLSA program is yet another in a long list of innovative large-scale planning options that the state has made available to local governments (Chapin, 2009; Chapin, Higgins, and Rosenberg 2007). The state's DRI process, created in the early 1970s in order to provide regional and state scrutiny of projects with inter-county impacts, is detested by the development community—and many local governments—because it brings numerous state agencies to the table during the development review process. In the late 1990s Florida added an optional sector planning (OSP) process to the mix in order to guide the development of large-scale development projects. While a DRI is typically a single, large project (such as a new airport or new town development), OSPs are designed to provide for a long-term conceptual land use plan within which many DRI-level projects may be built. While DRIs have proven to be a mainstay of Florida's growth management process, despite almost annual calls for limiting or even eliminating the scope of this planning process, the OSP process has generally remained on the fringes of the state's planning landscape (Chapin 2009; Chapin, Higgins, and Rosenberg 2007).

Implementation of the RLSA Program: Limited and Contentious

As designed, Florida's RLSA program offers the possibility of simultaneously addressing important growth management and land conservation goals, including the conservation of natural resources, the protection of active farmland and ranchland, and the encouragement of rural development in suitable locations. The program is meant to work in concert with existing local, state, and federal regulations, with sufficient incentives that landowners voluntarily pursue this program, rather than avoid or work against it. In many ways, Florida's RLSA program lies at the nexus of growth management and land conservation, as growth is to be allowed in areas of lower natural resource value, while areas of high value are to be permanently protected from development.

By 2010, two counties in the state, Collier County and St. Lucie County, actively pursued an RLSA program while six other counties considered this planning approach before eventually abandoning these efforts. At the height of interest in the RLSA program in 2007, when a total of eight counties appeared to be ready to adopt this planning tool, the acreage that would have been managed by a rural land stewardship program was 800,000 acres. However, a combination of an internally inconsistent set of program goals, an overly complex RLSA model, and aggressive oversight by DCA has effectively hobbled this planning initiative. The following section describes Collier County's successful RLSA and St. Lucie County's ultimately doomed RLSA effort. Subsequently sections summarize other RLSA efforts that were pursued but ultimately scuttled, as well as DCA's role in limiting the spread of the RLSA program in the state. This material is taken in part from work undertaken by the authors as part of a project funded by the Florida Department of Community Affairs (Chapin and Higgins, 2007).

RLSA Success: Collier County's RLSA Experience

After many years of development, Collier County's RLSA was adopted in October, 2002. The RLSA boundary encompasses approximately 195,000 acres located in the northeastern portion of the county around the community of Immokalee, a poor and largely Hispanic unincorporated area of roughly 20,000 residents. Immokalee is the epicenter of the southwest Florida tomato industry, which is a major economic engine for the region, and a locus of farmworker activism. Of note, the RLSA boundary did not include Immokalee, the primary small town in this part of the county. In 2002 several large landowners held the majority of the land within the RLSA. Agricultural uses prevail in this part of the county, with roughly 90 percent of the area in improved agriculture, associated water retention areas, or under grazing leases at the time the RLSA was created.

Under Collier County's program landowners that decide to enter the RLSA program must have their lands designated as either a Stewardship Sending Area or Stewardship Receiving Area. SSAs are the primary conservation tool in Collier County's RLSA, functioning by credit generation and transfer. In exchange for a perpetual stewardship easement, landowners receive stewardship credits that can have monetary value if developers are required to purchase these credits in order to move their projects forward. Stewardship easements are written in favor of Collier County and the Florida Department of Agriculture and Consumer Services, functioning similar to agricultural or conservation easements. In effect, landowners encumber their property in perpetuity by permanently giving up rights to develop development and land use rights. The easement agreement spells out the rights the landowner gives up and those retained.

For lands within the overlay that are not designated as SSAs or SRAs, existing land development regulations remain in place. As per the language adopted by the County Commission and approved by DCA no changes to the underlying density and intensity of land within the RLSA are allowed unless a property owner elects to enter the stewardship program. Land zoned as agricultural before the implementation of the overlay retains that zoning until the landowner decides to participate in the RLSA. However, some changes have been made to the underlying land entitlements within the most environmentally sensitive areas. After implementation of the RLSA lands are mostly restricted to uses directly related to farming, ranching, or silviculture. More intensive uses, such as residential and mining that were previously permitted as part of agricultural zoning are no longer allowed.

To effect a transfer of development out of SSAs and into SRAs, stewardship credits are provided to participating landowners. These stewardship credits are legally valid entitlements to development, with no restrictions on their sale, ownership, or holding period. The county has designed its stewardship credit system so that the most environmentally sensitive lands are likely to be protected first. Stewardship credits are allocated based upon the characteristics of the subject properties on an acre-by-acre basis. For any acre within the RLSA overlay, two primary factors explain the total number of stewardship credits that a given property can generate: 1) the release of rights to develop certain land uses and 2) an index of documented natural resources present on the land.

Under Collier County's approach, individual acres can have as many as eight different layers of land use entitlements, ordered from the most to the least intensive. The most intensive entitlement is residential, while the least intensive is conservation (which effectively is not a development entitlement). The landowner may remove individual land use layers successively, beginning with residential and moving through the other layers until reaching the last layer, conservation, which entitles no development. With each successive move to a lower development entitlement, stewardship credits are generated. Under the Collier County model, landowners willing to give up only the residential entitlement and retaining the rights to the other uses on their land (e.g., to farm the land) will generate fewer stewardship credits than landowners willing to forego all of their land use entitlements.

The second attribute used to generate stewardship credits on the land, the natural resource index (NRI), is simple in concept but complex in calculation. The NRI aims to capture the value of the natural resource attributes of a particular piece of land. The NRI is based upon a number of environmental and ecological factors, including proximity to existing conserved lands, presence of listed species habitat, presence and quality of soils and surface water, and existing land cover. For acreage within SSAs, index values are calculated for individual factors and are summed to create a total index value that is then translated into a number of stewardship credits. Under the county's system, a property could potentially generate as many as three stewardship credits per acre for these attributes, but this is true for only extremely sensitive property and located near existing conserved lands.

In March 2004, the county designated the Town of Ave Maria as the RLSA's first stewardship receiving area. Initially, an SRA of 960 acres was approved so that construction of Ave Maria University could commence. In June, 2005, the county approved an expanded SRA and concomitantly approved the Town of Ave Maria DRI (despite not technically having to do so under state law), expanding the SRA to over 5,000 acres. The fact that Ave Maria moved through both the RLSA and DRI processes is telling, as it indicates that both the developer and regulators distrusted the RLSA model. The willingness of the developers of Ave Maria to endure the expensive and time consuming DRI review process illustrated that they were unsure that development entitlements would result from the RLSA process. DCA's push to see Ave Maria go through a DRI review demonstrated that state regulators were not convinced that the RLSA model could yield desirable development outcomes.

Once approved, plans for the Town of Ave Maria include 11,000 dwelling units, almost 700,000 square feet of retail/service uses, over 500,000 square feet of office uses, 35,000 square feet of medical facilities, roughly 150,000 square feet of civic uses, 400 hotel rooms and various private school uses, including a Roman Catholic university. To support development of Ave Maria, over 17,000 acres have been preserved within the RLSA in existing SSAs. As per guidelines developed by the county and reviewed by DCA development within SRAs is to take the form of a "town, village, or hamlet", and reflect the tenets of smart growth, including compact development, high relative densities for rural areas, centralized water and wastewater, and the inclusion of a commercial and employment within town centers or along main streets.

As of this writing, sixteen SSAs have been approved in Collier County, with over 50,000 acres enrolled in the program and having some form of conservation easements in place. Another 40,000 acres have been identified as likely SSAs, although they have yet to be officially designated as such. The county has identified over 43,000 acres of land within the RLSA overlay that will likely become SRAs, although only the Ave Maria SRA has been approved by the County Commission.

As required by their agreement with DCA concerning their non-compliant comprehensive plan, in 2007 a Collier County Rural Lands Stewardship Area

Review Committee (CCRLSAC) began an official review of their RLSA program. Their final report was issued in January 2009. This Committee concluded that the RLSA program had generally been an effective tool for managing development and protecting agricultural and environmentally sensitive lands within the RLSA. The CCRLSLAC did make a number of recommendations for improving the program, most of them minor. The primary substantive recommendations of the Committee were to place a cap both the total SRA acreage within the overlay and the number of credits that could be generated within the SSAs. With broad backing from a range of groups, the County Commission voted to support these changes but have yet to implement them.

Despite ample signs of success in Collier County, the RLSA program has not been without its detractors. While substantial agricultural and resource rich acreage has been preserved, critics have noted that this has come at the cost of substantial new development in this formerly quiet and undeveloped part of the county. Additionally, the development of Ave Maria has required substantial infrastructure investments in the form of new and expanded roads, new water and sewer systems, and other urban services. Given these investments, there is a concern that Ave Maria will spur further development in a portion of the county that the comprehensive plan envisions as rural and in undeveloped portions of neighboring counties, turning this once rural landscape into a patchwork of suburban subdivisions and that the RLSA program is an inadequate tool to control such development. Lastly, unincorporated Immokalee has generally not benefitted from the massive public and private investment in northeastern Collier County. This area of the county is developing into two separate, unequal places: poor, largely Latino Immokalee and wealthy, predominately white Ave Maria.

Indicative of the conservation-development tension, there continues to be an ongoing debate in Collier County about the design and implementation of its RLSA program. While the program has remained in place and continues to be supported by landowners, environmental interests have begun to question the balance of developed and preserved acres in the RLSA overlay. As will be detailed, Collier County's experience contributed to DCA looking very closely at the RLSA program and working more actively with interested parties. Ultimately, concerns about urban sprawl and the ratio of developed and preserved acres led DCA to develop and promulgate new guidelines about the design and implementation of any newly proposed RLSA programs.

RLSA Failure: The Case of St. Lucie County

The only other place in Florida that has pursued and passed an RLSA program is St. Lucie County, on the state's east coast. A moderately fast growing county (by Florida standards), St. Lucie is home to over 250,000 residents, with most located in small to medium sized communities on or near the Atlantic Coast. Much like Collier County, St. Lucie County pursued the RLSA program as a means to protect large areas of land in the county's interior. Unlike Collier County, though, St.

Lucie's RLSA program ultimately failed, in large part because of concerns over land conservation versus land development.

With approval from the state, in November, 2006 St. Lucie County became the first county to adopt an RLSA under the state's legislation (recall that Collier County's RLSA was developed pre-statute). St. Lucie's RLSA encompasses over 22,000 acres, divided between Adams Ranch, a working cattle ranch that has been in operation since 1937, and Cloud Grove, a property that includes cankered citrus groves and a large water retention area. The approved RLSA overlay called for Adams Ranch to be the SSA and Cloud Grove to be the SRA.

Unlike Collier County, where the primary intent of the RLSA was to protect environmentally sensitive lands and active agricultural lands, St. Lucie County's RLSA grew out of a desire to protect beautiful ranchlands in the interior of that county. Initial interest in the program began with Bud Adams, a second-generation rancher who wanted to see his ranchland protected over the long term for his family. Adams Ranch includes more than 65,000 acres spreading across St. Lucie, Osceola, and Okeechobee counties, in an area long untouched by Florida's population boom. However, the ranch sits in the likely path of development that is slowly spreading inland from coastal areas in St. Lucie County and moving southward as the Orlando metropolitan area expands. Although this land is almost certainly many years from experiencing development pressure, the opportunities to develop a long-term vision for portions of the property and to provide protection to the ranch's operations made the RLSA option attractive to Adams.

In terms of the receiving area, Cloud Grove is a 5,918-acre managed citrus grove located in the north-central part of the county. The property also contains a large reservoir that has served as storage for grove operations in the area. The property has little environmental value, having been tailored to citrus operations years ago, with acres and acres of citrus trees set in rows. In addition citrus canker came to Cloud Grove a number of years ago, which required clearing approximately 2,000 acres on the site. In December of 2004, Lennar Corporation and Centex Homes, two large homebuilding firms, bought Cloud Grove and continue to maintain ownership of the property. The long-term plans for this property are for a large-scale, mixed-use development including more than 13,000 homes and several million square feet of office, commercial, and industrial space.

The intention of St. Lucie's Rural Land Stewardship Overlay Zone is to conserve and protect natural resources and retain and promote agriculture, while promoting sustainable mixed-use development in desirable areas. Along most dimensions, St. Lucie County's RLSA program mirrors Collier County's program. Landowners voluntarily enter the RLSA program and their properties must be designated as an SSA or SRA. Within SSAs stewardship credits are allocated based upon the land use and natural resource value inherent in the landscape. Within SRAs development must take on smart growth attributes.

As per Florida's RLSA statute, St. Lucie's program was designed to capture the unique characteristics of the RLSA lands within unincorporated St. Lucie County. The primary differences between the Collier and St. Lucie RLSA programs rest in the calculation of stewardship credits and the non-contiguity of the sending and receiving areas within the RLSA overlay. In Collier County stewardship credits focus primarily upon resource rich lands and lands under active agricultural use. In contrast, St. Lucie County's program allocates the most credits to agricultural uses, including (not surprisingly) ranchlands. St. Lucie's program also allocates credits to "cultural heritage" lands—lands that have been recognized as being culturally significant to St. Lucie County, have historically significant structures, and/or encompass areas identified by the State Historical Commission. Under credit formulas established by the program, the SSA acres could generate 35,000 stewardship credits. This would enable the plans for Cloud Grove to proceed. Of note, although Cloud Grove was eligible to be waived from the state's DRI review process, the landowners voluntarily decided to pursue this process.

As the St. Lucie County RLSA was being pursued, there was substantial debate about employing this rural land planning tool. On the positive side, this initiative fit well with ongoing comprehensive planning efforts in the county, including the development of an award-winning plan based upon a "Towns, Villages, and Countryside" (TVC) concept. The TVC plan provided "a strategy for development in the existing rural agricultural areas that will ensure that future growth is sustainable, predictable, protects and enhances the natural environment, and improves the citizens' quality of life", and corresponding with the goals of the RLSA program, the TVC concept "encourages a pattern of development that will preserve the rural character while still providing for future growth" (TCRPC, 2006, p. 3). In addition to the planning opportunity, St. Lucie benefitted from the presence of key actors supportive of the program: one landowner (Bud Adams) willing to strip his development rights via a stewardship credit scheme and others (the Cloud Grove landowners) willing to purchase these credits to entitle further development on their property.

Despite these local advantages, St. Lucie's RLSA program struggled to gain support from elected officials, neighboring landowners, and the public. Concerns were raised about employing a planning tool to benefit two specific landowners in what looked to outsiders like a pre-arranged deal. Some other landowners complained about their exclusion from the RLSA process. A few commissioners raised concerns about urban sprawl issues, as Cloud Grove is located well inland from existing development and many miles outside of an established urban service area in the eastern part of the county. Major new roadways and long water and sewer lines would be required to connect Cloud Grove to the developed portions of the county, indicating that the project would result in leapfrog development discouraged by the state. Once this transportation and water/sewer infrastructure was in place, there were also concerns about the county's ability (and willingness) to limit development along these infrastructure corridors.

These concerns contributed to close scrutiny from DCA, which became involved in commenting upon the RLSA program and reviewing the Cloud Grove DRI. DCA raised objections to Cloud Grove on many of the above issues, expressing particular concerns about urban sprawl and the ratio of preserved land to developed land under St. Lucie's RLSA program. DCA provided strong signals that it would be challenging Cloud Grove on many fronts and sent a clear message to St. Lucie County planning staff that the RLSA approach was a poor method for achieving the goals of the TVC concept plan.

After several years of community debate—and at the urging of DCA—in 2008 St. Lucie County decided not to pursue its RLSA program (FDCA, 2009). At this time the county's RLSA program remains in limbo, with the language still on the book but with no current interest in employing this planning approach. Cloud Grove's landowners continue to work through the lengthy DRI process, with DCA remaining an opponent of the project. The future of Adams Ranch remains a concern for its owners and for proponents of retaining the ranchlands of western St. Lucie County. The recession of the late 2000s crippled Florida's housing industry and halted many proposed projects in their tracks, including Cloud Grove, so the development pressure of recent years has abated. As the economy recovers and Florida experiences renewed population growth, it is likely that St. Lucie County will again struggle with the conservation-development tension on its western lands. Planning staff members continue to work with landowners to develop policies and programs that promote rural development, but in a form and in locations that meet the goals of the county's TVC plan. In the meantime, a $1.6 million payment by the state for a conservation easement, financed by Florida Forever funds, will allow the Adams family to continue ranching on their property and to continue to breed their prized Bradford Cattle.

Other RLSA Efforts in Florida

Although no other RLSA programs have been established, in 2006 and 2007 a number of counties announced their intentions to pursue this rural land planning approach. Proposed RLSAs were planned for large tracts of land in Collier, Highlands, Osceola, and Glades counties in the central part of the state's southern peninsula, properties that included very important environmentally sensitive lands; Florida panther habitat lands; and large, active agricultural properties. In Glades County alone over 250,000 acres were to be included in a proposed RLSA. Two coastal counties, Brevard and Manatee, also indicated interest in pursuing RLSA, and held public meetings to educate the residents about the concept.

However, despite substantial interest on the part of these communities and months of work by local planning staffs and consultants to landowners, none of these RLSA programs were ever established. Only Osceola and Highlands counties went so far as to request permission from DCA to designate an RLSA overlay zone, originally receiving permission to do so. In subsequent months, as DCA finished an evaluation of the RLSA program the tenor of the agency changed. DCA staff began sending signals to interested counties that the RLSA program was not one they were likely to support, at least not until the agency had finished developing new guidelines and rules on the design and implementation of the program. More recently, the economic downturn and a remarkable slowdown in the state's population growth also contributed to the loss of momentum for the program.

DCA's Role in Limiting the Spread of the RLSA Program

While RLSA offered opportunities to develop long-range, conceptual land use plans for rural areas of the state, it was a planning tool that was never well-received nor actively supported by the state's land planning agency, DCA. Although DCA was a major player in the work of Collier County in developing an RLSA solution, and the DCA Secretary at the time served on the GMSC, this was not an initiative that was developed in-house at DCA. The legislation that was ultimately passed in 2001 was problematic for DCA on many fronts and, in subsequent years the Department backed several changes to the statutory language. As evidenced by the experiences in both Collier and St. Lucie counties, RLSA is also a planning process that can work at cross-purposes with local comprehensive plans, the primary planning instrument under DCA's purview. DCA worked extensively with staff in Collier and St. Lucie to integrate their RLSA programs into their comprehensive plans, often struggling to balance the goals of land conservation and rural development. Ultimately the combination of a planning approach that was developed outside of the agency's control and the program's frequent conflicts with existing comprehensive plans contributed to DCA's efforts to limit the spread of the RLSA program.

DCA's response to the RLSA program also stemmed in part from the appointment of a new DCA Secretary. Thomas Pelham took over DCA for a second time in January 2008 at the request of the new governor, Charlie Crist. A land use and development attorney, Pelham was DCA Secretary in the late 1980s during a key period in the state's planning history, when Florida was implementing its 1985 Growth Management Act. Unlike other recent agency heads, Pelham saw DCA's role primarily as a regulator and enforcer of the state's land planning laws. Under prior Governor Jeb Bush, a pro-development advocate and a developer himself, DCA secretaries tended to be much more supportive of a technical assistance role for the agency and less of a regulatory one.

Almost immediately upon taking over, Pelham announced that the agency would closely review any proposed RLSA programs. Under his direction, DCA staff aggressively pursued new rulemaking on the RLSA program that had begun just prior to his return. This work yielded new guidance from DCA in the state's Administrative Code, language that became official in October 2009. These changes established a clear process for creating RLSAs, articulated DCA's role in reviewing and commenting upon any proposed RLSA programs, and offered guidance on the conservation-development linkage that lies at the heart of the program. The new rule also required that any proposed RLSA yield development in the form of new towns surrounded by greenbelts, articulating with more clarity the form of any new development that would result from the implementation of this program. Under Pelham's direction DCA staff also discouraged local governments from the

RLSA program, directing them instead to address their land use, conservation, and rural development issues through their comprehensive plans.

Taken as a whole, these actions had a clear chilling effect on the spread of RLSA programs in the state. Whereas as many as eight counties had indicated plans for pursuing the RLSA option, all but Collier County ultimately abandoned their efforts. As a consequence Florida's RLSA program is now effectively on life support. The RLSA legislation remains on the books and counties still have the option to pursue this program. However, there is every reason to believe that the RLSA program will operate only at the margin of the state's planning approaches. While Collier's RLSA program still remains in place, even within that county concerns have been raised about the value of the program in yielding desirable development and conservation outcomes (CCRLSARC, 2009). It is conceivable that a reinvigorated housing market and/or a change in leadership at DCA will lead to a renaissance for the RLSA program. However, given the underlying tensions between conservation and development that came up over and over again during the planning process, the RLSA program seems insufficient for solving these problems and successfully balancing these competing forces.

Assessing Florida's RLSA Program: Is Balancing Conservation and Development Possible?

Florida's Rural Lands Stewardship Area program represents one of the more progressive attempts to link land conservation and growth management. Rather than treating land conservation and growth management as separate and disconnected processes, often managed by different state agencies and departments in local governments, the RLSA program attempts to simultaneously solve for conservation and development in rural areas of the state. As designed, the program is to provide a long-term conservation and development blueprint for these areas. If implemented successfully, the RLSA program would yield a mix of conservation easements and development entitlements that balanced the desire for economic development and the need to protect and preserve sensitive or agriculturally productive lands in rural landscapes. From an environmental perspective, what is particularly compelling about the program is that it has the potential to preserve the most important rural lands, as defined by each county. While development could occur, it would to located only in areas with little impact on ecological and agricultural resources, and per rules passed by DCA, would take the form of compact, mixed-use towns or villages.

While ambitious and well-intentioned, Florida's RLSA program has proven to be a flawed and ultimately failed policy initiative. To date only Collier County has successfully created and implemented a rural land stewardship program. This program is still an active part of that county's planning toolbox and internal evaluations point to some success in meeting its goals. However, outside of Collier County the RLSA program never gained a foothold in the state's planning landscape. Despite signs that the RLSA program was going to be employed in many of the peninsula's coastal and central counties, areas of the state that have been under intense development pressure, almost these efforts have been abandoned and the RLSA program appears to be little more than a footnote in the state's storied planning history.

A review of the program's history finds that the rise and fall of Florida's RLSA program is best explained by two factors, one programmatic and one fundamental to the design of the program. First, the substantial complexity of the stewardship credit portion of the program proved to be problematic, leading to increased scrutiny from DCA and hindering the program's expansion (Chapin and Higgins, 2007). While Collier County and St. Lucie County created schemes for establishing and transferring stewardship credits, these schemes require substantial data on the RLSA landscapes and complex formulas for calculating stewardship credits. The assignment of stewardship credits is also based in part upon subjective valuation of attributes of properties. Taken together, these rather opaque stewardship credit processes were expensive, data intensive, and difficult to employ in counties with limited resources.

While implementation proved problematic, the evidence indicates that the RLSA program failed primarily because it never overcame the inherent tension between land conservation and land development. Consistent with the goals of the enabling statute, the RLSA program was designed to simultaneously promote rural economic development, contain urban sprawl, and protect environmentally sensitive and active agricultural lands. RLSA was based upon the idea that rural areas could best be protected and preserved only by allowing some development to occur on the least important lands in these areas. If implemented successfully, the economy and the environment would mutually reinforce each other, providing monetary value for land that would remain undeveloped and creating development entitlements that could be transferred to more desirable locations.

While fine in concept, in practice the idea that more rural development could promote rural sustainability proved beyond the capacity of the state's planning regime. In St. Lucie County, concerns about urban sprawl and the provision of infrastructure in undeveloped areas saw that county's RLSA program die on the vine. Concerns about too much development within rural areas and the amount of conservation required to enable this development led DCA to aggressively work to develop stricter guidelines for the program and to limit the spread of the RLSA model to other counties. Even in Collier County, the cradle of the RLSA program, concerns have been raised about the scope and scale of its RLSA program. As the Town of Ave Maria has grown and the rural character of Collier County's RLSA zone has changed, calls have been made to cap the amount of development allowed through this program. Reflective of a longer term narrative in Florida (and many other places), the goal of balancing conservation and development proved unworkable, as the development of land usually trumped the conservation of it (Chapin, 2009; Chapin, Connerly, and Higgins, 2007; Higgins and Paradise, 2007; Mormino, 2005; Ziewitz and Wiaz, 2004).

In closing, Florida's experience with its Rural Lands Stewardship Areas program provides a cautionary tale about the ability to link land conservation and land development through public policy. This innovative, ambitious program operates on the assumption that balancing land conservation and land development is possible in both practice and theory. In practice the complexity of the program has proved daunting to local governments and often impenetrable to DCA staff and local landowners. However, this problem could be overcome by a simplified credit generation and credit transfer system, an issue raised by DCA staff during their review of Collier County's program. More problematic is the assumption that land conservation and land development can work synergistically to the benefit of both. Despite Florida's strong foundation for being able to make a program like this work, including a well-resourced planning regime, a culture of public investment in land conservation, and a sophisticated development industry that understands the economic value of preserved landscapes, the RLSA program could not overcome this tension. This suggests that the successful linkage of land conservation and land development is perhaps best achieved through smaller, incremental policies and programs instead of large-scale, statewide programs.

References

Chapin, T. 2009. Large Landowners as Plan Makers: St. Joe and the Future of the Florida Panhandle. In R. Bostic's *The Impact of Large Landowners on Land Markets*. Cambridge, MA: Lincoln Institute of Land Policy, pp. 137–63.

Chapin, T., C. Connerly, and H. Higgins. 2007. *Growth Management in Florida: Planning for Paradise*. Aldershot: Ashgate.

Chapin, T., and H. Higgins. 2007. *Rural Land Stewardship Area (RLSA) Program Case Studies: Collier County & St. Lucie County*. Tallahassee, FL: Florida Planning and Development Laboratory.

Chapin, T., H. Higgins, and E. Rosenberg. 2007. *Comparison of Florida's Approaches to Large-Scale Planning: DRIs, RLSAs, OSPs, AWDRIs, and SAPs*. Tallahassee, FL: Florida Planning and Development Laboratory.

Collier County Rural Lands Stewardship Area Review Committee. 2009. *Five-Year Review of the Rural Lands Stewardship Program*. Naples, FL: Author.

Florida Department of Community Affairs. 2007. *Rural Land Stewardship Area Program 2007 Annual Report.* Author: Tallahassee, FL.

Florida Department of Community Affairs. 2009. *Rural Land Stewardship Area Program 2008 Annual Report.* Author: Tallahassee, FL.

Florida's Growth Management Study Commission. 2001. *A Liveable Florida for Today and Tomorrow* [Online]. Available at: http://floridagrowth.org/gmsc.pdf [accessed: 4 June 2010].

Growth Policy; County and Municipal Planning; Land Development Regulation, Fla. Stat. §§ 163.3177(11)(d)(2). 2001. [Online: Online Sunshine]. Available at:http://www.leg.state.fl.us/Statutes/index.cfm?App_mode=Display_

Statute&URL=Ch0163/part02.htm&StatuteYear=2001&Title=%2D%3E2001%2D%3EChapter%20163%2D%3EPart%20II [accessed: 4 June 2010].

Higgins, H. and N. Paradise. 2007. Paying for the "priceless": Florida Forever, managing growth, and public land acquisition, in *Growth Management in Florida: Planning for Paradise*, edited by T. Chapin, C. Connerly and H. Higgins. Aldershot: Ashgate, pp. 241–60.

Mormino, G. 2005. *Land of Sunshine, State of Dreams*. Gainesville, FL: University Press of Florida.

Pelham, T. 2007. A historical perspective for evaluating Florida's evolving growth management process. In T. Chapin, C. Connerly, and H. Higgins, *Growth Management in Florida: Planning for Paradise*. Aldershot: Ashgate.

Treasure Coast Regional Planning Council. 2006. *Towns, Villages, and the Countryside: A New Pattern of Settlement for North St. Lucie County*. Fort Pierce, FL: Author.

Ziewitz, K., and J. Wiaz. 2004. *Green Empire: The St. Joe Company and the Remaking of Florida's Panhandle*: Gainesville, FL: University Press of Florida.

PART II
Challenges and Opportunities

Chapter 6
Preservation Backfired? Open Space Acquisition and Its Impacts on Land Markets

Yan Song

Most existing open space preservation programs in the U.S. have established non-economic criteria for land acquisition based on the ecological value of the land to be protected. In this chapter, a case study of Portland's land market is employed to demonstrate that open space preservation affects the surrounding land market economically in two ways, by creating an enhancement value of nearby properties and by inducing more urban development. These findings are of interest because of their implication for open space policies. A more comprehensive open space acquisition program is called for to account for the effects open space have on a land market and to minimize the possibility of inducing further land conversions close to the preserved land.

Introduction

Recognizing that the loss of open space poses a threat to the health and sustainability of ecosystems and human habitats, communities across the United States continue to adopt strategies to protect open space, parks, and farmland and preserve the ecological value of the natural system. According to statistics from the Trust for Public Lands, there were 139 open space related ballot measures in the U.S. in 2005; and 111 of these passed, generating $2.7 billion in total funds. The selection, creation, and implementation of public open space preservation programs are generally based on the needs and concerns of local citizens and governments, focusing on political, community, financial, and legal issues during the planning and implementation process of a preservation program. It is recommended that, as the first step to pursue with open space preservation, a community develop a plan that outlines the areas for protection and determines the implementation tools and financing strategies to protect these areas.

In implementing open space conservation programs, criteria have been developed to govern the allocation of resources for land acquisition and development. A meta-analysis of a variety of open space conservation programs in the U.S. suggests that the following lands have been given priority: lands rich in natural resources including ecologically sensitive lands (such as watersheds and waterways, wetlands, slopes, wildlife habitat, large and connected open spaces), forest lands, and lands with geological significance such as high ridges. The preservation of watersheds and/or waterways would maintain the potable water supply for public health. The protection of wetlands and slopes avoids disturbances to these areas and buffer areas surrounding them, preventing flooding, erosion, increased water pollution, and loss of wildlife and vegetation. Conservation of the wildlife habitat maintains healthy environments for diverse communities of plants and animals, enabling the survival of many unique and endangered species and promoting higher biodiversity. Protection of large areas of open lands containing many smaller natural communities and/or connected open lands can potentially increase the effectiveness of these protected lands in providing important services to their ecosystems. Finally, conservation of forest lands and lands with geologically significant features is essential for protecting valuable natural areas.

The methods used to target areas for acquisition and conservation, as shown above, are mostly noneconomic. Conservation groups increasingly develop tools from decision theory to help identify priority areas for preservation based on scoring those areas for their ecological and biological values, conservation costs, and threat level (Armsworth et al. 2006). These tools typically ignore land market dynamics. However, the supply and demand for land in local land markets will be affected by preserved open spaces. Public land acquisition sites and their associated amenities could generate price premiums for their adjacent properties. A range of previous studies have observed that permanently-protected open land uses increase values of residential property nearby (Irwin and Bockstael 2001). This observation raises one crucial question for conservation planning: Given that public land acquisition sites have the potential to increase adjacent property values, would public land acquisition sites induce faster conversion of adjacent lands? In other words, when the overall attractiveness of the area is improved by a land acquisition site, will developers be more likely to seek to capitalize the amenities in the area?

To answer this question, I will explore the issue of land market feedback brought about by open space preservation. A rich dataset of land information over time from the Portland, Oregon metropolitan area is employed. I first use a hedonic price analysis to examine the price premium incurred by locating closer to land acquisition sites in a local housing market in 2000. Using a Geographic Information System (GIS) dataset, I also explore cases of land conversions surrounding preserved open spaces between 2000 and 2007. Finally I employ a land conversion model to test whether proximity to preserved open spaces is one of the determinants of land development.

In what follows, I first summarize findings from previous studies on how preserved open spaces could affect the land market. In the next section, I describe two models: a hedonic price model employed to examine the price premium associated with conserved open space in residential sales transactions and a land conversion model used to explore whether areas closer to conserved open lands are more likely to be developed into residential use. In the final section, I present the conclusions and implications of the research findings.

Existing Studies

There are three sets of studies that are relevant to this research: those that examine the impact of preserved open space on the values of surrounding properties, those that identify determinants contributing to land use change or conversion, and those that consider the association between open space conservation and land market dynamics.

Studies on Open Space and Property Values

The hedonic price method has been used extensively by researchers to estimate the value of open spaces. This section outlines key contributions relevant to this study without attempting to replicate the thorough literature reviews by previous researchers. McConnell and Walls (2005) undertake a massive literature review synthesizing the results of hedonic studies on the value of open space. They note in their conclusions the difficulty of generalizing results amongst these studies since each deals with a particular open space area or set of areas that are unique to a particular region and time period. They suggest that, nevertheless, some general results can be gleaned from the literature about the direction of particular effects and the differences across the methods used to estimate values.

Another review (Henderson and Song 2008) has grouped studies into into three categories, according to the choice of open space variables. These studies use: binary variables indicating whether a property is within a certain distance buffer of an open space; continuous distance variables measuring the distance from a property to the nearest open space; and magnitude variables estimating the amount of open space in the neighborhood surrounding a property.

Many studies employ binary variables to examine the amenity effects of open spaces. Some of these studies measure only direct adjacency to open spaces, while others use the binary variables to test the effect of certain distance ranges or "zones." Bolitzer and Netusil (2000) examine the effect of open space within 1500 feet of homes on their sale prices in Portland, OR. Using a similar approach, Earnhart (2001) examines the amenity value of adjacency to various water and land open space features in Fairfax, CT.

Studies also use straight-line distance measures to evaluate the effect of open space proximity on housing value. For example, Schultz and King (2001) use 1990 U.S. Census data to construct a hedonic model for the Tuscon, AZ area. The authors measure the straight-line distance to the nearest large resource area and Class I/II wildlife habitat. They find that proximity to large protected areas and Class II wildlife habitats raises values, but proximity to Class I habitats lowers values. In another study, Song and Knaap (2004) analyze the impact of mixed neighborhood land uses on the prices of single family houses and find that housing prices increase with proximity to the nearest protected public park.

A third group of studies uses magnitude variables to examine the impact of surrounding land cover on property value. These variables measure the percentage of a set of land uses surrounding each house. Each study defines the relevant neighborhood differently, though several use a ¼-mile neighborhood radius. For example, Bockstael (1996) considers the effect on home sale price of several variables including the percentages of forest, agricultural cropland, agricultural pasture land, and preserved open space within the 250 acres surrounding each house. The author finds that a large proportion of surrounding open space registers as a significant amenity in this seven county region of Maryland. Similarly, Irwin and Bockstael (2001) study the effect of several neighborhood variables on the sale of nearly 56,000 homes in four Maryland counties from January 1995 to December 1999. They define three open space variables: 1) privately-owned, developable (crop, pasture, and forest land); 2) protected by easement; and 3) publicly-owned. The authors find that the privately-owned and protected by easement or conservation and the publicly-owned open space have a significant positive impact on housing price. In another study, Irwin (2002) conducts a hedonic price study on the same four-county region. Irwin specifies all open space variables within the surrounding neighborhood, defined by a 400 m radius around the center point of each residential parcel in the study. In this study the author also incorporates private open spaces such as cropland, pastureland, forestland, and easement land and for publicly-owned military and non-military land. She finds positive and significant amenity effects associated with proximity to privately-owned conservation lands, public non-military open space, and developable forests. More generally, the amenity effects from preserved open spaces are significantly greater than those associated with developable farmland and forestland, and private protected lands are a greater amenity than public protected lands. Researchers continue to investigate the amenity difference between permanently protected and developable open space. For example, Geoghegan et al. (1997) find a positive and significant effect on house prices associated with proximity to permanently protected open space in Howard and Calvert Counties in Maryland. The agricultural and forest land coefficients are negative or insignificant in both counties.

In summary, many previous studies suggest that there is a price premium associated with preserved open spaces. The sources of the price premium possibly derive from the views of open space and the recreational opportunities brought by the open space.

Studies on Determinants of Land Conversion

Geographers, natural scientists, landscape ecologists, and economists have developed models of spatial land use change (Chakir and Parent 2009, Carmen and Elena 2004, Verburg et al. 2004, Agarwal et al. 2002, Irwin and Geoghegan 2001). Land use change patterns are the result of complex interactions between the human and the physical environments. Studies of the determinants of open space conversion can help analyze what factors triggered conversion and evaluate whether open space preservation programs are effectively implemented.

For example, through land use change analysis, researchers are able to identify the factors responsible for urban land use conversion (Chakir and Parent 2009, Carmen and Elena 2004). Land use changes can be identified by using satellite images or land parcel data; binary logistic regression can be used to model the probability of observing urban development as a function of explanatory variables. In predicting land conversion from a non-developed state to a developed state, empirical studies of discrete choice models of land conversion have included several categories of explanatory variables: biophysical land characteristics such as slope, soil, elevation, aspect, and location; economic considerations such as distance to urban centers (Irwin and Geoghegan 2001); characteristics of land managers such as family size, off-farm income, education level, wealth, and ability to bear risk; and land cost (David et al. 2006). Most previous findings suggest that the loss of open space is due to urban development pressure.

Studies on Open Space and Land Market Dynamics

Armsworth et al. (2006) argue that the supply of and demand for land will be affected by large areas of preserved land. Land market dynamics can make conservation purchases backfire, resulting in more biodiversity being lost than saved. Specifically, there are a couple of land market feedbacks which determine the effectiveness of conservation efforts. First, with the preservation of land taking place, land prices increase in the local market. The increase of land prices will make future investments in preserving lands more expensive. Second, conservation of lands can displace development pressure to locations that are adjacent to the conserved lands, because real estate developers seek to capitalize on amenities brought by conservation efforts. In essence, Armsworth et al. suggest that in the process of determining locations of lands for conservation, ignoring the laws of supply and demand may waste limited conservation resources and cause more harm than good.

Several researchers have begun to develop models to examine the impacts of open space policies (Walsh 2007, David et al. 2006). For example, Walsh argues that the partial equilibrium analysis, which is intended to inform us about the value of open space amenities, fails to examine the long run landscape patterns and welfare consequences associated with open space protection policies. Using data from Wake County, NC, he combines a locational equilibrium model of household preferences for landscape amenities and an empirical model of land conversion decisions to develop a general equilibrium model of this land market. Walsh (2007) concludes that when endogenous adjustments in privately held open space are accounted for, increasing the quantity of land in public preserves may lead to a decrease in the total quantity of open space in a metropolitan area.

A Case Study of the Impact of Portland's Open Space Preservation Program

In this section, I employ Portland's open space preservation program as a case study to illustrate the methods which can be used to explore the impacts of a preservation program on the land market. Specifically, this research employs a hedonic price model and a land conversion model. The study area is Washington County, the western portion of the Portland metropolitan area. The county is the most rapidly growing of the three counties within Metro's jurisdiction.

Residents of the Portland metropolitan area are using ballot measures to express their desire for more parks and open spaces. In May of 1995, voters in the Portland, Oregon metropolitan area approved a $135.6 million general obligation bond measure to purchase land for regional parks, natural areas, trails, and greenway corridors. As of 2006, there were close to 8,650 acres that had been purchased through Metro's Opens Spaces, Parks and Streams Bond Measure. In the study area, there were close to 2,200 acres of acquired open lands by 2006. A quick examination of these acquired open lands shows that most are small in size, with an average of 11 acres in the metropolitan area and an average of 22 acres in Washington County.

In order to implement the hedonic model and the land conversion model, I use data from four primary sources: (1) tax assessment files from Washington County, 2000 and 2007; (2) sales transaction files from Washington County, 2000 and 2007; (3) Regional Land Information System (RLIS) data from Portland, 2000 and 2007; and (4) census data from the U.S. Census Bureau. In this study, only those single-family residential properties sold in the year 2000 are included. Prior to estimation, invalid transactions and multiple sales were omitted to ensure that sales reflect market clearing prices.[1] The cleaned dataset contains 4,314 real estate sales transactions in the study area. The average sale price in this period is $187,095, with prices ranging from $68,000 to $800,000.

Hedonic Analysis

Researchers use hedonic modeling to estimate the marginal implicit prices of characteristics of a differentiated market good such as housing. The hedonic price function is implemented by treating price as a function of the quantities of a good's characteristics. Below is the basic hedonic price function model and the control variables used in this study. A simple hedonic housing price function in semi-log form is specified as

$$\ln P_i = f(X_i, OPENLAND_i) + \varepsilon_i \tag{1}$$

where P_i, the dependent variable, is the sale price of the ith house, and $OPENLAND_i$ is preserved open space variables associated with the ith house. In this analysis,

1 Non-arms-length transactions are removed. Transactions that have a sale price that is 60 percent greater than the assessed value or that is less than 60 percent of the assessed value are deleted from the data set. In addition, properties with lots greater than two acres or older than 80 years are excluded to maintain a homogenous pool of transactions. Furthermore, I removed transactions if the assessed value of the land is less than $1.00 per square foot or the assessed value of improvements is less than $25.00 per square foot.

Table 6.1 Results from spatial hedonic analysis for transactions, 2000

Variable	Coefficient	Std. Err	t statistics
LOTSIZE	0.000010	0.00000	29.57*
FLOORSPACE	0.000291	0.00000	25.12*
AGE	-0.007685	0.00041	-18.60*
AGESQUARE	0.000052	0.00000	38.71*
INCITY	0.006949	0.00338	2.06***
SAT	0.001997	0.00015	13.31*
TAXRATE	-0.003106	0.00095	-3.27*
HILLCBD	-0.000000	0.00000	-3.08*
BEAVCBD	0.000007	0.00000	30.08*
PORTCBD	-0.000008	0.00000	-34.26*
MARRDDIS	0.000009	0.00000	5.98*
MOUTVIEW	0.078641	0.00493	15.95*
OPENSIZE	0.000010	0.00000	12.32*
OPENSDIST	-0.000008	0.00000	-3.25*
CONSTANT	10.750910	0.59229	18.15*

(spatial lag) Not significant; (spatial error) = 0.001**
N = 4,314
R^2 =0.86
Adjusted R^2 =0.83

Note: *** Significant at 10 percent level; ** Significant at 5 percent level; * Significant at 1 percent level.

I only include permanently preserved open space[2] to test its impacts on land market. For each sales transaction, I compute the following open space measures: OPENDIST, distance from a house to the nearest permanently preserved open space; and OPENSIZE, size of the nearest public open space. In other words, this model can evaluate the effect of open space, both in terms of size and distance, on housing sale prices.

2 There are other types of open spaces including, for example, golf courses and privately owned agricultural, forest, and horticultural lands. Endogeneity might exist when surrounding open space is privately held and developable. Proximity to open space influences house price, but house prices in turn influence how much open space remains in the vicinity. If open space can be developed for residential use, then it is part of the market for residential land and therefore subject to the same economic forces that decide the value of residential land at that location. In this situation, ordinary least squares (OLS) estimates fail to account for the fact that the location and the amount of developable open space are endogenously determined. I do not include those in this study. For this reason, the problem of endogeneity is less of a concern.

In equation (1), ε_i is a vector of errors and X_i is a vector of control variables associated with the ith house in the following categories: property structural features, public sector characteristics, accessibility measures, and amenity features (Song and Knaap 2003). Property structural attributes, taken from the Washington County tax data, include: lot size (LOT), age of the house (AGE), and age of the house squared (AGESQUARE). Public services within the neighborhood affect housing values; I therefore include a binary variable indicating if the house is located within an incorporated municipality and has access to municipal services (INCITY), mean SAT score (SAT), and the adjusted property tax rate (TAXRT). According to economic theory, location with respect to employment centers is a fundamental determinant of location rents. To capture these effects I include measures of distance to three central business districts: Portland (PORTCBD), Hillsboro (HILLCBD), and Beaverton (BEAVCBD). Because some households are willing pay a premium for improved access to major transportation routes, I include distance to major arterial roads (MRJRDDIS). To capture amenities I include a dummy variable indicating whether the property has a mountain view (MOUNTNVW).[3]

The results from the hedonic analysis are presented in Table 6.1.[4] Of most interest, the negative coefficient on the variable OPENSDIST signifies that housing price increases with shorter distance to an acquired open land. In addition, housing

3 Since the socioeconomic characteristics of households within the census block group are hypothesized to influence housing prices, I also include median household income in the census block group (MEDINC) and percent of the population that is non-white (NONWHITE). However, these variables are not significant in the model. Thus I do not provide related discussions here in the text.

4 Spatial effects may arise while using the above specified hedonic housing price analysis. The first type of spatial effect is the spatial lag effect. With a spatial lag effect, housing price at one location is correlated with housing price at another location within a certain distance. This spatial lag effect might exist because of procedures used to construct explanatory variables at the neighborhood level or because of overlapping market areas of nearby properties. Unless corrected, the spatial lag leads to biased parameter estimates. The second type of spatial effect is the spatial error effect. With a spatial error effect, the error term at each location is correlated with values for the error term at other locations. There are two possible explanations for this. First, potential measurement errors in the dataset could spill over across the spatial units since some data are collected and constructed at an aggregate scale. Second, spatial error effect might arise from similarities in housing market characteristics not explicitly captured by the explanatory variables. For example, some of the omitted variables, such as exterior material and other physical characteristics of the house, may be correlated spatially. The existence of spatial errors leads to biased standard errors. This study incorporates spatial effects into the hedonic price structure explicitly to investigate this issue. Maximum likelihood models are estimated to account for possible spatial effects. The results of the hedonic price analysis incorporating spatial effects are presented in Table 6.1.

price also increases if the size of the acquired open land is larger.[5] These results indicate that open space has a significant impact on the values of nearby residential properties: Consumers are willing to pay higher prices for houses closer to preserved open land.

Land Conversion Model

To test if the lands closer to the preserved open spaces are more likely to be developed, I employ a conceptual model of land owners choosing to develop land when the present value of the future stream of net returns generated by land in an urban land use less conversion costs rises above the present value of the future stream of net returns generated by the land remaining in its current non-urban land use (Bockstael 1996).

Empirically estimating this model requires specification of appropriate explanatory variables triggering land use conversion. Following Bockstael (1996), I assume that the developer predicts the value of residential use by looking at current residential transactions. Assuming it is possible to estimate a hedonic model that is an approximation of how developers view the market conditions at time *t*, I can use the predictions of prices as proxies for expectations of returns from land conversion. Therefore, the empirical framework includes two steps. The first step estimates the value of land in alternative uses (see Table 6.2 in the appendix for the results estimating land values in alternative uses). The second step estimates the probability of a given parcel being converted, conditional on the value of its alternative uses, its costs of conversion, and its distance to the preserved open lands.

5 The other results indicate that the parameter estimate for λ is significant, implying the presence of spatial error dependence in the model. For the results of the control variables, as expected, LOTSIZE and FLOORSPACE are positively related to house price. The expected negative coefficient on AGE reveals that an older home is worth less than a newer home, and the positive coefficient of AGESQUARE indicates that the relationship between house value and house age is not linear. Public services are capitalized into property values. INCITY is positively related to house price, reflecting the value of services provided by cities. The expected negative sign of TAXRT reveals that property taxes are capitalized in property values. The positive coefficient of SAT indicates that school districts with higher SAT scores are associated with higher value of sales. Location matters. Negative coefficients for the variables HILLCBD and PORTCBD indicate that housing prices fall with distance from the Portland and Hillsboro CBDs. Since the CBDs of Portland and Hillsboro are major employment centers, this was expected. The coefficient on the variable BEAVCBD, however, is positive. Though not expected, this likely reflects the character of downtown Beaverton as more of an automobile-oriented retail center than an employment center. The positive coefficient on MAJRDDIS indicates that housing price increases with distance from major roads. Amenities affect housing prices as expected. The positive coefficient on the binary variable MOUTNVW indicates that a view of the mountains increases property value.

Table 6.2 Results from estimating land in alternative residential use, 2000

Variable	Parameter Estimate	Standard Error	t-statistics
INTERCEPT	12.292999	1.222371	10.06*
LOT SIZE	-0.292626	0.004942	-59.21*
INCITY	0.073233	0.018283	4.01*
DISTANCE-HILLSBORO	-0.002189	0.000689	-3.18*
DISTANCE-BEAVERTON	0.001824	0.000112	16.29*
DISTANCE-PORTLAND	-0.000018	0.000001	-18.00*
DISTANCE-MJRD	-0.012457	0.001647	-7.56*
MOUNTAINVIEW	0.268487	0.025327	10.60*
% ZONED LOW DENSITY	-0.139843	0.042245	-3.31*

Dependent Variable is sale price/acre.
N = 4,314
R^2 =0.5655
Adjusted R^2 =0.5639

Table 6.3 Probit analysis of land conversion decision

Dependent variable = 1 if the parcel was converted to residential use between 2000 and 2007
Dependent variable = 0 if the parcel was not converted to residential use between 2000 and 2007

Variable	Estimate	Standard Error	z	Prob > z
INTERCEPT	-2.599155	0.0524	-49.59	0.000
EXPVALUE	1.916412	0.1964	9.76	0.000
AGVALUE	-0.000012	0.0000	-5.24	0.000
STEEPSLOPE	-0.005265	0.0004	-13.21	0.000
POORSOIL	0.000067	0.0002	0.34	Not sig.
CONSERVED	-0.003025	0.0003	-8.75	0.000

N = 3,498
Log Likelihood = -298.42
Likelihood ratio test = 200.29
Pseudo R2 = 0.54

Specifically, the land use conversion model is estimated using all parcels that as of 2000 could be considered as developable for residential use. To be considered as developable, land should be under private ownership, should not have been developed as a residential use, and should not be constrained by zoning or conservation area regulations. Based on this set of criteria, there were 3,498 such developable parcels in 2000. In the land conversion model, the dependent variable is a dummy variable. A value of 1 indicates that the parcel or some portion of the parcel has been developed into residential use between 2000 and 2007. The

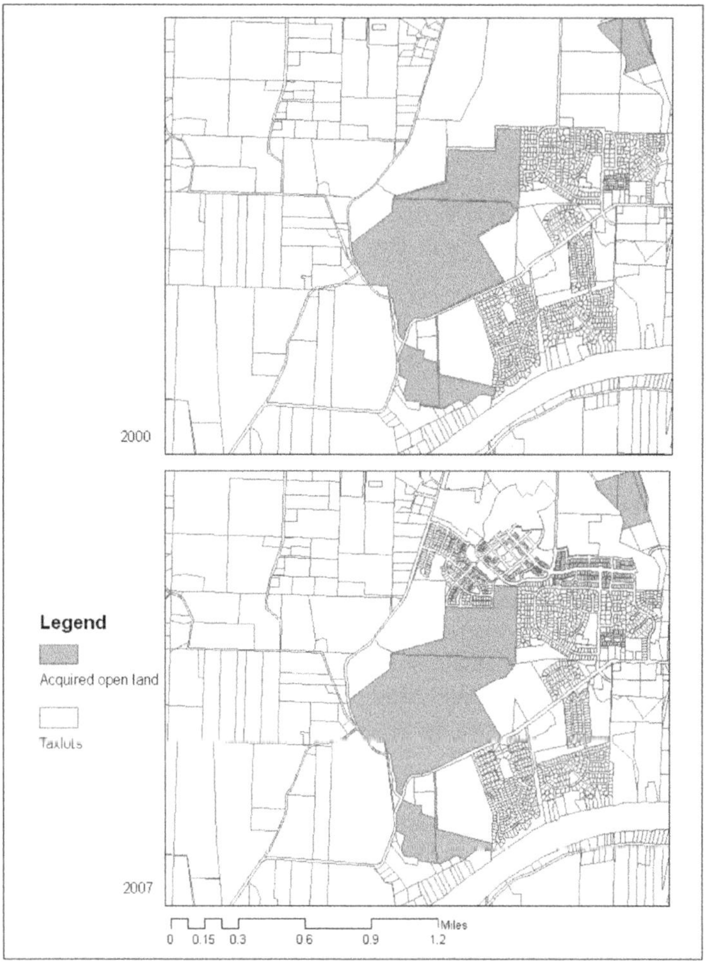

Figure 6.1 Land conversion in proximity areas of conserved open space

independent variables include the estimates of the land values in alternative residential use as predicted from the hedonic model (EXPVALUE), land values in agricultural use (AGVALUE), proxies for conversion costs including slope (STEEPSLOPE) and soil quality (POORSOIL), and distance to the nearest acquired open land (CONSERVED).

As shown in Figure 6.1, several land parcels closer to an acquired open land are converted to residential use between 2000 and 2007. Through the land conversion model, it is possible to explore whether this is a pattern throughout the study area. In other words, the study is able to test whether lands closer to conserved lands are generally more likely to be converted than lands that are farther away from the preserved open spaces.

The results from the land conversion model are presented in Table 6.3. Most variables are significant and of the expected signs. Specifically, the results show that parcels with higher predicted values in alternative residential use and lower value in agricultural land use are more likely to be developed. Steeper slopes are associated with a lower probability of being developed. Soil quality is not significant, probably due to the lack of variation in soil quality in the study area. Finally of most interest in this study, the results show that being closer to a conserved open space increases the likelihood that a land parcel is converted to residential land use.

Conclusions and Implications

Communities across the United States continue to adopt strategies to protect open space, parks, and farmland and preserve the ecological value of the natural system. A survey of open space preservation programs across the U.S. shows that most cities and towns have established the following criteria for open space: protection of land identified as being especially valuable for recreation, forestry, fishing, conservation of wildlife or natural resources; protection of habitat for native plant or animal species listed as threatened or endangered or of special concern; protection of a relatively undisturbed outstanding example of a native ecological community; enhancement and conservation of water quality; and preservation of local agricultural heritage. From this list, it is evident that most acquisition criteria do not include considerations of how protected land would affect further land development.

In this chapter, a case study of Portland's land market is employed to provide empirical evidence of the alterations that preserved open space could make to a land market. There are two main findings: first, residential sales are of higher prices with shorter distances to and greater amounts of preserved open space; second, developable parcels with shorter distances to preserved open space are more likely to be converted to residential land use. These results indicate that open space affects the surrounding land market in two ways, by creating an enhancement value and by inducing more development.

These findings are of interest because of their implication for open space policies.

Land use decisions on the allocation of scarce conservation budgets will be better informed if there is a more comprehensive understanding of the effects open space have on a land market. When designating open space for preservation and protection, we are not only specifying an area prohibited from future development but also generating an adjacent area with higher amenity values (Irwin and Bockstael 2001). When the incurred amenities brought by preserved open space attract urban developments close to the protected open lands, the conservation value of public land acquisition programs could be weakened, especially if the developments occur in the larger surrounding open areas within which the publicly acquired sites are situated. The results bring about a cautionary note for policy makers concerned with open space conservation: Policies that seek to protect open space may actually induce development of other undeveloped lands proximate to the conserved lands.

The research implies that the following factors should be considered in establishing criteria for open space acquisition and development. First, how to strategically allocate funds for acquisition of open space depends on the purpose of the acquisition program. If the purpose of an open space acquisition program is to maintain ecologically strong communities by preserving natural resources, it is more effective to preserve large natural areas to reduce the edge effects that adversely affect natural communities. If, on the other hand, the purpose of acquiring open space is to balance open space facilities throughout the planned area and to provide adequate and equal access to all urban residents, it is better to situate the acquired open spaces as recreational facilities in established residential areas. In other words, scattered small open spaces for recreational services need to be carefully located in areas already developed or to be developed, so that unintended land conversions could be minimized.

Second, many cities and towns have implemented information systems for open space management, including database functions to allow for an automated and centralized open space acquisition tracking system. Information such as location, size, ecological values, and land costs of open spaces are included in these databases. In order to have an information system which allows for evaluation of the effects of preserved open spaces on properties nearby, it is necessary to collect and store information on those properties. This comprehensive database will be able to track not only the status of open lands, but also the changes of land nearby brought about by preserved open spaces.

Finally, but certainly not least, in order to make more effective investment decisions on open space acquisitions, it is essential to develop a comprehensive strategy that is informed by an economic analysis examining the interplay between the acquired land and other lands. The current methods used to target areas for acquisition and conservation are mostly noneconomic. Given the strong evidence provided by this research and many previous studies, however, it is indispensable to take land market feedbacks into consideration when making decisions on open space acquisitions. In addition to protecting sensitive lands such as wetlands and water bodies, an effective conservation program must also link protected areas to surrounding areas to make sure that unintended urban growth will not be adjoining the preserved areas.

References

Agarwal, C., Green, G.M., Grove, J.M., Evans, T.P. and Schweik, C.M. 2002. *A Review and Assessment of Land-Use Change Models: Dynamics of Space, Time, and Human Choice* (Gen. Tech. Rep. NE-297), Newton Square, PA: U.S. Department of Agriculture, Forest Service, Northeastern Research Station.

Armsworth, P.R., Daily, G.C., Kareiva, P. and Sanchiroco, J.N. 2006. Land market feedbacks can undermine biodiversity conservation. *Proceedings of the National Academy of Sciences*, 103(14), 5403–08.

Bockstael, N.E. 1996. Modeling economics and ecology: The implications of a spatial perspective. *American Journal of Agricultural Economics*, 79(5), 1168–80.

Bolitzer, B. and Netusil, N.R. 2000. The impact of open spaces on property values in Portland, Oregon. *Journal of Environmental Management*, 59(3), 185–93.

Carmen, C.-F. and Elena, G.I. 2004. Determinants of residential land-use conversion and sprawl at the rural-urban fringe. *American Journal of Agricultural Economics*, 86(4), 889–904.

Chakir, R. and Parent, O. 2009. Determinants of land use changes: A spatial multinomial probit approach. *Papers in Regional Science*, 88, 327–44.

David, A.N., Peter, B. and Adina, M.M. 2006. Habitat and open space at risk of land-use conversion: Targeting strategies for land conservation. *American Journal of Agricultural Economics*, 88(1), 28–42.

Earnhart, D. 2001. Combining revealed and stated preference methods to value environmental amenities at residential locations. *Land Economics*, 77(1), 12–29.

Geoghegan, J., Wainger, L.A. and Bockstael, N.E. 1997. Spatial landscape indices in a hedonic framework: An ecological economics analysis using GIS. *Ecological Economics*, 23, 251–64.

Henderson, K.K. and Song, Y. (2008). Can nearby open spaces substitute for the size of a property owner's private yard? *International Journal of Housing Markets and Analysis*, 1(2), 147–65.

Irwin, E.G. 2002. The effects of open space on residential property values. *Land Economics*, 78(4), 465–80.

Irwin, E.G. and Bockstael, N.E. 2001. The problem of identifying land use spillovers: Measuring the effects of open space on residential property values. *American Journal of Agricultural Economics*, 83(3), 698–704.

Irwin, E.G. and Geoghegan, J. 2001. Theory, data, methods: Developing spatially explicit economic models of land use change. *Agriculture, Ecosystems and Environment*, 85, 7–23.

McConnell, V. and Walls, M. 2005. *The Value of Open Space: Results from Studies of Nonmarket Benefits* [Online: Resources for the Future]. Available at: http://www.rff.org/Documents/RFF-REPORT-Open%20Spaces.pdf [accessed: 28 January 2008].

Shultz, S.D. and King, D.A. 2001. The use of census data for hedonic price estimates of open-space amenities and land use. *The Journal of Real Estate Finance and Economics*, 22, 239–52.

Song, Y. and Knaap, G.J. (2003). New urbanism and housing values: A disaggregate assessment. *Journal of Urban Economics*, 54, 218–38.

Song, Y. and Knaap, G.J. (2004). Measuring the effects of mixed land uses on housing values. *Regional Science and Urban Economics*, 34(6), 663–80.

Verburg, P.H., van Eck, J.R.R., de Nijs, T.C.M., Dijst, M.J. and Schot, P. 2004. Determinants of land-use change patterns in the Netherlands. *Environment and Planning B: Planning and Design*, 31(1), 125–50.
Walsh, R. 2007. Endogenous open space amenities in a locational equilibrium. *Journal of Urban Economics* 61(2), 319–44.

Chapter 7
Green Infrastructure and Public Health: An Evaluation of the Florida Communities Trust Public Land Acquisition Program[1]

Christopher Coutts

Introduction

This study takes an explicit public health perspective on land conservation. This perspective asserts that conservation supports not only the most basic of human needs of water, air, and food but also myriad other conditions that are necessary for health. The social good of health is influenced by both the natural and built environments, and therefore should be a consideration in the development and conservation dichotomy. To date, largely untested is how land conservation efforts can be made more effective by combining them with social goals and programs (Daniels and Lapping, 2005).

The Florida Communities Trust (FCT) open space acquisition program is part of a larger growth management strategy in Florida. This program was evaluated to determine which criteria used to prioritize and fund land acquisitions are supporting health. This type of retrospective assessment is used to inform the ongoing development of existing work (World Health Organization [WHO], 2009), in this case, highlighting components of the FCT that supported community health and well being. The question this study addresses is as follows: Is there latent support for public health in communities funded by the FCT? This was answered by examining the response patterns of communities whose FCT applications were successfully funded and comparing these responses to those which were unfunded to determine if the differences between these two groups included criteria with public health significance. The results reveal that applicant communities proposing projects that support public health are indeed being funded, and the FCT is therefore supporting public health—one of the stated goals of growth management.

The chapter proceeds by first examining the larger umbrella program under which the FCT operates: Florida Forever. Next, evidence, both nascent and well established, is used to support the public health benefits of conservation. Then, after

1 This chapter was originally published in the *Journal of Planning Practice and Research*, 25(4), 439–59 (2010). Reprinted with permission.

the analysis of the FCT, this chapter concludes by offering a justification for giving greater priority to projects that can satisfy both ecological and public health goals.

Florida Forever

The Florida Forever program is the most recent and ambitious version among a series of land acquisition programs that started with the 1985 Growth Management Act. This Act, like most planning statutes across the country, requires that each city and county in the state create a local comprehensive plan that must aim to "preserve, promote, protect, and improve public health, safety, comfort, and good order" (Carriker, 2006). This Act also requires that local plans contain both a conservation element to protect natural resources and a recreation/open space element. With $3 billion devoted to Florida Forever over 10 years (2000–2010), the State of Florida now outpaces the federal government in resources devoted to land acquisition.

> With the passage of the Preservation 2000 [the predecessor program to Florida Forever] and Florida Forever Acts, the State of Florida has one of the most aggressive conservation and recreation land acquisition programs in the United States and the world. Over the past thirty years, Florida has invested approximately $6.8 billion to conserve approximately 3.7 million acres of land for environmental, recreational and preservation purposes. (Florida Department of Environmental Protection, 2007)

The structure and delivery of Florida Forever are such that the vast majority of funds, 70 percent, are devoted to managing lands (Department of Environmental Protection, Division of State Lands) and protecting watersheds (state water management districts). An additional 22 percent, or $66 million annually, is allocated to the Department of Community Affairs which administers the planning functions within the state including the Florida Communities Trust program.

The Florida Communities Trust

> Florida Communities Trust is a state land acquisition grant program that provides funding to local governments and eligible non-profit environmental organizations for acquisition of community-based parks, open space and greenways that further outdoor recreation and natural resource protection needs identified in local government comprehensive plans. (Florida Department of Community Affairs, n.d.)

The legislature created the FCT as a non-regulatory action to encourage local governments to comply with the conservation, recreation and open space, and coastal elements in their local comprehensive plans. Communities can take advantage of the technical and financial support provided through the FCT to conserve and restore public open space in order to satisfy their comprehensive planning goals and objectives.

Over $1 billion have come through the FCT to conserve over 80,000 acres since its inception in 1989, and there is still great demand for FCT support in local communities. In 2008, a record number of communities applied for FCT funding (Florida Department of Community Affairs, 2008). With the enormous resources and popularity of this program, there is great potential to impact residents throughout the state and, considering Florida as a popular location for tourists, people from throughout the world.

Planning for Public Health

There is a growing recognition in Florida, as elsewhere, that environmental issues span disciplinary bounds. In fact, the effect of green space on health has been used as a case study of multidisciplinary research in public health (Kessel et al., 2009). This has necessitated governmental departments breaching their traditionally confined roles. For example, the Florida Department of Health (FDOH) recently distinguished itself as the first public health agency to become a partner of the national Smart Growth Network. FDOH staffers also met with their counterparts at the Departments of Transportation, Community Affairs, and Environmental Protection to discuss the challenges of rapid growth in Florida. In an effort to build the public health capacities, urban planners in Florida have been trained in the use of Health Impact Assessments at the Centers for Disease Control and Prevention. These developments have increased the contact between public health and planning professionals and have subsequently created new needs for common methodologies to evaluate public health pertinence and prioritization.

As evidenced by a recent Protocol for Assessing Community Excellence in Environmental Health (PACE-EH) exercise in Wabasso, FL, community members did not fragment planning and public health issues when given an opportunity to express environmental concerns. In addition to their self-identified public health needs for street lights and sidewalks, empowered community members identified parks as important for community health. The communities for which both planners and public health professionals work recognize the connection between environmental improvements and their health and well-being.

The Public Health Benefits of Conservation

As McCally states, "at least since the time of Hippocrates's essay 'Air, Water, and Places,' humans have been aware of the many connections between health and the environment" (2002, p. 1). Despite this awareness of the environment as a major determinant of health (Cortese, 2004) and the recognition that protecting the environment is one of the most important public health challenges of this century (Koplan and Fleming, 2000), seldom do we create an environment optimal for achieving health and well-being.

The link between environmental quality and health was formalized decades ago in the World Health Organization's *Ottawa Charter for Health Promotion* (WHO, 1986). This Charter recognizes the necessity of supportive environments and the reciprocal maintenance between the human and natural environments (WHO, 2005). This health promotion perspective differs from a biomedical approach concerned with individual immunity and pathology or a health science perspective focused on the control of pathogens or hazardous substances. Rather, this paradigm promotes environmental improvements to address the root or "upstream" (Tabor, 2002) causes of disease.

> Health promotion is the process of enabling people to increase control over, and to improve, their health. To reach a state of complete physical, mental and social well-being, an individual or group must be able to identify and to realize aspirations, to satisfy needs, and to change or cope with the environment. (WHO, 1986, p. 1)

Among the fundamental conditions necessary for health are a stable ecosystem and sustainable resources, both of which are dependent on land conservation. The World Health Organization's publication *Ecosystems and Human Well-Being* (2005) represents an increased awareness of our place within and dependence upon ecosystems to deliver the goods necessary to support health. What is not explicit is the importance of land conservation in supporting ecosystem functioning and health.

Although there is a dearth of research devoted to studying the health benefits of conservation in the fields of either public health or conservation biology, there have been a handful of noteworthy attempts at ushering in the interdisciplinary collaboration necessary to address this complicated relationship. There is a considerable amount of work under the rubric of "conservation medicine" which connects ecosystem, animal, and human health (Aguirre et al., 2002), but this movement largely focuses on infectious diseases that are exacerbated by human encroachment into animal habitat. The approach taken in this study intersects conservation medicine in recognizing that there are human health ramifications to disrupting ecosystems, but diverges from it by focusing on the chronic conditions and human needs met by maintaining environmental integrity.

Ecotoxicology is another cross-over field which examines the relationship between ecosystems and human health (DiGiulio and Monosson, 1996). This is important for understanding the ecological products and mechanisms that make ecosystems and humans sick, but it doesn't offer a solution to fix ecosystems. How this study diverges from this approach is that it examines a policy solution for conserving the land on which ecosystems and humans depend. If we are to improve the quality of the environment and the intertwined ecological and social benefits that ensue, then we must not only understand the mechanisms but also the policy solutions and programs that will help us conserve and repair the landscape.

There has also been a movement in "health ecology" stemming from human ecology (Honari and Boleyn 1999). Health ecology is distinct from conservation medicine and ecotoxicology in that it makes ecology a humanistic endeavor. Health ecology places health as the core concept in human ecology, the ultimate aim of which "… is the creation and maintenance of healthy people in healthy environments" (Honari and Boleyn, 1999, p. 17). A humanistic approach informs this study as it makes explicit the reciprocal determinism between changes in the environment and changes in an organism (Wolonski, 1999), the organism in question here being human.

A consideration of ecological influences is part of a contemporary public health paradigm (Duhl and Sanchez, 1999) increasingly pertinent to environmental protection. This "ecological" approach in public health unfortunately has little to do with ecology and is more a consideration of a holistic approach to health promotion that includes the often overlooked environment, recognizing there are forces beyond individual level indicators such as personal lifestyle that influence health (Green and Kreuter, 1999). The adoption of the new public health paradigm recognizes the importance of the environment but has yet to put biological ecology and ecosystems into the ecological framework. The benefits of doing so are only now creeping into view amidst a nascent public health interest in sustainability (National Environmental Health Association, n.d.), but even here land conservation is currently overlooked.

These are a number of the paradigms getting us closer to making the connection between human well-being and landscape integrity. Some of these cross-over fields are doing meaningful work in beginning to untangle the intricacies of this complicated relationship, but there is still a limited amount of evidence supporting the importance of land conservation on health.

How conservation influences health Various forms of conserved lands, from neighborhood parks to national forests, support health and health behaviors in various ways. For example, protecting a wetland improves water quality and creating a park with amenities, such as soccer or softball fields, may act as a setting for social interaction and physical activity. Conserved land in the form of linear greenways has the potential to connect habitats and protect sensitive natural features while simultaneously providing a setting for recreational or utilitarian physical activity and the alleviation of psychological and social stressors. It is likely time to move beyond striving for an elusive and often esoteric "well-being" and "livability"—reflecting our inherently understood dependence on environmental quality—and become more specific about the public health goals that can be achieved through ecologically sensitive growth management practices.

When considering the myriad ways in which land conservation can support public health, we not only acknowledge the ways in which landscape integrity can satisfy human needs for water and air but also other emerging environmental and contextual variables being empirically linked to public health outcomes. Positive correlations found between self-reported health status and the amount of greenspace in one's immediate living environment (Maas et al., 2006, de Vries et al., 2003) demonstrates our tacit knowledge of the benefits of everyday exposure to nature beyond the services that nature and ecosystems provide. A more recent study reveals that objective measures of mortality also confirm the importance of green space whose benefits are distributed equally among all segments of a population (Mitchell and Popham, 2008).

The following subsections covering water, food, air, physical activity, mental health, social capital, safety, and ecological integrity represent a number of ways in which land conservation can support public health.[2] Most of what we know pertains to the effect of environmental modification on environmental elements, while the effect of environmental elements on human beings is often addressed separately. There is rarely a perspective which links the associative chain from environmental modification to human health impacts. The following sections are by no means meant to represent a comprehensive treatise on the ways in which the environment influences health. Rather, they are offered as a compendium of the many, and often interrelated, ways in which our health is dependent on maintaining environmental quality. They are presented to illustrate the many ways that land acquisition, and in particular actions taken under the auspices of the Florida Communities Trust, could influence health.

Water

We, as human organisms, maintain a daily need for the consumption of the most basic of life supporting elements: water. The quality and quantity of this resource is dependent upon the ability of the landscape to filter pollutants and facilitate the recharging of groundwater stores. Ecologically insensitive development

---

2 Unless otherwise noted, evidence for the following sections was derived from evidence summaries provided by the Metropolitan Design Center's Design for Health initiative (Metropolitan Design Center 2007), the National Association of County and City Health Officials (NACCHO 2003), and the Trust for Public Land (2006), and from reviews of environmental audit tools and guides which capture the public health impacts of development. These latter include the Design Guidelines for Active Michigan Communities (Alaimo et al. 2006) and the Healthy Development Tool (San Francisco Department of Public Health 2007). Specific to land conservation and health, a recently published literature review by Tzoulas et al. (2007) provides more references which support many of the health considerations listed in the individual subsections.

practices that consume and replace land area with impervious surfaces increase the levels of non-point source pollution in surface and groundwater (Arnold and Gibbons, 1996). Runoff carried unchecked over impervious surfaces and into lakes and streams carries with it the pollutants accumulated on these surfaces. Runoff that passes over permeable open space filters moderate levels of non-point source pollution and allows absorption into groundwater reservoirs. In addition to partially alleviating the deleterious health effects associated with exposure to toxic pollutants, the conservation of natural floodplains and riparian corridors also helps to control and absorb an overabundance of surface water. As witnessed most disparagingly in the devastation of Hurricane Katrina, but evidenced in many other areas of the world as well, consuming open space in floodplains can cause serious, if not fatal, injuries and infections. On the other end of the spectrum, land conservation can also reduce the severity of droughts. Where drought in the developed world is associated with the stress of altered diets and collapsing livelihoods, drought in much of the developing world results in starvation. Water is of course intertwined with another life sustaining element: food and food production.

Food

Not only is the conservation of the landscape vital to drought reduction, flood protection, pollution removal, and hydrological functioning on which productive agriculture relies, but it can preserve functioning ecosystems—also a key to agricultural production. For example, the natural qualities of conserved land are important to maintain habitat for insects that pollinate crops. This service alone is worth an estimated $217 billion worldwide (Helmholtz Association of German Research Centres, 2008) and $57 billion in the U.S (Cornell University, 2006). Maintaining ecological integrity may also increase the longevity of productive agriculture. Conversely, there is also the argument for protecting agriculture as an essential component of our green infrastructure (Cremer, 2009). Techniques that deplete the soil and otherwise create ecological imbalances exacerbate the need for herbicides, pesticides, and genetic engineering that pose both proven and suspected risk factors.

Air

Land conservation efforts can be complementary to efforts aimed at reducing airborne pollutants. Selected forms of vegetation, most notably trees, have the capacity to filter both gaseous and particulate airborne pollutants (Bealey et al., 2007, Nowak, Crane and Stevens, 2006). These pollutants exacerbate asthma, a growing malady among children in the U.S., and are associated with lung cancer and cardiopulmonary mortality (Pope et al., 2002). Conserving land and vegetation also plays a role in sequestering carbon (Nowak and Crane, 2002).

This action not only improves air quality but also helps to mitigate climate change.

The risks to health caused by the desertification and diminished biodiversity of global climate change include changing patterns of infectious disease (Frumkin et al., 2008; McMichael, Woodruff and Hales, 2006; Patz et al., 2003; Dobson and Carper, 1993) and threats to food security. Although it has been shown that local temperatures in urban environments can be partially reduced through the cooling effect of urban nature (Gill et al., 2007), it is less clear what effect a national or global land conservation effort may have on reducing temperatures within the biosphere as a whole.

Conservation of flora may also have some benefit for not only the remediation of pollutants but also the prevention of their release. Conserved space in the form of greenways and trails supports the substitution of motorized transport with walking and biking, thereby reducing emissions and increasing air quality. Better yet, the physical activity gained through non-motorized forms of transportation and recreation has substantial cumulative health benefits.

Physical Activity

Environmental supports for the performance of physical activity have been the focus of a considerable amount of research over the past decade (Frank, Engelke and Schmid, 2003; Kahn et al., 2002; Sallis, Bauman and Pratt, 1998). This thrust in research was spurred by the theory that physical activity is facilitated or hindered by environmental supports and barriers. Included in a supportive environment is the availability and accessibility of attractive public space which provides a setting for physical activity (Cohen et al., 2007; Bedimo-Rung, Mowen and Cohen, 2005; Coombes et al., 2010) and increases the likelihood of walking (Giles-Corti et al., 2005). An activity as simple as walking can help someone achieve the level of physical activity known to have health benefits. Even modest amounts of physical activity, such as the levels recommended by the Centers for Disease Control and Prevention (CDC), can prevent increases in visceral fat, a major risk factor for many diseases (Slentz et al., 2005). In addition, the regular physical activity that could be achieved by walking to the store or taking a stroll in a park could reduce the risk of cardiovascular disease, type 2 diabetes, selected forms of cancer, and osteoporosis, as well as improving mental health and mood and increasing general longevity (CDC, 2008).

Creating access to public space that could support physical activity means locating these spaces in areas where most of the population lives, namely urban and urbanizing environments. The importance of creating these settings within urban environments has gained recognition at the national scale, with four of the six newly designated National Recreation Trails in Florida planned for urban and urbanizing settings. Although termed "recreational" trails, these facilties also have the potential to be used for transportation. In other words, these are not just places to visit in order to recreate and be active but also spaces with utilitarian purposes. Facilities that have multiple purposes are likely to appeal to more people. The FCT recognized the importance of this and maintains a mandatory allocation of at least 30 percent of its funding to projects in metropolitan areas.

Mental Health

Beyond the implications that land conservation may have on physical health, exposure to and contact with nature also influence mental health. If we are to fully achieve health, defined by the World Health Organization as the "state of complete physical, *mental* [italics added] and social well-being and not merely the absence of disease or infirmity" (WHO, 1948), then mental health must be a component of environmental interventions aimed at improving overall health.

Modern tendencies towards what has been termed our "nature deficiency disorder" run counter to the biophilia hypothesis (Kellert and Wilson, 1993) or our innate connection to nature and natural elements. This hypothesis has been confirmed by research in the environmental psychology field which demonstrates that exposure to nature provides psychological regeneration (Kaplan and Peterson 1993). A more recent review of studies concluded that contact with nature has a wide variety of mental health benefits (Maller et al., 2006).

Social Capital

Social capital is the value of the relationships that exist between people in a community. Those bonds have been proven to be important indicators of many health outcomes fostered by the presence of shared public space. Creating appropriate spaces for human interaction is essential for creating a sense of community, as "... community cannot form in the absence of communal space ..." (Duany, Plater-Zyberk and Speck, 2000, p. 60). Parks and open space can provide gathering places for social interaction, recreation, and civic function. More specifically, public spaces with natural elements such as vegetation are an important indicator of the degree of social ties built by the use of these spaces (Kuo et al., 1998; Coley, Sullivan and Kuo, 1997).

Safety

There are two general ways that the built environment influences safety: injuries incurred from accidents and crime or violence. The relationship between conservation and violence, to the best of my knowledge, is remote and untested, but there is great potential for conserved lands to improve safety by reducing accidents between pedestrians and automobiles. Nationally, there are 5,849 pedestrians and cyclists killed and 64,000 pedestrians injured in traffic accidents every year (National Highway Transportation Safety Administration [NHTSA], 2005). In Florida in 2005, there were 3.24 pedestrian fatalities per

100,000 persons in the population. This was double the prevalence that occurred in the state of New York with a comparable total population. Until our roadways include amenities for pedestrians and cyclists, conserved lands in the form of multi-use greenways and parks can improve their safety by separating them from roadways.

Ecological Integrity

The dependency between ecological integrity and public health is likely the most complex, understudied, encompassing, and important factor presented here. This is an area of intersection for many disciplines including public health and urban planning. Recognizing that people suffer the consequences when ecosystems collapse was a significant contributor to a renewed collaboration between planners and public health practitioners (Jackson and Kochtitzky, 2001). The World Health Organization report, *Ecosystems and Human Well-Being* (2005), illustrates the complex way that our health and existence are linked to the integrity of ecosystems. The natural functions on which our health and ultimate existence depend are influenced by the structure of the natural landscape.

This is pertinent to both infectious and chronic disease. Urban sprawl has been considered for its propagation of infectious disease (Koontz and Daszak, 2005). While the relationship between ecosystem integrity and infectious disease is certainly worthy of further investigation, the chronic diseases associated with lifestyle choices are the leading causes of mortality in the developed world. Therefore, in these places and in addition to the basic needs of water, air, and food to which none are immune, land conservation that ensures ecological integrity should be explored for its ability to support the lifestyle choices (e.g., physical activity) that can alleviate chronic disease.

The importance of land conservation in the developing world may be even more acute to protecting public health. Without a robust infrastructure, the basic human needs of food and water are often precariously dependent on the local landscape and ecosystem integrity. There may be little hope for an attainable technological fix to temporarily overcome these basic needs. Therefore, land conservation is not only intimately entwined with health, but it may be the only reasonable way to sustain it.

A public health ecology approach (Coutts, 2010) is concerned with securing the landscape needed to ensure ecological integrity and the health of the humans and animals dependent upon it. As the human signature expands and the prospect of an increasingly tainted environment leads to greater risks to human health, this notion of public health ecology will become increasingly pertinent. It will become of increasing importance to think globally by planning locally in order to protect the landscape on which public health depends.

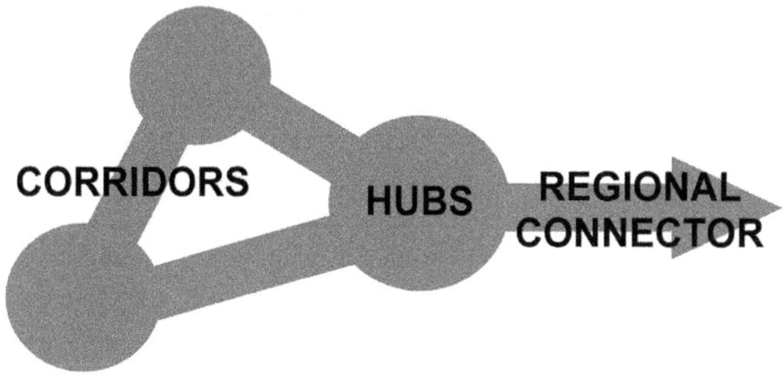

Figure 7.1 Green infrastructure

Landscapes that Support Public Health

Protecting public health is not the purpose of the Florida Communities Trust program, but public health is a community benefit of conservation. This is not to say that all forms of conserved land are equal in their ability to support public health. A small isolated patch of public open space is likely to have limited, albeit still important, benefits to both ecosystems and human health. Considering the form of conserved lands and how these individual pieces fit together is essential to provide the maximum benefit to natural systems and to create an environment that supports public health. This systems thinking requires the interspersion and mingling of conserved lands within developed areas as opposed to relying on larger green swaths in the hinterland separated from human settlements. Protecting public health and ecosystem integrity involves the creation of everyday green infrastructure within urban and urbanizing areas connected to regional systems. This green infrastructure is the "... interconnected network of natural areas and other open spaces that conserves natural ecosystem values and functions, sustains clean air and water, and provides a wide array of benefits to wildlife and people" (Benedict and McMahon, 2006, p. 1). Figure 7.1 displays the infrastructure approach to land conservation. Not only are patches or hubs essential (think city or county parks), but so are the corridors connecting these hubs to one another and to larger regional hubs. Distinct from a typology approach to open space that categorizes open space by function, this is a structural approach (Erickson, 2006).

Green infrastructure in the form of hubs and corridors add to the *composition* of land uses in the planned environment. Corridors which support landscape structure support not only the composition but also the *configuration* of the greenspace system by increasing connectivity. Parks and preserves have long been considered important components of land use planning and development, but the importance of connecting these conserved lands with conservation corridors is not commonly recognized. When corridors are planned, they often occur in the form of multi-use greenways. Multi-use greenways are an important form of open space, which can repair the fragmentation of green infrastructure (Forman, 1995; McHarg, 1992). When there is access to these conservation corridors in the form of a trail, they can simultaneously support ecological systems and provide public health benefits. For example, a greenway routed along a river corridor has the potential to protect water resources, provide a safe setting for physical activity, bestow the mental health benefits associated with exposure to nature, and create a public forum for social interaction while simultaneously creating the interconnected landscape structure necessary for ecological functioning. Environmentally sensitive growth management policies are important for these corridors to be realized (Ryder, 1995).

Preservation or conservation when supporting public health There is an inherent tension between preserving and conserving land. Preservation involves maintaining the land in its pristine state without consideration of the potential human benefits of doing so. Conservation, on the other hand, involves the sustainable use of natural resources to satisfy human needs. Preserving sensitive lands in a pristine state by limiting access may be critical in some circumstances to protect fragile ecosystems, but conservation that allows access, likely with site-specific limitations, will often be a necessary compromise to satisfy and balance a wider range of environmental and social goals.

Many of the public health benefits that conserved lands support stem from their ability to be accessed by the public. Once access is granted, there is another potential tension regarding the allowable *passive* and *active* uses of the public space.[3] Active recreation areas provide a setting for those forms of recreation where physical activity is performed. These forms of recreation can be highly intrusive on the land. A nature trail could be considered slightly intrusive while a park largely consisting of a soccer field could be considered very intrusive. While both provide access to conserved land and support community health, their contribution to land conservation goals varies. Although facilities such as sport fields are important to some communities and support community health, they do little to support the services of functioning ecosystems. On the other hand, a larger land acquisition that includes, but does not consist entirely of, sports fields may be beneficial to multiple realms of health and a useful compromise to multiple community interests. For the purposes of fostering the essential public and political will to make conservation happen, some level of access and facilities will likely

3 From an environmental sciences perspective, passive recreation involves low impact activities such as walking or hiking while active recreation involves climbing, hunting, horseback riding, and bike riding. This is very different from a public health perspective where recreation is considered "active" if physical activity results. Walking or hiking qualifies as passive within the rubric of environmental science but is active from a public health perspective. Conversely, horseback riding, considered active or invasive from an environmental sciences perspective, would be termed passive from a public health perspective because no physical activity is being achieved. For the purposes of this chapter, we will adopt the public health perspective of active and passive use.

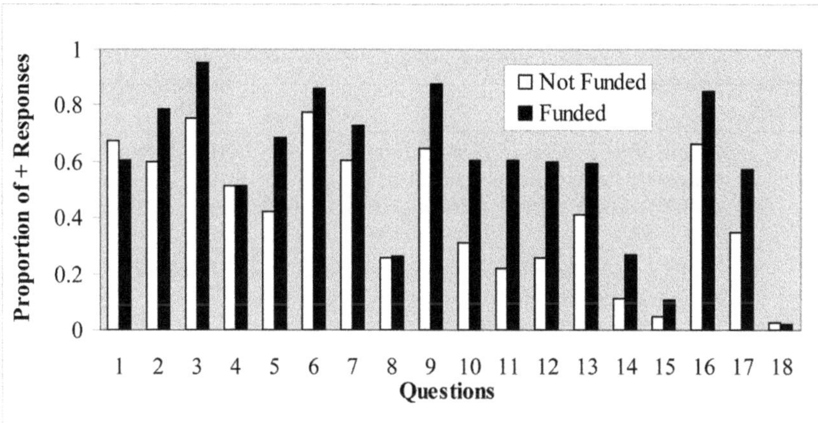

Figure 7.2 Proportion of positive responses to questions with public health significance in funded versus unfunded FCT applications 2001–2006

Note: Question 1 occurred only in 2005–2006.

need to be found in concert with landscape conservation. The multidimensional role of parks, including their support for both human and ecological health, is likely to be of an increasing necessity (Hough, 1994).

Is the Florida Communities Trust Supporting Public Health?

Now that we are aware of the many ways that land conservation and public health are connected, let us examine a large and well-established land acquisition program to determine how it is supporting health and how it can be improved further to achieve this goal. A total of 617 Florida Communities Trust (FCT) applications submitted between 2001–2006 were examined to determine in what ways the FCT is supporting public health. The FCT application questions with public health significance were those that contributed to at least one of the aforementioned aspects of public health. In reviewing the instrument that communities complete to apply for funding, it was determined that 18 out of the 60 questions total are pertinent to the health of the candidate communities. These questions related to the provision of recreational amenities, the protection of water quality and quantity, and the reduction of exposure to environmental hazards. A list of the questions with public health significance and their corresponding health component(s) is provided in Table 7.1.

Next, the proportions of positive responses to questions with public health significance in the funded and unfunded communities were plotted on a histogram

Table 7.1 FCT questions with public health significance

Question number	Question	Influence on public health
1*	Neighborhood access. The project site is accessible by an existing sidewalk or will be connected to an adjacent sidewalk within the next two years.	Air, PA, Safety
2	Will the project provide outdoor recreation areas or open space adjacent to existing publicly-owned upland area, such as, existing parks, museums, schools, libraries, affordable housing, or transit stations?	Air, PA, SC
3	Will the project include two or more resource-based outdoor recreation facilities, such as a nature trail, picnic pavilion, fishing pier, wildlife observation platform, boardwalk, camping area or canoe launch?	PA, Mental health, SC
4	Will the product include two or more user-oriented outdoor recreation facilities, such as, playgrounds, basketball courts, tennis courts, bocci ball courts, shuffleboard courts, volleyball courts or fitness trail?	PA, SC
5	Will the project provide access to a shoreline or beach and be managed for recreation uses?	PA, EI
6	Is the project site located within an existing urban service area, as defined in Rule 9K-7.002(40) F.A.C.?[1]	Many
7	Is the project site located within an urban service area and also within ½ mile of a built-up commercial or high density mixed use area?	Many
8	Is the project site located within an urban service area and is also within a built-up commercial or high density mixed use area?	Many
9	Will the project include new or enhance land-based nature, bike or equestrian trails that are at least ¼ mile in length?	PA, Safety
10	Will the project enhance or connect local, regional or statewide land-based recreational trail systems by extending an exiting trail system or by providing trailhead or trailside facilities?	PA
11	Will the project enhance or connect local, regional or statewide network greenways by expanding existing greenways, such as wildlife corridors or canoe trails?	Water, Air, PA, Mental health, EI

12	Will the project further a locally adopted greenway, water trail, or land-based recreational trail system plan for the community?	Water, Air, PA, Mental health, EI
13**	Will the quality of the surface waters occurring on or adjacent or in close proximity to the project site be improved by the elimination of existing pollution sources from the project site, removal of impervious surfaces, or other means?	Water
14	Will acquiring the project site protect adjacent Outstanding Florida Waters,[2] as designated by the Department of Environmental Protection?	Water
15	Will acquiring the project site protect adjacent Class I Waters,[3] as identified by the Department of Environmental Protection, or is the project site in a locally designated wellfield protection zone?	Water
16	Flood Hazard Area. Will the project provide recreational opportunities and open space areas that direct residential and commercial development away from a coastal high hazard area or a 100-year flood plain?	Water, Safety
17	Local Mitigation Strategy Priority. Is the project site located within an area identified in the County's adopted Local Mitigation Strategy[4] as a mitigation priority?	Safety
18	Designated Brownfield Area. Will the project provide recreational opportunities or open space areas within a state designated brownfield[5] area?	Safety, EI

Note: *2005–06 only, **2001 does not make the "from the project site" specification; 2005–06 makes specification for the inclusion of stormwater facilities that create open space. PA = Physical activity; SC = Social capital; EI = Ecological integrity; Many = Supportive of most aspects, depending on type of project.

[1] The Florida Adminsitrative Code (FAC) defines Urban Service Areas as "...built-up areas where public facilities and services such as sewage treatment systems, roads, schools, and recreation areas, are already in place. For the purpose of this rule, it may also include other similar designations that have been formally adopted by a local government on its Future Land Use Map..."

[2] "An Outstanding Florida Water, (OFW), is a water designated worthy of special protection because of its natural attributes. This special designation is applied to certain waters, and is intended to protect existing good water quality."

[3]Class 1 Waters are potable supplies.

[4]Local Mitigation Strategy plans are intended to reduce the vulnerability to disasters and identify opportunities for post-disaster mitigation in Florida communities.

[5]Existing commercial and industrial sites that are abandoned or under used due to environmental hazards.

Table 7.2 Summary of funded and unfunded FCT applications, 2001–2006

Funding Year	n	Funded (%)	Unfunded (%)
2001	138	88 (64)	50 (36)
2002	114	42 (37)	72 (63)
2003	97	55 (57)	42 (43)
2004	76	47 (62)	29 (38)
2005	77	35 (45)	42 (55)
2006	115	31 (27)	84 (73)
Total	617	298 (48)	319 (52)

(Figure 7.2). Proportions were used to normalize the varied number of applications submitted in different year.

Table 7.2 reveals a noticeably varied percentage of projects being funded from year to year. This was due to the fact that in some years more costly projects were funded and they consumed more of the finite budget allocation. There was a steady decrease in the number of applications submitted between 2001 and 2005, with a subsequent upturn in 2006. The upturn in 2006 resulted in a low percentage of projects being funded.

The total number of points a community received on their FCT application determined whether they were funded or not. The FCT application was structured in such a way that negative or "no" responses to questions resulted in zero points. Positive or "yes" responses resulted in the allocation of five points. Responses to all questions were recoded as a binary response (0,1) where 1 was assigned if any points were given and 0 if none. Only projects that were either funded or not funded were included in the analysis. Projects classified as either "withdrawn" or "ineligible" were excluded.

Funded communities gave a higher proportion of positive responses on almost all questions. This was expected because funding decisions are based on cumulative point totals; the more positive responses, the more points a prospective community earns. Table 7.3 provides the results of a test determining if statistically significant differences existed between funded and unfunded communities in the proportion of positive responses to public health significant questions. There were only four questions (1, 4, 8, 18) with no statistically significant difference between the funded and unfunded groups.

Question 1 determines if the project is connected to a sidewalk or will be within two years. This is important to increase pedestrian accessibility and safety, and a large proportion of both funded and unfunded applications provided a positive response to this question. Noting below that very few funded projects are located within built-up commercial or high density mixed use areas (Question 8), one may

Table 7.3 Differences in questions with public health significance between funded and unfunded groups

Question	Proportion Funded n=298	Proportion Unfunded n=319	Difference	σp	p
1*	0.61	0.67	-0.06	0.07	0.344
2	0.79	0.6	0.19	0.04	>0.001
3	0.95	0.74	0.21	0.03	>0.001
4	0.51	0.51	0	0.04	0.951
5	0.68	0.42	0.26	0.04	>0.001
6	0.86	0.77	0.09	0.03	0.003
7	0.73	0.6	0.13	0.04	0.001
8	0.26	0.25	0.01	0.04	0.824
9	0.87	0.64	0.23	0.03	>0.001
10	0.6	0.31	0.29	0.04	>0.001
11	0.6	0.22	0.38	0.04	>0.001
12	0.6	0.26	0.34	0.04	>0.001
13	0.59	0.41	0.18	0.04	>0.001
14	0.27	0.11	0.16	0.03	>0.001
15	0.11	0.05	0.06	0.02	0.005
16	0.85	0.66	0.19	0.03	>0.001
17	0.57	0.34	0.23	0.04	>0.001
18	0.02	0.03	-0.01	0.01	0.898
Mean	0.58	0.42	0.16	X	X

Note: *Question 1 appeared only in the 2005–06 year-group cycle (Unfunded n=126, Funded n=66).

conclude that many sidewalks are being built or are planned to be built into the many forms of lower density development.

Question 4 relates to the inclusion of recreation facilities in the proposed project. The results indicate that approximately half of the funded and unfunded applications included the provision of these facilities. Therefore, the inclusion of recreational facilities was not associated with a successful application, and the potential public health benefits of facilities that may attract users was not present. Three questions address the location of the proposed project in an urban area. Although it is promising that funded projects were more likely to be located in urban service areas (Question 6) and within ½ mile of a "… built-up commercial or high density mixed use area" (Question 7), it is somewhat discouraging that proposed projects were not incorporated within built-up commercial or high density mixed use areas (Question 8). It is possible that there were not many high density mixed use areas to locate these projects within. A failure to incorporate conserved spaces within built-up commercial areas is a missed opportunity to connect green infrastructure and provide utilitarian and recreational opportunities. Having both higher population density and land use mixture and connecting greenways to parks are important to maximize use for physical activity (Coutts, 2008, 2009).

Although there are 165 state designated brownfields in the state of Florida totaling almost 150,000 acres (Department of Environmental Protection, 2008), the results of Question 18 reveal that almost none of the applications, funded or unfunded, proposed reclaiming them.

Some other selected points of interest include:

- 95 percent of funded communities provided a positive response to Question 3 which asks if the proposed project includes recreational facilities such as trails, picnic pavilions, or campsites.
- There was a large difference between funded and unfunded communities in the cluster of Questions 9–12. Funded communities were much more likely to propose trails and greenways projects. This is promising to the creation of a green infrastructure system and the myriad public health benefits of establishing a sound landscape structure.
- The large difference between funded and unfunded applicants in Question 5 indicates that many more funded communities proposed providing access to a shoreline or beach. In Florida, waterfronts are year-round attractive public spaces.

Summary

The results indicate that the FCT is supporting public health. Communities funded by the FCT are providing positive responses to almost all of the FCT criteria with public health significance. Based on the positive responses to 2001–06 FCT application criteria, public health is being supported through open space acquisition in the following ways:

- Physical activity gained through nonmotorized recreational and/or utilitarian activity is supported by increasing pedestrian accessibility through acquisitions located ½ mile or closer to built-up commercial or high density areas.
- Creating trail and greenway systems provides opportunities for physical activity and contributes to the green infrastructure needed for ecological integrity and the filtering of ambient pollution. Recreation in green settings also provides psychological benefits.

- The creation of attractive public space that contains recreational facilities for active uses increases the potential for both spontaneous and organized social interaction.
- The quantity and quality of surface waters is protected and the percolation of water into aquifers is enhanced.
- The mitigation of potential hazards improves public safety by preventing injury and death.
- Supporting ecosystems by providing the landscape structure on which they depend reduces the likelihood of the deleterious effects of ecosystem collapse.

There is certainly room for optimism regarding the accomplishments of the FCT, but there are a handful of considerations which may further improve the public health impact of this program and possibly others like it:

- An explicit statement of the ecological and social benefits stated adjacent to application criteria would not only make the state's awareness of these benefits clear, but it may also be educational to the communities completing the FCT application.
- Giving public health significant questions more weight, to reward communities that satisfy multifaceted ecological and social goals, is more congruent with the FCT mission of considering both outdoor recreation and natural resource protection needs.
- A wider dispersal of funds to a larger number of smaller projects may have greater public health benefits. Large swaths of conserved land are undoubtedly important, but everyday nature connected to these hubs is also important. A larger number of smaller projects could bring these public facilities within closer proximity to where greater numbers of people live and work.

The environmental supports provided through land conservation are absolutely necessary, but not sufficient, to foster community health and well-being. A comprehensive health promotion framework is necessary which captures not only the environment but also the intra-and inter-personal, community, and policy levels of intervention (Green and Kreuter, 1999). Accepting that, it is still the natural environment and the ecosystems it supports which is the foundation to which all other levels of intervention should be subordinate (Coutts, 2010). "The state of one's environment is one of the most important determinants of health" (Cortese, 2004, p. 27), and protecting the environment is one of the most important public health challenges for the new century (Koplan and Fleming, 2000).

Health has a historically significant role in justifying planning actions (Shilling and Linton, 2005; Hebbert, 1999; Ashton and Ubido, 1991) and this relationship has recently undergone a rebirth (Frank and Kavage, 2008). What is not currently clear is if it still carries weight or has regained a legitimate place in the planning discourse when considering, for example, the extent and pattern of a state level open space system. Health might very well provide a justification for conservation, offering the humanistic impetus to increase public support—leading to political support—for green infrastructure projects. The health of our communities might become an indicator of how well we understand and subsequently protect the landscape on which we ourselves and ecosystems depend, making the benefits of conservation more tangible to the public at large and to legislators prioritizing projects.

It is through their influence on public health that ecosystem management and sustainability relate to comprehensive planning (DeGrove, 2005). The stated justification for growth management is to "preserve, promote, protect, and improve public health" and land conservation is integral to supporting health. Therefore, the protection of open space in growth management is necessary to achieve its stated goal.

Although conserved lands support the health of the public that governments are chartered to protect, local governments and developers have little incentive to create these spaces (Daniels and Lapping, 2005). Therefore, programs such as the Florida Communities Trust are essential to the conservation of public lands. Further, other departments and agencies receiving funds through the Florida Forever program, such as the Department of Environmental Protection and the state water management districts, can also aid conservation and support public health in various ways.

Finally, there is the issue of equity, as there are greater benefits to those nearer and having greater access to green spaces. The concept of green infrastructure overcomes this through its dispersion over the landscape, making it more likely that some part of the system will be proximal to more people. As a health promotion strategy, green infrastructure benefits everyone regionally and globally, although those persons closer and with greater access benefit more. A protected river corridor and cleaner water and air know no age, race, income, nationality, or ethnicity, as the benefits of local efforts are spread spatially. Most persons become free-riders to the health benefits of land conservation.

References

Aguirre, A., Ostfeld, R., Tabor, G., House, C. and Pearl, M. (eds) (2002) *Conservation Medicine: Ecological Health in Practice*. New York: Oxford University Press.

Alaimo, K., Bassett, E., Wilkerson, R., Smiley, M., Warbach, A., Hines, A. et al. (2006) *Design Guidelines for Active Michigan Communities.* Available at http://www.mihealthtools.org/communities (accessed 31 August 2007).

Arnold, C. and Gibbons, J. (1996) Impervious surface coverage: The emergence of a key environmental indicator. *Journal of the American Planning Association*, 62(2), 243–58.

Ashton, J. and Ubido, B. (1991) The healthy city and the ecologic idea. *Journal of the Society for the Social History of Medicine*, 41, 173–80.

Bealey, W.J., McDonald, A.G., Nemitz, E., Donovan, R., Dragosits, U., Duffy, T.R. et al. (2007) Estimating the reduction of urban PM10 concentrations by trees within an environmental information system for planners. *Journal of Environmental Management*, 85(1), 44–58.

Bedimo-Rung, A.L., Mowen, A.J., and Cohen, D.A. (2005) The significance of parks to physical activity and public health: A conceptual model. *American Journal of Preventive Medicine*, 28(2S2), 159–68.

Benedict, M.A. and McMahon, E. (2006) *Green Infrastructure: Linking Landscapes and Communities*. Washington, D.C.: Island Press.

Carriker, R. (2006) *Florida's Growth Management Act: An Introduction and Overview.* Available at http://edis.ifas.ufl.edu/FE643#FOOTNOTE_2 (accessed 14 July 2006).

CDC (2008). *Physical Activity and Health.* Available at http://www.cdc.gov/physicalactivity/everyone/health/index.html (accessed 14 August 2009).

Cohen, D., McKenzie, T., Sehgal, A., Williamson, S., Golinelli, D. and Lurie, N. (2007) Contribution of public parks to physical activity. *American Journal of Public Health*, 97(3), 509–14.

Coley, R., Sullivan, W. and Kuo, F. (1997) Where does community grow? The social context created by nature in urban public housing. *Environment and Behavior*, 29(4), 468–94.

Cornell University (2006) Value of services performed by insects tops $57 billion in United States. *Science Daily*. Available at http://www.sciencedaily.com/releases/2006/04/060401104604.htm (accessed 13 August 2009).

Cortese, A. (2004) Redesigning environmental health, in: K. Ausubel and J.P. Harpignies (eds) *Ecological Medicine: Healing the Earth, Healing Ourselves*, pp. 26–31. San Francisco: Sierra Club Books.

Coutts, C. (2008) Greenway accessibility and physical activity behavior. *Environment and Planning B: Planning and Design*, 35(3), 552–63.

Coutts, C. (2009) Locational influence of land use type on the distribution of uses along urban river greenways. *Urban Planning and Development*, 135(1), 31–8.

Coutts, C. (2010) Public health ecology. *Journal of Environmental Health*, 72(6), 53–5.

Cremer, J.T. (2009) Tractors versus bulldozers: Integrating growth management and ecosystem services to conserve agriculture. *Environmental Law Reporter*, 39(6), 10541–54.

Daniels, T. and Lapping, M. (2005) Land preservation: An essential ingredient in smart growth. *Journal of Planning Literature*, 19(3), 316–29.

DeGrove, J.M. (2005) *Planning Policy and Politics: Smart Growth and the States.* Cambridge, MA: Lincoln Institute of Land Policy.

Department of Environmental Protection. 2008. *Designated Brownfields Areas and Acreage*. Available at http://www.dep.state.fl.us/waste/quick_topics/publications/wc/brownfields/processes/Areas.pdf (accessed 11 January 2008).

Di Giulio, R.T., and Monosson, E. (eds) (1996) *Interconnections between Ecosystem and Human Health*. London: Chapman and Hall.

Dobson, A. and Carper, R. (1993) Biodiversity. *The Lancet*, 342(8879), 1096–99.

Duany, A., Plater-Zyberk, E. and Speck, J. (2000) *Suburban Nation*. New York: North Point Press.

Duhl, L.J. and Sanchez, A.K. (1999). *Healthy Cities and the City Planning Process: A Background Document on Links Between Health and Urban Planning*, WHO Publication No. EUR/ICP/CHDV 03 04 03. Copenhagen: WHO Regional Office for Europe.

Erickson, D. (2006). *MetroGreen: Connecting Open Space in North American Cities*. Washington D.C.: Island Press.

Florida Department of Community Affairs (n.d.) *What is Florida Communities Trust?* Available at http://www.floridacommunitydevelopment.org/fct/index.cfm (accessed 20 July 2006).

Florida Department of Community Affairs (2008) *Florida Communities Trust*. Available at http://www.floridacommunitydevelopment.org/fct/about.cfm (accessed 17 July 2008).

Florida Department of Environmental Protection (2007) *February 2007 Report of the Florida Forever Program, 2007 Florida Forever Five Year Plan*. Available at http://www.dep.state.fl.us/lands/FFAnnual/default.html (accessed 18 June 2006).

Forman, R.T. (1995) *Land Mosaics: The Ecology of Landscapes and Regions*. New York: Cambridge University Press.

Frank, L.D., Engelke, P.O. and Schmid, T.L. (2003) *Health and Community Design: The Impact of the Built Environment on Physical Activity*. Washington, D.C.: Island Press.

Frank, L. and Kavage, S. (2008) Urban planning and public health: A story of separation and reconnection. *Journal of Public Health Management Practice* 14(3), 214–20.

Frumkin, H., Hess, J., Luber, G., Malilay, J. and McGeehan, M. (2008) Climate change: The public health response. *American Journal of Public Health*, 98(3), 435–45.

Giles-Corti, B., Broomhall, M.H., Knuiman, M., Collins, C., Douglas, K., Ng, K. et al. (2005) Increasing walking: How important is distance to, attractiveness, and size of public open space? *American Journal of Preventive Medicine*, 28(2S2), 169–76.

Gill, S., Handley, J., Ennos, A. and Pauleit, S. (2007) Adapting cities for climate change: The role of the green infrastructure. *Built Environment*, 33(1), 115–133.

Green, L.W. and Kreuter, M.W. (1999) *Health Promotion Planning: An Educational and Ecological Approach*. Mountain View, CA: Mayfield.

Hebbert, M. (1999) A city in good shape: Town planning and public health. *Town Planning Review*, 70(4), 433–53.

Helmholtz Association of German Research Centres (2008) Economic value Of insect pollination worldwide estimated at U.S. $217 billion. *ScienceDaily.* Available at http://www.sciencedaily.com /releases/2008/09/080915122725.htm (accessed: 13 August 2009).

Honari, M. and Boleyn, T. (1999) *Health Ecology: Health, Culture, and Human-Environment Interaction.* London: Routledge.

Hough, M. (1994) Design with city nature: An overview of some issues, in: R. Platt, R. Rowntree and P. Muick (eds) *The Ecological City: Preserving and Protecting Urban Biodiversity*, pp. 40–8. Amherst, MA: The University of Massachusetts Press.

Jackson, R.J. and Kochtitzky, C. (2001) *Creating a Healthy Environment: The Impact of the Built Environment on Public Health.* Available at http://www.sprawlwatch.org/health.pdf (accessed 23 July 2002).

Kahn, E.B., Ramsey, L.T., Brownson, R.C., Heath, G.W., Howze, E.H., Powell, K.E., et al. (2002) The effectiveness of interventions to increase physical activity: A systematic review. *American Journal of Preventative Medicine* 22(4S), 73–107.

Kaplan, S. and Peterson, C. (1993) *Health and Environment: A Psychological Analysis.* Amsterdam: Elsevier Scientific Publishing Company.

Kellert, S.R. and Wilson, E.O. (1993) *The Biophilia Hypothesis.* Washington, D.C.: Island Press.

Kessel, A., Green, J., Pinder, R., Wilkinson, P., Grundy, C. and Lachowycz, K. (2009) Multidisciplinary research in public health: A case of research on access to green space. *Public Health*, 123, 32–8.

Koontz, F. and Daszak, P. (2005) Sprawl and disease, in: E. Johnson and M. Klemens (eds) *Nature in Fragments: The Legacy of Sprawl*, pp. 144–54. New York: Columbia University Press.

Koplan, J.P. and Fleming, D.W. (2000) Current and future public health challenges. *Journal of the American Medical Association*, 284(13), 1696–98.

Kuo, F.E., Sullivan, W.C., Coley, R.L. and Brunson, L. (1998) Fertile ground for community: Inner-city neighborhood common spaces. *American Journal of Community Psychology*, 26(6), 823–51.

Maas, J., Verheij, R.A., Groenewegen, P.P., de Vries, S. and Spreeuwenberg, P. (2006) Green space, urbanity, and health: How strong is the relation? *Journal of Epidemiology and Community Health*, 60(7), 587–92.

Maller, C., Townsend, M., Pryor, A., Brown, P., and St Leger, L. (2006) Healthy nature, healthy people: 'Contact with nature' as an upstream health promotion intervention for populations. *Health Promotion International*, 21(1), 45–54.

McCally, M. (2002) Environment, health, and risk, in: M. McCally (ed) *Life Support: The Environment and Human Health*, pp. 1–14. Cambridge, MA: MIT Press.

McHarg, I.L. (1992) *Design with Nature.* New York: J. Wiley.

McMichael, A.J., Woodruff, R. and Hales, S. (2006) Climate change and human health: Present and future risks. *The Lancet*, 367(9513), 859–69.

Metropolitan Design Center (2007) *Design for Health, General Health Issues*. Available at http://www.designforhealth.net/techassistance/generalhealthissues.html (accessed 19 June 2007).

Mitchell, R. and Popham, F. (2008) Effect exposure to natural environment on health inequalities: An observational population study. *The Lancet*, 372(9650), 1655–60.

NACCHO (2003) *Public Health in Land Use Planning and Community Design Checklist*. Available at http://archive.naccho.org/Documents/LandUseChecklist-03-10-03.pdf (accessed 14 June 2006).

National Environmental Health Association (n.d.) *Sustainability Library Resources*. Available at http://www.neha.org/sustainability/index.html [accessed 12 December 2008].

National Highway Traffic Safety Administration (2005) *Traffic Safety Facts*, Publication no. HS 810 624. Available at http://www-nrd.nhtsa.dot.gov/Pubs/810624.PDF (accessed 6 July 2006).

Nowak, D. and Crane, D. (2002) Carbon storage and sequestration by urban trees in the USA. *Environmental Pollution*, 116, 381–89.

Nowak, D., Crane, D. and Stevens, J. (2006) Air pollution removal by urban trees and shrubs in the United States. *Urban Forestry and Urban Greening*, 4, 115–23.

Patz, J., Githeko, A., McCarty, J., Hussain, S., Confalonieri, U. and de Wet, N. (2003) Climate change and infectious disease, in: A. McMichael, D. Campbell-Lendrum, C. Corvalán, K. Ebi, A. Githeko, J. Scheraga et al. (eds) *Climate Change and Human Health: Risks and Responses*, pp. 102–32. Geneva: World Health Organization.

Pope, C.A., Burnett, R.T., Thun, M.J., Calle, E.E., Krewski, D., Ito, K. et al. (2002) Lung cancer, cardiopulmonary mortality and long-term exposure to fine particulate air pollution. *Journal of the American Medical Association*, 287(9), 1132–41.

Ryder, B. (1995) Greenway planning and growth management: Partners in conservation? *Landscape and Urban Planning*, 33, 417–32.

Sallis, J., Bauman, A. and Pratt, M. (1998) Environmental and policy interventions to promote physical activity. *American Journal of Preventive Medicine*, 15(4), 379–97.

San Francisco Department of Public Health (2007) *Healthy Development Tool*. Available at: http://www.thehdmt.org/ (accessed 31 August 2007).

Slentz, C.A., Aiken, L.B., Houmard, J.A., Bales, C.W., Johnson, J.L., Tanner, C.J. et al. (2005) Inactivity, exercise, and visceral fat. STRRIDE: A randomized, controlled study of exercise intensity and amount. *Journal of Applied Physiology*, 99(4), 1613–18.

Shilling, J. and Linton, L. (2005) The public health roots of zoning: In search of active living's legal genealogy. *American Journal of Preventive Medicine*, 28(2S2), 96–104.

Tabor, G. (2002) Defining conservation medicine, in: A. Aguirre, R. Ostfeld, G. Tabor, C. House and M. Pearl (eds) *Conservation Medicine: Ecological Health in Practice*, pp. 8–16. New York: Oxford University Press.

Trust for Public Land (2006) *The Health Benefits of Parks: How Parks Help Keep Americans and their Communities Fit and Healthy*. Available at http://www.tpl.org/tier3_cd.cfm?content_item_id=21053&folder_id=175 (accessed 1 September 2007).

Tzoulas, K., Korpela, K., Venn, S., Yli-Pelkonen, V., Kaźmierczak, A., Niemela, J. et al. (2007) Promoting ecosystem and human health in urban areas using Green Infrastructure: A literature review. *Landscape and Urban Planning*, 81, 167–78.

de Vries, S., Verheij, R.A., Groenewegen, P.P. and Spreeuwenber, P. (2003) Natural environments—healthy environments: An exploratory analysis of the relationship between greenspace and health. *Environment and Planning A*, 35(10), 1717–31.

WHO (1948) *Preamble to the Constitution of the World Health Organization*. Available at http://www.who.int/about/definition/en/print.html (accessed 10 October 2004).

WHO (1986) *Ottawa Charter for Health Promotion*. Available at http://www.who.int/hpr/NPH/docs/ottawa_charter_hp.pdf (accessed 17 January 2008).

WHO (2005) *Ecosystems and Human Well-Being: Health Synthesis*. Available at http://www.who.int/globalchange/ecosystems/ecosys.pdf (accessed 19 February 2010).

WHO (2009) *Health Impact Assessment*. Available at http://www.who.int/hia/about/glos/en/index2.html (accessed 12 August 2009).

Wolonski, N. (1999). Human health as an ecological problem, in: M. Honari and T. Boleyn (eds) *Health Ecology: Health, Culture, and Human-Environment Interaction*, pp. 79–111. London: Routledge.

Chapter 8
The Role of Local Governments in Open Space Preservation and Land Acquisition in Florida

SeJin Lee and Richard C. Feiock

Introduction

The provision of local public goods has been a central focus of the urban political economy literature since Tiebout (1956) introduced the idea that governments compete for residents through provision of services, including environmental amenities such as open space (see also Schneider 1989, Peterson 1981). In contrast to traditional types of growth management controls that place regulatory restrictions on new development, open space preservation protects land from future development by the outright purchase of land or development rights. What are the political and policy implications of this approach? How does it differ from conventional growth management politics?

We begin to answer these questions by casting open space preservation efforts as the product of interactions among political actors in the context of local political institutions. Below we present a political market explanation (Feiock et al. 2010 Lubell et al. 2009) that conceptualizes open space acquisitions as the result of political decisions made within a set of formal political institutions.

We present a theoretical framework to investigate the choices of Florida counties and cities to supply environmental public goods in the form of land acquisitions for parks, recreation, and open space conservation. This allows us to bring insights from institutional and political economy theories to bear on the broader questions of local land use and the provision of environmental public goods. The important theoretical and empirical contribution of this chapter is to clarify the role of local political institutions in growth management and the local provision of environmental public goods by describing the political market for environmental public goods.

The Political Market

Provision of an intergenerational good such as open space is influenced by constituency demands and governmental incentives and commitment (Lowry

1998). The political market approach offers an integrated theoretical framework in which political institutions mediate the demands of private actors and the willingness of public officials to supply land use policies they desire (Lubell et al. 2009, Jeong 2006, Clingermayer and Feiock 2001). Policy choices are represented as an equilibrium resulting from the interplay between the aggregate demand for environmental goods by residents, businesses, environmental interest groups, and homeowners, and the aggregate supply of growth management by government officials (Lubell et al. 2009, Alston 1996). Local government institutions play a decisive role in organizing local land use decision making. Institutions operating at the local level determine the rules of the game, create incentives, and provide opportunities for collective action to bring about policy changes (Clingermayer and Feiock 2001).

The political market framework conceptualizes provision of environmental public goods as the result of a dynamic contracting process between the suppliers and demanders of policy change in a community (Lubell et al. 2005). As stated above, the demanders are the private interests in society, and the suppliers are the government authorities (Feiock 2004, Schneider 1989). Interest group demands are driven by local economic changes such as land scarcity. In return for political resources, elected officials will support land use policies that affect the utility of vested social interests. Local government institutions constitute the arena in which political contracting occurs. Political institutions combine with the structure of interest organizations and the economics of land use to influence policy outcomes. Different types of political institutions favor different types of interests, either enhancing or reducing the ability of interests to influence land use policy. In other words, the structure of local political institutions determines the winners and losers.

This political market framework builds upon three distinct traditions: a consideration of local politics, the urban growth machine, and progressive reform and political institutions. The first tradition extends contemporary theories of local politics and governance that focus on property rights and the role of political processes and institutions in aggregating individual and group preferences. The second tradition, the growth machine perspective, intersects planning and political science by focusing on the political economy of growth and land use decisions. The third tradition is derived from the study of the Progressive reform movement of the early 20th century and the institutional reforms in government structure that it produced (Ruhil 2003, Schneider 1989, Ostrom, Bish, and Ostrom 1988, Lineberry and Fowler 1967). We describe how the political market integrates these traditions before examining the efforts of Florida local governments to conserve land through the Florida Community Trust.

Environmental Demands and Local Politics

Citizen and interest group support for the provision of environmental public goods emerges from scarcity and the overconsumption of common-pool resources (Lubell et al. 2005, Libecap 1989). Land is a common-pool resource for local communities, and as land becomes scarce, there are Pareto benefits to open space preservation that protects environmental values. The benefits of environmental public goods are related primarily to the extent to which existing growth patterns increase the scarcity of local land and infrastructure resources (Lewis and Neiman 2002, Steinacker 1998). As growth pressures intensify, so do demands for policies that preserve environmental resources. Thus, we expect measures of land scarcity, sprawl, and population pressure to be positively related to demands for open space preservation.

Population growth patterns have been linked to open space preservation as well as to growth controls more generally. Several studies report a positive relationship between patterns of community growth or growth rates and support for growth controls (Anglin 1990, Protash and Baldassare 1983, Baldassare and Protash 1982). Howell-Moroney (2004) examines taxes and bonds for open space preservation in the Philadelphia area and reports that population growth predicts open space preservation efforts.

Efforts to restrict development or provide environmental public goods sometimes pit high and low SES populations against each other. The literature has sometimes described growth management as exclusionary, elitist, and status-biased (Navarro and Carson 1991). Like growth controls more generally, open space preservation has been linked to income and community social status. Romero and Liserio's investigation of open space preservation finds that community status is a significant predictor of open space preservation votes: The "smaller, wealthier and whiter areas were the most likely to include openspace preservation measures" (Romero and Liserio, 2002: 343). Howell-Moroney (2004) also reports a positive relationship between community status measures and adoptions of open space taxes or bonds.

High social status communities may support growth controls in order to exclude lower income groups (Feiock 2004, Maser, Riker, and Rosett 1977). Low income populations also tend to be less concerned with environmental amenities not because minority and low SES populations do not prefer environmental policies, but instead because they lack political resources to articulate political demand (Ihlanfeldt 2004, Lubell et al. 2002, Pendall 2000, Danielson 1976). Recent work stresses the fact that some interests are better at organizing for collective action, and therefore better able to articulate policy preferences and participate in political decision making. Hence, the relative political powers of the demanders and the willingness of government authorities to supply favorable policies to various interests are each important. Groups that are better able to deliver political resources to local elected officials are more likely to receive their preferred policies, but public entrepreneurs can sometimes mobilize diffuse public interests to influence public decisions (Lewis and Neiman 2002, Elkins 1995, Goetz 1990, 1994). Generally, interest group models have a pluralist perspective that views policy change as a result of group competition.

We expect community characteristics such as wealth, education, and race to influence the demand for environmental public goods. If the politics of open space preservation is similar to that of growth controls more generally, high socioeconomic status communities may use environmental amenities to increase surrounding land values and create barriers to entry for lower SES groups (Navarro and Carson 1991). Higher income and education groups also tend to place higher value on protection of the natural environment and join environmental groups (Dunlap and Mertig 1992). Thus, we expect greater open space land acquisition in communities with higher per capita personal income and educational attainment levels. We also expect race may be a predictor of open space preservation because minority populations are often environmentally disadvantaged (Lubell et al. 2002).

The Urban Growth Machine

A second perspective sees land use decision making as a growth machine controlled by a political alliance between local government officials and development interests (Logan and Molotch 1987). Development interests have the upper hand in local politics because they receive concentrated benefits for pro-development policies and are well organized. Environmental interests on the other hand tend to be fragmented. The literature portrays environmental interests as a diffuse, unorganized constituency that favors some general form of environmental protection (Lubell et al.2002).

Thirty years ago, Harvey Molotch (1976) drew attention to the role of development interest groups in local arenas and their efforts to capture the benefits and avoid the costs of local growth. According to this perspective, private actors, such as local real estate and construction interests, use their political power to influence the costs and benefits of growth (Logan and Molotch 1987, Vogel and Swanson 1989). Political institutions are largely not transparent in the underlying demands driving land use policy in the urban politics and political economy literatures. This is a critical oversight because political institutions are crucial mediators of political and economic demands (Clingermayer and Feiock 2001).

Economic and development interests have a substantial stake in land use decisions. Development interests are often organized and well financed, making them powerful articulators of political demand. These characteristics give development interests an advantage in translating their preferences into policy. Another advantage that business interests possess is their perceived importance to local economies (Schneider 1989). A number of studies suggest a substantial degree of cooperation between business and public officials (Stone 1989, Fleischmann 1986). The growth machine perspective often portrays local policy regimes as an alliance between government officials and interest groups from the development and real estate/finance industries.

Environmental interests may come together and be organized on a geographic basis. Many such interests are territorial groups with links to a specific location (Lubell et al. 2005). These groups are often main players in Not-In-My-Backyard politics, and include neighborhood organizations, homeowners associations, and citizen activists located within geographically defined constituencies. These groups resist locally unwanted land uses or clamor for environmental amenities like parks and open space in their neighborhoods.

Development interests, on the other hand, tend to be defined along functional or occupational lines. Such groups might include developers, realtors, contractors, construction trade unions, and financial institutions. Occupationally organized interests seek economic opportunities across the entire community, and are less concerned with a particular location. Geographically-based environmental interests may not be able to compete in the political market with well-organized development interests unless political entrepreneurs help environmental interests mobilize (Clingermayer and Feiock 2001).

Progressive Reform and Political Institutions

Political institutions determine the rules and procedures for making collective choices (Clingermayer and Feiock 2001). Form of government plays an important role by enhancing public managers' credibility in collaborative settings and by reducing uncertainty (Smith 2009, Feiock, Jeong, and Kim 2003). Institutional influences on fiscal policy outcomes have been the subject of many empirical studies over the last forty years. Although consensus is still lacking, most report that differences in form of government lead to differences in policy outputs (Clingermayer and Feiock 2001, Morgan and Kickham 1999, DeSantis and Renner 1994, Lineberry and Fowler 1967). Recent work highlights the role of local government institutions in shaping growth management decisions (Jeong 2006, Lubell et al. 2005).

The reform movement of the early 20th century brought about significant changes in local government institutions. Reformers centralized executive leadership at the city and county levels, allowing local governments to respond more efficaciously to the service needs of rapidly growing populations (Benton 2002). At the city level, the goal of reform was to increase the efficiency, professionalism, and technical competence of local government administration (Morgan 1997). Reformers wanted to achieve the separation of powers and the insulation of the administration from undue interference by elected officials, while simultaneously guaranteeing that it was subject to democratic control (Svara 1998). The creation of the council-manager form of government was a response to this need to centralize executive authority and insulate public decisions from partisan politics and interest group pressures.

Government reform followed a different path in county governments where the commission form of government without executive authority predominated (DeSantis and Renner 1994). Reformed or modernized counties opted for either commission-administrator or commission-elected executive forms that provided separation of powers and greater executive authority (Benton 2002). Professional county administration has been linked to greater emphasis on the role of local land use planning and provision of environmental public goods (Benton and Feiock 2008, Feiock 2004).

Both executive and legislative institutions shape the responsiveness of land use policy to environmental pressures and interests (Hinds and Ordway 1986, Denzau and Weingast 1982, Maser, Riker, and Rosett 1977). The structure of the executive branch defined in a city or county charter affects incentives to supply environmental public goods (Feiock 2004, Feiock and Taveras 2002, Schneider and Teske 1993). Two alternatives hypotheses have been advanced regarding the role of appointed managers in environmental and land use decisions (Lubell et al. 2009). The insulation hypothesis argues that city and county managers are insulated from citizen pressures and environmental interests and thus promote efficiency and economic development over provision of environmental amenities.

In contrast, the planning hypothesis states that the professional socialization of managers in council-manager government systems makes them more sensitive to environmental, growth management, and sustainable development concerns, leading to conservation measures and the provision of environmental public goods (see Lubell et al. 2005). Professional local government managers are frequently trained in public administration and planning programs where they learn the skills necessary to operate within the political environment and to distance themselves from partisanship (Renner 2001). About 60 percent of city managers hold master's degrees in such fields as public or business administration, policy, or planning (Renner 2001). In theory, professional managers are less risk averse and are able to transcend the political transactions engaged in by elected officials. Thus they can afford to invest in policies with longer term benefits such as environmental protection and preservation Zhang 2007, Nalbandian 1989).

Legislative reforms focused on creating a small legislative body, typically consisting of only five members, and structuring representation on an at-large rather than district basis.

While a small body may reduce bargaining and decision costs, it may also be a barrier to the representation of diffuse and organized interests (Feiock et al. 2008). Cooter (2000) argues that representatives have better information and better represent constituents' preferences as the size of the body increases. Similarly, at-large representation has been generally linked to responsiveness to business and economic interests over citizen and neighborhood interests (Clingermayer and Feiock 2001).

Application of the Political Market to Open Space Conservation

This section describes the Florida Communities Trust (FCT) land acquisition grant program and examines city and county government efforts to preserve open space through FCT-funded acquisitions from 2001 through 2007. We investigated the characteristics of city and county governments submitting applications for matching funds for open space preservation. The social, economic, and political attributes of local governments seeking open space preservation grants were then compared to attributes of governments that did not seek these grants.

Florida's statewide land acquisition programs, Preservation 2000 and Florida Forever, have been phenomenal successes in terms of acquiring land and protecting open space. Although scaled back enormously in 2009, the programs bonded $300 million each year between 1990 and 2008 and a dedicated revenue source for debt service is provided by a documentary stamp tax. Over 2 million acres of environmentally important lands in Florida have been acquired. Florida Forever is recognized as the largest land acquisition program in the country. Its success has focused popular and scholarly attention on the large-scale state land acquisitions it has supported. Much less attention has been given to the small-scale open space preservation activities funded by FCT and the roles of local governments in managing and preserving public land.

FCT provides funds for acquisition of community-based parks, open space, and greenways that further outdoor recreation and natural resource protection needs identified in local government comprehensive plans. Annually, 22 percent of the revenue ($66 million) funds the Florida Communities Trust (FCT) were directed to small-scale local grants. The 1985 State Growth Management Act requires every city and county to create and update a comprehensive growth management plan to guide land use decisions. The plan provides a legally binding constraint on development decisions because local zoning codes, land development regulations, and permit decisions must conform to the provisions and designations of the plan. The plan must contain certain elements, including a conservation element. The Florida Statutes prescribe a conservation element as follows:

> *(d) A conservation element for the conservation, use, and protection of natural resources in the area, including air, water, water recharge areas, wetlands, waterwells, estuarine marshes, soils, beaches, shores, flood plains, rivers, bays, lakes, harbors, forests, fisheries and wildlife, marine habitat, minerals, and other natural and environmental resources* (Growth Policy; County and Municipal Planning; Land Development Regulation, Fla. Stat. § 163.3177(6)(d)).

The Trust for Public Lands reports that about 70 percent of its work in Florida is with local governments. State funding for these local land acquisitions is through FCT grants. Projects must address needs that are identified in the local government comprehensive plan and the program has emphasized funding projects in low income or otherwise disadvantaged communities and built-up urban areas.

The FCT requires local matching funds. Counties with populations greater than 75,000 and municipalities with populations greater than 10,000 are required to provide a minimum match of 25 percent of the total project cost. However, small counties and cities that are under these thresholds, and eligible nonprofit environmental organizations, may apply for a 100 percent grant award.

Table 8.1 Land acquisition applications by jurisdiction

	Cities	Counties	Total
Number of Applications	2.59	5.91	3.32
Number Pre-Acquired	.61	2.28	1.00
Average Acres	.96	1.00	.97
Average Local Match	.76	.81	.77

Florida provides an ideal research setting for studying the provision of environmental public goods through open space acquisition. We first examined the characteristics of the proposed land acquisitions by local governments participating in the FCT program. While only 140 cities applied to the program, the majority of counties (43) participated and 15 had multiple applications.

Table 8.1 compares the characteristics of the submitted land acquisition applications by cities and counties. Counties not only submitted a greater average number of applications, they were more likely to pre-acquire the land. While the average acreage was almost the same, counties had a higher local match.

Data and Measures

The descriptive analysis presented above provides new insight into how land acquisition functions as a growth management tool by identifying the type of lands that local governments target for conservation and how these acquisitions are linked to comprehensive planning goals. We next applied the political market framework to determine if the same political forces that affect regulatory approaches to growth management influence local land acquisition choices.

Local government open space preservation efforts were measured by applications for land acquisition grant support from the Florida Communities Trust. Measures for most of the independent variables are available from U.S Census Bureau products, primarily the 2000 Population Census and the annual County Business Patterns series. These were collected for all cities and counties submitting applications from 2001 through 2007. From the 2000 Population Census, we measured proportion of the county population that is black, proportion with at least some college education, and median income. We assumed that local governments with higher socioeconomic status are both more likely to express environmental preferences and better able to absorb the transaction costs of political participation. Growth machine interests were measured by the proportion of business establishments in the jurisdiction in construction and real estate at the county level from County Business Patterns and aggregated to the city level from Zip Code Business Patterns. Environmental support was gauged by the amount of environmental specialty license tag revenues per capita in each county.

Data on local government political institutions were collected in five stages. First, information on form of government and provisions for appointed manger

Table 8.2 Comparisons of governments with and without land acquisition applications

	Land Acquisition Application	
	No	**Yes**
Number of Counties	23	43
Number of Cities	268	140
Percent White	73.08	74.66
Percent Black	14.73	13.34
Percent Hispanic	9.78	10.50
Percent College Degree	20.46	22.63
Percent below Poverty	15.14	12.86
Population Change 2000–2006	2154.71	8996.61
Population 2000	15599.94	67656.36
Land Area in acre mile	51.83	184.70
Population Density	1931.84	2200.25
Median Income	39757.19	38653.45
Median Housing Value	112749.7	102381.4
Mayor Council	106	30
Manager Council	163	143
Commission	13	6
Total Number of Council Seats	5.14	5.49
Proportion Seats Elected by District	.1469	2913

positions were collected for all Florida cities from directories of the Florida League of Cities. Second, charter provisions regarding mayoral powers, district and at-large council representation, and direct democracy provisions were recorded for the Florida respondents to the International City Managers Association's 2001 Form of Government survey. Third, online charter documents available from the Municipal Code Corporation were used to identify powers and provisions for cities and counties that did not respond to the ICMA survey. Fourth, the city and county clerks for the jurisdictions were contacted to complete the data set for any remaining missing information. Finally, we had staff at the Florida League of Cities and Florida Center for Excellence in City Management review the accuracy of our coding based on their understanding of the structure of these cities.

We first explored differences between jurisdictions that engage in conservation land acquisition and those that do not. Table 8.2 provides comparisons of governments with and without land acquisition efforts. While racial composition was similar, areas pursuing land acquisition had a slightly higher proportion of the population with a college degree. Jurisdictions pursuing land acquisition were much larger in population and land area, more densely populated, and experienced more rapid growth since 2000. Form of government made a substantial difference. Jurisdictions with council-manager forms of government were much more likely to

Table 8.3 Logit regression of FCT land acquisitions

Variables	Coefficient	Std. Error
Population	**-659*****	.121
Population Change	-.016	.009
Land Area	.004	.002
Open Space Area	.007	.059
Non-Hispanic White	-.000	.006
College Degree	**.021***	.012
Proportion below Poverty	.022	.043
Median Income	.507	.891
Median Housing Value	-.450	.507
Environmental Tag Revenue (ETR)	**.722****	.320
Construction Industry	-1.610	2.23
Real Estate Industry	4.055	3.67
Municipal Government	**-1.277*****	.202
Council Manager Government	**.687*****	.257
Total Number of Council Seats	**.181*****	.045
Proportion of Seats elected by Districts	.101	.191
LR chi^2	80.48	
McFadden's R^2	.119	
Observations	437	
Zero Observations	171	

participate in land acquisition than jurisdictions with mayor-council or commission forms. District representation was also associated with land acquisitions.

We next estimated a logit model to predict the likelihood that a Florida government unit would submit an FCT application, based on the demand and supply factors suggested by the political market framework.

Findings

The likelihood of land acquisition applications was estimated based on population, land characteristics, demographics, and political institutions. The results provide strong support for several of the hypothesized relationships. Land acquisition activities were the product of environmental demands and local political institutions. These results are reported in Table 8.3.

Based on Table 8.3, decreased population reduces the likelihood of land acquisition. Except for college degree, the community SES indicators and exclusion preferences, as indicated by demographic variables, were unrelated to open space conservation. Environmental interests, as indicated by per capita revenue from environmental license tag sales, had a positive relationship with open space acquisition efforts. Construction and real-estate interests did not have any significant influence.

Some of the strongest effects relate to form of government and political institutions. Cities were less likely to engage in land acquisition than counties, and local governments with council-manager governments were more active. The size of the council also had a significant effect. As council size increased, it became more likely that land acquisition efforts were undertaken. District representation, on the other hand, had little effect.

Conclusions

This chapter introduced a political market framework to investigate the choices of Florida counties and cities to supply environmental public goods in the form of land acquisitions for parks, recreation, and open space conservation. The theoretical contribution this makes is to enhance understanding of the role of local political institutions in growth management and the local provision of environmental public goods.

The voluntary nature of open space preservation contrasts with traditional types of growth controls such as zoning or subdivision/land development regulations which rely on coercive regulatory mechanisms to restrict new development. Open space preservation restricts new development by the purchase of land or development rights, not coercion. Because extant work has applied the political market framework to explain regulatory approaches to land use policy, we have a unique opportunity to compare the politics of these two policy approaches.

While the statistical model is almost certainly underspecified, the results provide important insights for understanding the politics of growth management. Open space acquisition has been seen as fundamentally different from other local growth control efforts because it relies on voluntary mechanisms rather than the coercive force of regulatory restrictions, and the configuration of actors and interests involved is different. The empirical analysis presented here finds the politics of open space preservation shares some, but not all, of the characteristics of growth regulation. For instance, population and population growth are important drivers of growth control in general, but open space preservation is not confined to high SES communities. We also find that environmental interests are more important than development interests. Counties are more important players than cities in open preservation, and the structure of local political institutions makes a substantial difference. Professional managers and larger councils appear to insulate local government from pro-growth pressures and facilitate open space preservation.

The analysis demonstrates the usefulness of a political market approach that integrates urban politics and political economy perspectives into the structure of local political institutions. We find that open space preservation efforts are generally consistent with local comprehensive plan goals and that the structure of local political systems influences the level of land acquisition activity. Local political institutions matter by shaping the dynamics of the political market. We also find that rapid growth stimulates demand for land conservation, and both council-manager government and larger council size increase the frequency of conservation efforts. This influence of professional managers is consistent with the planning hypothesis. The finding that larger council size increases the provision of environmental public goods is consistent with recent evidence that the vast majority of cities are below the optimal sized council which would best represent community preferences (Feiock et al. 2008).

Where open space preservation most differs from land use regulation is the lack of influence exerted by development or growth machine interests. We do not find that construction and real estate constituencies reduce growth management. Perhaps this is because open space preservation relies on market mechanisms to achieve its goals. Additionally, the provision of environmental public goods can enhance surrounding land values in ways that benefit these pro-growth groups. On the other hand, the scope of environmental conservation constituencies, as indicated by environmentally themed specialty license tag revenues, has the predicted positive influence on open space preservation. While this is similar to growth regulation generally, the positive effects found here are especially strong.

Overall, the findings and methodologies in this chapter are viewed as the initial step in establishing a research agenda on the role of formal and informal institutions in the supply of environmental public goods. Future work can build upon this foundation to investigate the link between open space preservation and regulatory approaches to growth control taken by Florida local governments. Future research should also explore non-additive relationships between institutions and interest group demands. The political market framework (Feiock and Lubell forthcoming) suggests that institutions mediate the influence of group demands.

References

Alston, L.J. 1996. Empirical work in institutional economics: An overview, in *Empirical Studies in Institutional Change*, edited by L.J. Alston, T. Eggertsson, and D.C. North. Cambridge: Cambridge University Press, 25–30.

Anglin, R. 1990. Diminishing utility: Effects on citizen preferences for local growth. *Urban Affairs Quarterly*, 25, 684–96.

Baldassare, M. and W. Protash. 1982. Growth controls, population growth, and community satisfaction. *American Sociological Review*, 47, 339–46.

Benton, J.E. and Feiock, R.C. 2008. Local governments in Florida: Institutions of local governance and service delivery Agents, in J. Edwin Benton (ed.), *Government and Politics in Florida,* Gainesville, FL: University Press of Florida, 240–64.

Benton, J.E. 2002. County service delivery: Does government structure matter? *Public Administration Review*, 62(4), 471–9.

Clingermayer, J.C. and Feiock, R.C. 2001. *Institutional Constraints and Local Policy Choices: An Exploration of Local Governance*.Albany: State University of New York Press.

Cooter, R. 2000. *The Strategic Constitution*. Princeton, NJ: Princeton University Press.

Danielson, M. 1976. *The Politics of Exclusion*. New York, NY: Columbia University Press.

Denzau, A.T. and Weingast, B.R. 1982. The political economy of land use regulation. *Urban Law Annual*, 23, 385–405.

DeSantis, V. and Renner, T. 1994. The impact of political structures on public policies in American counties. *Public Administration Review*, 54(3), 291–5.

Elkins, D. 1995. Testing competing explanations for the adoption of type II polices. *Urban Affairs Quarterly*, 30, 809–39.

Feiock, R.C. 2004. Politics, institutions and local land-use regulation. *Urban Studies*, 41(2), 363–77.

Feiock, R.C., Jeong, M. and Kim, J. 2003. Credible commitment and council-manager government: Implications for policy instrument choices. *Public Administration Review*, 63(5), 616–25.

Feiock, R.C., Lubell, M. and Lee, I. 2010. The political market framework: Property rights, interest groups and institutions. working paper.

Feiock, R.C. and Taveras, A.F. 2002. County government institutions and local regulation in *Analysis of Local Markets and the Impact of Market Regulations*. Paul Cheshire and Stephen Sheppard (eds.) Cambridge: Lincoln Land Institute.

Feiock R.C., Ihlanfeldt K. and McDonald L. 2008.Housing values and the density of political representation at the local level. Paper presented at the annual meeting of the Midwest political science association, Chicago, April 19, 2008.

Fleischmann, A. 1986. The goals and strategies of local boundary changes: Government organization or private gain. *Journal of Urban Affairs*, 4, 63–75.

Goetz, E. 1990. Type II policy and mandated benefits in economic development. *Urban Affairs Quarterly*, 26(2), 170–90.

Goetz, E. 1994. Expanding possibilities in local development policy: An examination of U.S. cities. *Political Research Quarterly*, 47(1), 85–110.

Growth Policy; County and Municipal Planning; Land Development Regulation, Fla. Stat. §§ 163.2511–3247. 2008. [Online: Online Sunshine]. Available at: http://www.leg.state.fl.us/STATUTES/index.cfm?App_mode=Display_Statute&URL=Ch0163/part02.htm&StatuteYear=2009&Title=%2D%3E2009%2D%3EChapter%20163%2D%3EPart%20II [accessed 10 March 2010].

Hinds, D.S. and Ordway, N. 1986. The influence of race on rezoning decisions: Equality of treatment in black and white census tracts, 1955–1980. *The Review of Black Political Economy*, 14(4), 51–63.

Howel-Moroney, M. 2004. Community characteristics, open space preservation and regionalism: Is there a connection? *Journal of Urban Affairs*, 26(1), 109–18.

Ihlanfeldt, K. 2004. Exclusionary land-use: Regulations within suburban communities: A review of evidence and policy prescriptions. *Urban Studies*, 41(2), 261–83.

Jeong, M. 2006. Local choices for development impact fees. *Urban Affairs Review*, 41(3), 338–57.

Lewis P. and Neiman, M. 2002. *Cities Under Pressure: Local Growth Controls and Residential Development Policy.* San Francisco: Public Policy Institute of California.

Libecap, G. 1989. *Contracting for Property Rights*. New York: Cambridge University Press.

Lineberry, R.L. and Fowler, E. 1967. Reformism and public policy in American cities. *American Political Science Review*, 61, 701–15.

Logan, J. and Molotch, H. 1987. *Urban Fortunes: The Political Economy of Place.* Berkeley: University of California Press.

Lowry, W.R. 1998. *Preserving Public Lands for the Future: The Politics of Intergenerational Goods*. Washington, D.C.: Brookings Institution Press.

Lubell, M., Feiock, R.C. and Ramirez, R. 2005. Political institutions and conservation by local governments. *Urban Affairs Review*, 40(6), 706–29.

Lubell, M., Feiock, R.C., and Ramirez, R. 2009. Local institutions and the politics of urban growth. *American Journal of Political Science*, 53(3), 649–65.

Lubell, M., Schneider, M., Scholz, J., and Mete, M. 2002. Watershed partnerships and the emergence of collective action institutions. *American Journal of Political Science*, 46(1), 148–63.

Maser, S., Riker, W., and Rosett, R. 1977. The effects of zoning and externalities on the price of land: An empirical analysis of Monroe County, New York. *Journal of Law and Economics*, 20, 111–32.

Molotch, H.L. 1976. The city as a growth machine: Toward a political economy of place. *American Journal of Sociology*, 86, 1387–400.

Morgan, D. 1997. Structural arrangements in local government: Organizing for effective management. In *Handbook of Local Government Administration*, ed. J.J. Gargan. New York: Marcel Dekker, Inc., 129–58.

Morgan, D. and Kickham, K. 1999. Changing the form of county government: Effects on revenue and expenditure policy. *Public Administration Review*, 59(4), 315–24.

Nalbandian, J. 1989. The contemporary role of city managers. *American Review of Public Administration*, 19, 261–77.

Navarro, P. and Carson, R. 1991. Growth controls: Policy analysis for the second Generation. *Policy Sciences*, 24, 127–52.

Ostrom, V., Bish, R.L., and Ostrom, E. 1988. *Local Government in the United States*.San Francisco: Institute for Contemporary Studies Press.

Paul, P.E. 1981. *City Limits*. Chicago: University of Chicago Press.

Pendall, R. 2000. Local land-use regulation and the chain of exclusion. *Journal of the American Planning Association*, 66(2), 125–42.

Protash, W. and Baldassare, M. 1983. Growth policies and community status. *Urban Affairs Quarterly*, 18, 397–412.

Renner, T. 2001. The local government management profession at century's end, in *The Municipal Yearbook*. Washington, D.C.: ICMA Press, 35–46.

Romero, F. and Liserio, A. 2002. Saving open spaces: Determinants of 1998 and 1999 "antisprawl" ballot measures. *Social Science Quarterly*, 83(1), 341–52.

Ruhil, A.V.S. 2003. Structural change and fiscal flows: A framework for analyzing the effect of urban events. *Urban Affairs Review*, 38, 396–414.

Svara, J.H. 1998. The politics-administration dichotomy model as aberration. *Public Administration Review*, 58(1), 51–8.

Schneider, M. 1989. *The Competitive City: The Political Economy of Suburbia.* Pittsburgh, PA: University of Pittsburgh Press.

Schneider, M. and Teske, P. 1993. The antigrowth entrepreneur: Challenging the "equilibrium" of the growth machine. *The Journal of Politics*, 55(3), 720–36.

Smith, C.R. 2009. Institutional determinants of collaboration: An empirical study of county open-space protection. *Journal of Public Administration Research and Theory*, 19, 1–21.

Steinacker, A. 1998. Economic restructuring of cities, suburbs, and non-metropolitan areas, 1977–1992. *Urban Affairs Review*, 34, 212–40.

Stone, C.N. 1989. *Regime Politics: Governing Atlanta 1946–1988*. Lawrence: University of Kansas Press.

Tiebout, C. 1956. A pure theory of local expenditures. *Journal of Political Economy*, 64, 416–24.

Vogel, R. and Swanson, B. 1989. The growth machine versus the anti-growth coalition. *Urban Affairs Quarterly*, *25*, 63–85.

Zang. Y. 2007. *Local Official's Incentives and Policy-Making: Through the Lens of the Politics-Administration Relationship*. Ph.D. Dissertation, Florida State University.

Chapter 9

Understanding Public Support for Land Acquisition and Growth Management: The Case of Florida

Timothy S. Chapin

Fundamental to the long-term success of any initiative to link growth management efforts and public land acquisition programs is the support of the state's citizens. The purchase of environmentally sensitive lands requires extensive public sector resources that usually come from taxes or fees. A lack of broad public support can hinder, if not terminate, any program aimed at protecting environmentally sensitive lands through the acquisition of land (or of development rights) by the public sector. Similarly, the management of growth typically requires the public sector to regulate the location, timing, and form of development, an activity that cannot succeed without public support for developing and implementing land use regulations and growth management processes.

To date there has been some scholarly attention paid to the issue of citizen support for growth management and environmental protection. This work has identified several factors that influence citizen attitudes on these issues, including income levels, demographics, and political orientation. However, no study has yet assessed whether citizen support for land conservation and for growth management emanates from the same base. Instead, studies typically treat these as related, but fundamentally different issues. Consequently there is little understanding of the amount and form of the overlap in support for these initiatives within the citizenry.

Given this, the question driving the work in this chapter can be summarized as: *Are the coalitions supportive of land conservation and growth management based in the same subsets of the population?* To answer this question survey data from Florida on citizen support for spending for environmental programs and citizen support for managing growth are analyzed. This work is intended to determine the level of support for these initiatives within subsets of the population, with particular attention paid to the amount of overlap in support across these subgroups.

The evidence indicates that the bases of support for growth management and for environmental programs overlap in some ways, but with key differences. Growth management finds greater support among whites, homeowners, and individuals in higher socioeconomic classes. In contrast, environmental programs receive greater support from a more traditionally politically liberal base, which includes blacks, younger adults, females, and renters.

Following this introduction, the chapter begins with a brief overview of the Florida context, demonstrating the state's long commitment to both growth management and land conservation. The following section briefly reviews the literature on citizen attitudes towards environmental and growth management issues, highlighting those factors that have been found to influence these attitudes. The chapter then turns to the empirical work, summarizing the data and methods employed and then laying out the results from the analyses. A final section summarizes the key findings of this work and identifies their possible implications.

The Florida Context

The state of Florida has a long history of innovative policy in the areas of environmental conservation and growth management. In terms of land conservation, Florida has several decades of investment in well-supported, successful programs for purchasing environmentally sensitive lands (McLeod this volume; Higgins and Paradise, 2007). Early examples of this commitment to land conservation include Land Conservation Act funding passed by the Legislature in 1972 and The Conservation and Recreational Lands Trust Fund established in 1979. In 1990, a ten year, $3 billion program called Preservation 2000 placed Florida at the forefront of state efforts to purchase sensitive lands. More recently in 2000 the Legislature reauthorized this program, renamed Florida Forever, allocating another $3 billion in state revenues for land acquisition. Florida Forever had been passed overwhelmingly by voters in 1998, with support from 72 percent of the electorate. These four programs, which total over $7 billion in current dollars, have preserved over 2.5 million acres of land in the state. McLeod's chapter (this volume) details the great successes of the Preservation 2000 and Florida Forever programs, but also documents the recent and long-term fiscal and programmatic challenges to land conservation efforts in the state.

Beyond these state-level efforts at land conservation, local governments in Florida have also shown substantial commitment to design and fund local land conservation programs. Data obtained from The Nature Conservancy reveals that since the mid-1980s at least 28 counties have passed local referenda to support the acquisition of environmentally sensitive lands, provide parks and open spaces, and/or protect active farmlands. The total amount of funding authorized by these local referenda comes in at over $2 billion. Most of these counties are located in the peninsula, in more urbanized areas of central and south Florida and not in the traditionally more politically conservative panhandle.

In addition to a lengthy history with land conservation, Florida also has almost forty years invested in state-led growth management efforts. While state-level growth management efforts began back in the early 1970s, most notable in Florida's growth management history was the passage of the 1985 Growth Management Act (GMA). The GMA has been termed a near perfect version of the planning profession's comprehensive planning model (Chapin, Connerly, and Higgins 2007), placing comprehensive planning and the planning process at the core of all local, regional, and state land use decisions. As originally called for in the GMA, every local government must prepare a comprehensive plan to guide development in the near and medium terms, up to twenty years into the future. These plans are to be implemented by local governments through land development regulations that *must* reflect the long-term vision laid out in these plans. Unlike other states, in Florida there is a strong state role in the review of these plans and any changes to them, activities undertaken by the Florida Department of Community Affairs (Pelham 2007).

Although in many ways a landmark piece of legislation, Florida's Growth Management Act has not been without its problems. Initially heralded around the country as one of the most comprehensive and potentially most effective attempts at managing growth, this system has experienced only mixed success (Chapin and Ihlanfeldt 2009, Chapin, Connerly, and Higgins 2007, Weitz 1999, Porter 1998). Over time criticisms have prompted reforms to the state's growth management system, including relaxation of transportation concurrency standards to promote infill development and more attention to issues of affordable housing and rural economic development (Chapin and Ihlanfeldt 2009, Chapin, Connerly, and Higgins 2007, Porter 1998).

Despite the challenges to funding and implementing these environmental and growth management programs and laws, Florida is by most accounts a national leader in each of these areas. There is also general evidence of widespread citizen support for these efforts, in the form of referenda on state and local land conservation initiatives and continued support for state efforts to manage growth (Chapin and Connerly, 2004). However, it remains unclear whether or not support for these initiatives stems from the same base. Before this issue is assessed empirically, factors that the scholarly literature has identified as important to shaping citizen attitudes towards these issues will be identified and the evidence on these factors will be summarized.

Summary of the Literature on Citizen Attitudes

There is a rich literature that has investigated citizen attitudes towards growth management and environmental protection. While not always consistent, this literature has yielded some findings of interest to planners supportive of growth management policies and environmental advocates interested in land conservation. More specifically, this research finds that attitudes towards these issues vary along several key dimensions: 1) Socioeconomic variables, 2) Demographic variables, 3) Political variables, and 4) Contextual variables. Below I briefly summarize this literature.

Among those social class variables that have been identified as potentially significant in shaping attitudes are income, education, and homeownership. It has been argued that members of higher social classes have the means (disposable income), the capacity (education), and the motive (home and real estate ownership) that predispose them to become familiar with and supportive of growth management efforts. Fischel (2005) has termed this the "homevoter hypothesis," arguing that taxation and land development policies are shaped by citizens interested in protecting their most important economic asset, the value of their residences. While intuitively this seems a sound hypothesis, some studies have not found a relationship between these class variables and attitudes towards growth (Knaap 1987, Connerly and Frank 1986, Protash and Baldassare 1983, Gottdiener and Neiman 1981, VanLiere and Dunlap 1980, Buttel and Flinn 1978). However, several recent studies have identified socioeconomic status as having a positive relationship with support for planning initiatives, including growth management, regional planning, and rural open space preservation (Mohamed 2008, Wassmer and Lascher 2006, Chapin and Connerly 2004).

Demographic factors have also been hypothesized as potentially important in understanding resident attitudes. Respondent age has been identified as having a statistically significant influence on attitudes towards growth management and the environment, although the direction of this relationship remains unclear (Mohamed 2008, Wassmer and Lascher 2006, Chapin and Connerly 2004, Connerly and Frank 1986, Baldassare 1984). Race has also been investigated as a potentially influential variable, with some studies finding that African Americans are less likely to support growth management efforts (Mohamed 2008, Chapin and Connerly 2004, Connerly and Frank 1986), while Wassmer and Lascher (2006) found that African Americans are more supportive of growth management efforts in California. In terms of nativity, Connerly and Frank (1986) determined that being a Florida native is irrelevant to predicting support for growth management in that state, whereas Gale and Hart (1992) and Chapin and Connerly (2004) found differences in support between natives and nonnatives. Some recent studies have also found statistically significant gender differences, with females indicating greater support for these policies (Wassmer and Lascher 2006, Chapin and Connerly 2004).

Political orientation has also been hypothesized as influencing attitudes towards planning. It is believed that because political conservatives generally favor a *laissez-faire* approach to governance, planning interventions, such as growth management, are not popular with them. Political liberals are generally more supportive of government intervention, so it has been hypothesized that Democrats would be more supportive of growth management and public land acquisition. Despite this expectation, research has not consistently borne out this relationship, as several studies found no relationship between political views and support for planning initiatives or environmental programs (Chapin and Connerly 2004, Connerly and Frank 1986, Gottdiener and Neiman 1981, Buttel and Flinn 1978). However, other studies have determined that political orientation is significantly correlated with attitudes towards growth controls and environmental programs, with those holding more liberal views evincing greater support for these initiatives (Mohamed 2008, Wassmer and Lascher 2006, Gale and Hart 1992, Bollens 1990).

Table 9.1 Summary of variables influencing citizen attitudes towards land conservation and growth management

Key Variables of Interest	Hypothesized Relationship	Relationship as Indicated in the Literature
Race: White	Positive	Mixed
Ethnicity: Hispanic	Unknown	Unknown
Gender: Male	Strong Negative	Negative
Native of Area	Positive	Positive
Age of Respondent	Mixed	Mixed
Educational Attainment	Strong Positive	Mixed, but Positive
Housing Income	Strong Positive	Mixed, but Positive
Household Tenure	Strong Positive	Mixed, but Positive
Politics: Democrat	Strong Positive	Mixed, but Positive
County Population Size	Positive	Mixed
County Growth Rate	Strong Positive	Mixed

Lastly, the context of an individual's community has been hypothesized to shape attitudes towards growth management and land conservation. Individuals living in communities that are undergoing rapid changes because of substantial new development are thought to be more likely to support growth management and land conservation efforts. Surprisingly, research has yielded no consistent conclusions on this hypothesis. Some studies have found that community characteristics are not useful for understanding variations in attitudes towards growth controls (Mohammed 2008, Gale and Hart 1992, Connerly and Frank 1986), whereas others have found this relationship to be in evidence (Wassmer and Lascher 2006, Knaap 1987, Dowall 1980).

Table 9.1 provides a summary of this literature, listing the key variables of interest. The table also summarizes the direction and magnitude of the hypothesized relationships, as well as the form of the relationship as indicated by empirical work to date.

Data and Methods

The data employed in this study come from the Florida Annual Policy Survey (FAPS), conducted by the Florida State University Survey Research Lab in almost every year since 1979. This survey is intended to monitor the policy interests and attitudes of Floridians on issues of importance to state and local governments. Responses to the survey are generated from a random digit dial telephone survey of Floridians 18 years or older. In 2004, survey results were obtained from a representative sample of 967 Florida residents. While these data are several years old, an advantage of employing data from this period is that they pre-date the recent massive economic downturn, which has affected Florida's economy more than almost any other state in the nation. As such, this survey captured citizen attitudes towards land conservation and growth management during a time of relative prosperity in Florida, when respondents could think more broadly about state priorities.

In addition to questions typically included in the FAPS, the 2004 survey incorporated questions of specific interest to this study. One question queried respondents on citizen willingness to support publicly-funded land acquisition programs. This question read: *Should funding for programs to protect the environment be a) Increased, b) Kept at the present level, or c) Decreased?* The responses to this question allowed for analysis of the first dependent variable, citizen support for funding allocated to environmental programs. Because general support for environmental spending was so high (90 percent or more of every subgroup of the population supported at least maintaining these levels of funding), this dependent variable took the form of increased environmental spending (the variable *IncEnv$* in the analyses that follow). Support for increased spending on environmental programs was used as a proxy for support for spending on land acquisition programs.

A second question focused upon the level of citizen support for managing growth in their communities, reading as follows: *Do you feel growth in your community should be stopped, limited, or not controlled at all?* The responses to this question provide the foundation for empirical analysis of the second dependent variable, citizen support for growth management. Note that those respondents who indicated they believe growth should be stopped or limited were coded as supportive of growth management (the variable *SupportGM* in the analyses that follow).

These FAPS data were used to analyze citizen support for growth management and environmental programs across subgroups of the Florida population. Table 9.2 summarizes independent variables employed in this study, as well as how they were operationalized in the analyses that follow. As described in the previous section, these variables are drawn from the literature on citizen attitudes towards growth and environmental issues. They include key demographic variables (race, ethnicity, and gender), important socioeconomic factors (income and education), political orientation, and local community context (population size and growth rate). Note that the population growth rates for Florida's counties were all positive in the 1990s, and many experienced very high growth rates during that decade.

Once these data were obtained and unusable records were discarded, percent support for the dependent variables, *IncEnv$* and *SupportGM*, was calculated both for the entire sample and for subgroups. Additionally, chi-square analyses were completed for independent variables where possible, which provides more compelling evidence as to any variations across these subgroups. Lastly, logistic regression analyses were carried out to identify those variables that were significant predictors of the two dependent variables, as well as those variables that contributed substantially to the overall explanatory power of these models.

Table 9.2 Summary of Primary Independent Variables of Interest

Descriptions	Variable Name(s)
Race of Respondent	White or Black
Ethnicity of Respondent	Hispanic
Gender of Respondent	Male or Female
Florida Native	Yes or No
Age of Respondent	Categories: 18–29, 30–45, 46–59, 60 or older
Educational Attainment	Categories: No College, Some College, College Graduate
Housing Tenure	Homeowner or Renter
Household Income	Low Income: Less than $30k Medium Income: $30k–$60k High Income: $60k–$90k Very High Income: Greater than $90k
Political Affiliation	Republican, Democrat or Independent
County Population Size in 2000	Small: Less than 50,000 residents Medium: 50,000–150,000 residents Large: 150,000–500,000 residents Very Large: greater than 500,000 residents
County Growth rate 1990–2000	Low: Less than 20% Medium: 20–30% High: Greater than 30%

Results from the analyses are presented in the following section. These analyses allowed for a more complete understanding of the relative importance of the independent variables in explaining variations in support for land conservation and growth management.

Results from the Analyses

Table 9.3 summarizes results from an analysis of citizen support by respondent subgroup and the chi-square analyses for selected subgroups. This table shows the percentage of respondents that indicated they supported increased funding for environmental programs (the *IncEnv$* columns) and efforts to manage growth in their communities (the *SupportGM* columns). The very first set of values reveal that 59.2 percent of all respondents supported greater funding for environmental programs and 70.8 percent supported managing growth in their communities. These data illustrate that Floridians remain strongly behind state and local government efforts to protect the environment and to manage growth in this fast-growing state. These findings reinforce the findings of previous work (Chapin and Connerly 2004, Connerly and Frank 1986) and illustrate generally broad-based support for these initiatives in Florida.

Table 9.3 Support for increased environmental funding and growth management

	Inc Env$	Support GM		Inc Env$	Support GM
All Respondents	59.2%	70.8%			
Race			*Gender*		
Whites	57.3%	73.1%	Males	55.1%	69.9%
Blacks	71.1%	56.0%	Females	61.7%	71.3%
Chi-Sq Test[2]	**	***	*Chi-Sq Test*[2]	**	n/s
Ethnicity			*Age*		
Hispanics	64.3%	62.6%	18–29	66.1%	53.6%
Non-Hispanics	58.7%	72.2%	30–45	62.0%	71.0%
Chi-Sq Test[3]	n/s	**	46–59	54.0%	79.1%
Florida Native			60+	57.1%	71.5%
Yes	62.0%	68.6%	*Chi-Sq Test*[2]	*	***
No	58.3%	71.4%			
Chi-Sq Test[2]	n/s	n/s			
Educational Attainment			*Household Income*		
No College	62.5%	67.2%	Low (<$30k)	64.8%	67.8%
Some College	55.8%	69.4%	Medium ($30–60k)	59.7%	65.6%
College Grad	57.9%	75.8%	High ($60–90k)	50.9%	71.9%
Chi-Sq Test[2]	n/s	*	Very High (>90k)	51.6%	77.9%
			Chi-Sq Test[2]	**	n/s
Housing Tenure					
Own	55.5%	73.2%			
Rent	69.6%	62.8%			
Chi-Sq Test[2]	***	***			
Political Affiliation					
Republican	50.6%	70.9%			
Independent	57.3%	73.1%			
Democrat	66.0%	69.9%			
Chi-Sq Test[2]	***	n/s			
County Population Size			*County Growth Rate*		
Small (0–50k)	50.0%	69.0%	Low (0–20%)	59.4%	71.5%
Medium (50–150k)	58.1%	68.5%	Medium (20–30%)	58.6%	70.5%
Large (150–500k)	59.9%	68.6%	High (>30%)	59.6%	70.2%
Very Large (>500k)	60.2%	73.3%	*Chi-Sq Test*[2]	n/s	n/s
Chi-Sq Test[2]	n/s	n/s			

* Significant at .90 level, ** Significant at .95 level, *** Significant at .95 level

Table 9.3 also summarizes the level of support for each of these two issues by population subgroups. A close reading of this table reveals some interesting themes. Support for these two issues differs along racial and ethnic lines, as blacks and Hispanics were more supportive of increased environmental spending, while whites and non-Hispanics were more supportive of growth management. Similarly, there are key differences along socioeconomic lines as more highly educated respondents were more supportive of growth management, while lower income respondents were more supportive of increased support for environmental programs. Results also indicate that women were more supportive than men of both issues, reinforcing prior scholarship that finds a growing gender gap on many planning issues (Wassmer and Lascher 2006, Chapin and Connerly 2004). The age variable also reveals an interesting finding, as younger respondents were more supportive of increased environmental funding, while older respondents were more supportive of efforts to manage growth. In terms of the political variable, the results suggest that Republicans were less supportive of increased funding for environmental programs, but that political affiliation and support for growth management were unrelated. The contextual variables reveal no clear themes, as county population size and population growth rates appeared non-factors in understanding attitudes on these two issues.

Beyond summarizing the levels of support for these issues, Table 9.3 presents the results of a set of chi-square tests for each of the independent variables, indicated in the "Chi-Sq Test" rows. The chi-square analysis found a statistically significant difference for whites and blacks on the two dependent variables, with blacks more supportive of increased spending on environmental programs and whites more supportive of growth management. For ethnicity the chi-square test found a statistically significant difference only for the *SupportGM* variable, with non-Hispanics being more supportive of this initiative, while support for increased environmental spending was not related to ethnicity. As suggested earlier, gender and age are indeed important factors in understanding attitudes towards these issues. Women were found to be more supportive of increased environmental spending than men, although not for the *SupportGM* variable. Age was found to be related to both dependent variables, with older residents showing greater support for growth management and younger residents showing more support for greater funding for environmental programs.

The chi-square tests for the socioeconomic variables yield a very interesting mix of findings. The socioeconomic variables generally behave as expected, as higher socioeconomic status (homeownership, and higher education) was generally found to be positively related to the *SupportGM* dependent variable. These findings reinforce the "homevoter hypothesis" put forward by Fischel and supported by several recent studies of citizen attitudes towards growth and development. However, for the *IncEnv$* dependent variable this hypothesis is not supported. Generally speaking, the findings of the chi-square analyses indicate that lower socioeconomic classes were more supportive of increased spending on environmental programs.

Table 9.4 Regression results for support for increased environmental spending

Variables	B	S.E.	Wald	Sig.		Exp(B)
White	-0.260	0.203	1.646	0.200		0.771
Male	-0.182	0.154	1.405	0.236		0.834
Age	-0.004	0.004	1.008	0.315		0.996
Education	-0.093	0.088	1.108	0.292		0.912
Homeowner	-0.413	0.185	4.969	0.026	**	0.662
Democrat	0.458	0.154	8.833	0.003	***	1.580
Pop2000	0.000	0.000	0.111	0.739		1.000
Constant	1.123	0.345	10.618	0.001		3.073
Nagelkerke R-Squared		0.046				

* Significant at .90 level, ** Significant at .95 level, *** Significant at .95 level

For the political and contextual independent variables, the results of the chi-square analyses offer some limited support for the hypothesized relationships. The findings support the hypothesis that political orientation matters, but only for the *IncEnv$* variable. Democrats were found to be more supportive of increased environmental spending, but political orientation was not determined to be related to support for growth management. In contrast, the hypothesis that local context shapes citizen attitudes is not supported at all by the findings. Citizen support for these two initiatives did not vary significantly by county population size and population growth rate.

Lastly, logistic analyses were completed to identify the core constituencies for the two dependent variables, *IncEnv$* and *SupportGM*. The results from these logistic regression analyses are presented in Tables 9.4 and 9.5. First, it is worth noting that neither of these regression analyses yields a particularly robust model (as evidenced by the very low Nagelkerke R-Squared values in the tables). Clearly, citizen attitudes are influenced by a wide array of factors, the vast majority of which are not captured in this dataset.

Nonetheless the results of these analyses do offer insights into the form of the constituencies supportive of either increased environmental spending or growth management. Table 9.4 illustrates that the *IncEnv$* constituency rests in lower socioeconomic groups (as evidenced by renters) and Democrats. The other coefficients indicate that the base is also more likely found in non-whites, females, and younger individuals. In almost direct contrast, the regression results in Table 9.5 suggest that the growth management constituency rests in older, white residents of higher socioeconomic status (homeowners and the higher educated). Also of interest, in this regression model county population size (Pop2000) was determined to be a positive predictor of support for growth management; residents

Table 9.5 Regression results for support for growth management

Variables	B	S.E.	Wald	Sig.		Exp(B)
White	0.560	0.199	7.940	0.005	***	1.750
Male	-0.103	0.164	0.394	0.530		0.902
Age	0.009	0.005	4.083	0.043	**	1.010
Education	0.130	0.095	1.864	0.172		1.139
Homeowner	0.238	0.188	1.604	0.205		1.269
Democrat	0.006	0.165	0.001	0.970		1.006
Pop2000	0.000	0.000	2.792	0.095	*	1.000
Constant	-0.568	0.351	2.629	0.105		0.566
Nagelkerke R-Squared		0.049				

* Significant at .90 level, ** Significant at .95 level, *** Significant at .95 level

in more populous, more urban counties were found to be more supportive of growth management than residents in less populated, more rural areas. Also of interest, while not significant, the results for the Male variable are negative in both tables, indicating less male support for government intervention in the form of greater spending on environmental programs and programs to manage growth.

When taken as a whole, these findings offer compelling evidence that support for increased environmental spending and for initiatives to manage growth do not emanate from the same core constituency. Within Florida it appears that advocates for greater funding for land conservation programs can find their greatest support amongst younger, non-white, and lower socioeconomic residents. The opposite largely holds true for growth management, as support emanates primarily from older residents, whites, and individuals in higher socioeconomic classes. The implications for these findings are discussed in the concluding section.

Conclusions and Implications

This chapter began with the question: *Are the coalitions supportive of land conservation and growth management based in the same subsets of the population?* In other words, do the constituencies for these issues emanate from the same base? Generally speaking, there is substantial evidence that the bases of support for increased environmental funding and for growth management are quite different. Environmental programs receive greater support from non-whites, younger adults, females, renters, and Democrats. In contrast, growth management finds greater support among whites, homeowners, and higher educated and older individuals, as well as those living in more populous counties.

Echoing the findings of Chapin and Connerly (2004), Wassmer and Lascher (2006), and Mohamed (2008), these data indicate increasing polarization within the citizenry on planning and environmental issues. For example, Chapin and Connerly (2004) expressed concern that growth management was becoming more of a class-based issue, with homeowners and higher income households supporting these efforts as a means of maintaining their high quality of life and home values. These results very much reinforce this concern and reaffirm Fischel's homevoter hypothesis (2005), in which individuals are likely to support taxation and development policies that enhance the values of their homes and the land that they own.

In contrast, support for environmental programs appears to be a function of both class and politics, with Democrats indicating much stronger support for "green" investments by the public sector. Additionally, findings hint that support for environmental programs may be a generational issue, with younger cohorts—most notably individuals under 30—being more supportive of environmental programs than preceding cohorts. With the rise of recycling programs, water conservation efforts, clean commute campaigns, and a myriad of other pro-environment programs, these younger adults have grown up during a time in which environmental issues and long-term sustainability are part of their everyday experience. It will be interesting to see whether the strong support of these younger cohorts for increased environmental spending is maintained over time. One possibility is that there has indeed been a sea change in citizen attitudes towards the environment, with increasing support for pro-environmental programs. However, it is also conceivable that this finding is instead simply a life-cycle issue, and that as individuals age and obtain greater economic resources, increasing their socioeconomic status in the process, their views towards increased spending on environmental (and other) programs also change. It will be fascinating to see which of these hypotheses wins out in the long-run.

In terms of the issue at the heart of this edited volume, evaluating efforts to link land acquisition and growth management, the work of this chapter suggests that forging this link may be problematic for planners, environmentalists, and other advocates for these initiatives. Simply put, while advocates see great opportunities for synergies between land acquisition and growth management programs, results indicate that residents do not see these programs as being similar in their form and function. While detailed data on the thinking behind citizen support for these initiatives are lacking, these survey results do provide evidence that the public at large sees efforts to manage growth and funding for environmental programs as distinctly different. As a consequence, the support for these initiatives stems from very different bases within the population.

This suggests that planners and environmental advocates that see great opportunity in forging stronger linkages between environmental programs and growth management policies need to identify the benefits of a combined approach and then successfully educate the population about these benefits. Given an increasingly fractious political environment, programs to fund land acquisition by the public sector and public sector initiatives to manage growth will almost certainly require substantial support from the public in order to be enacted, implemented, and funded. While smart growth advocates and survivors of the many growth management and land conservation wars that have been fought in Florida (and elsewhere) may see the connections between these initiatives, it would appear that the public at large does not. These findings signal that there is much work to be done to educate and inform the broader public about the many benefits that can flow from successfully linking land acquisition and growth management initiatives.

References

Baldassare, M. 1984. Predicting local concern about growth: The roots of citizen discontent. *Journal of Urban Affairs*, 6, 39–49.

Bollens, S. 1990. Constituencies for limitation and regionalism: Approaches to growth management. *Urban Affairs Quarterly*, 26(1), 46–67.

Buttel, F. and Flinn, W. 1978. Social class and environmental beliefs: A reconsideration. *Environment and Behavior*, 10(3), 433–50.

Chapin, T. and Connerly, C. 2004. Attitudes towards growth management in Florida: Comparing resident support in 1985 and 2001. *Journal of the American Planning Association*, 70(4), 443–52.

Chapin, T., Connerly, C., and Higgins, H. 2007. *Growth Management in Florida: Planning for Paradise*. Aldershot: Ashgate.

Chapin, T. and Ihlanfeldt, K. 2009. State of Florida case study, in *Smart Growth Policies: An Evaluation of Programs and Outcomes*, edited by G. Ingram, A. Carbonell, Y. Hong and A. Flint. Cambridge, MA: Lincoln Institute of Land Policy, 152–65.

Connerly, C. and Frank, J. 1986. Predicting support for local growth controls. *Social Sciences Quarterly*, 67(3), 572–86.

Dowall, D. 1980. An examination of population-growth-managing communities. *Policy Studies Journal*, 9(3), 414–27.

Fischel, W. 2005. *The Homevoter Hypothesis: How Home Values Influence Local Government Taxation, School Finance, and Land-Use Policies*. Cambridge, MA: Harvard University Press.

Gale, D. and Hart, S. 1992. Public support for local comprehensive planning under statewide growth management: Insights from Maine. *Journal of Planning Education and Research*, 11, 192 205.

Gottdiener, M. and Neiman, M. 1981. Characteristics of support for local growth controls. *Urban Affairs Quarterly*, 17(1), 55–73.

Higgins, H. and N. Paradise. 2007. Paying for the "priceless": Florida Forever, managing growth, and public land acquisition, in *Growth Management in Florida: Planning for Paradise*, edited by T. Chapin, C. Connerly and H. Higgins. Aldershot: Ashgate, 241–60.

Knaap, G.J. 1987. Self-interest and voter support for Oregon's land use controls. *Journal of the American Planning Association*, 53(1), 92–7.

Mohamed, R. 2008. Who would pay for rural open space preservation and inner-city redevelopment? Identifying support for policies that can contribute to regional land use governance. *Urban Studies*, 45(13), 2783–803.

Pelham, T. 2007. A historical perspective for evaluating Florida's evolving growth management process, in *Growth Management in Florida: Planning for Paradise*, edited by T. Chapin, C. Connerly and H. Higgins. Aldershot: Ashgate, 7–19.

Porter, D. 1998. The states: Growing smarter? In *Smart Growth: Economy, Community, Environment*, edited by the Urban Land Institute. Washington, D.C.: Urban Land Institute, 28–35.

Protash, W. and Baldassare, M. 1983. Growth policies and community status: A test and modification of Logan's theory. *Urban Affairs Quarterly*, 18(3), 397–412.

VanLiere, K. and Dunlap, R. 1980. The social bases of environmental concern: A review of hypotheses, explanations, and empirical evidence. *Public Opinion Quarterly*, 44, 181–97.

Wassmer, W. and Lascher, E. 2006. Who supports local growth and regional planning to deal with its consequences? *Urban Affairs Review*, 41(5), 621–45.

Weitz, J. 1999. *Sprawl Busting: State Programs to Guide Growth*. Chicago: American Planning Association.

Chapter 10

Incorporating Land Values to Improve Targeting Schemes for Land Acquisition: An Application to Maryland's GreenPrint Program

Karen Palm Szobota and Lori Lynch

At least 38 states in the United States have statewide land conservation programs which focus on saving valuable ecological lands. These programs collect data on a plethora of land characteristics to rank parcels' ecological importance but seldom include acquisition costs in determining which parcels should be selected. This study focuses on improving targeting strategies by incorporating acquisition costs along with ecological benefits in land parcel rankings. This can be a challenging task. The market value of rural and ecologically important land can be difficult to obtain since these lands are not sold frequently. And because of use-value or preferential property tax schemes, assessed values often do not reflect market values. Therefore we recommend programs estimate hedonic models on recent land sales using the land and neighborhood characteristics they have already collected and then use the estimated model parameters to predict market land values for other parcels. To illustrate this approach, we estimate hedonic models to predict the market values of land parcels larger than 10 acres in three Maryland counties. We then use these estimated market land values in three targeting schemes, along with the parcels' ecological scores, to rank parcels. Our results suggest the current land targeting scheme in Maryland's GreenPrint Program can be improved by incorporating parcel acquisition costs in the ranking schemes.

Incorporating Land Value to Improve Targeting Schemes for Land Acquisition

Natural lands produce ecosystem services for which the private landowners receive little or no economic return. These services are not priced in a private land market because they provide benefits to one person without hindering the benefits received by another (non-rival) and it is difficult to prevent someone from benefiting easily (non-excludable). Erosion control, sediment retention, wildlife habitat, and recreation opportunities are examples of some of the positive benefits having land remain in a natural state might provide. Other ecosystem services could include filtering and cooling of water, carbon sequestration, cleaning air, and genetic resource preservation.

Although no market exists in which to purchase these goods, people have expressed a willingness to pay for ecological attributes and the benefits they provide in a variety of studies: Households are willing to pay between $67 and $215 for improvements in wetland habitat (Pate and Loomis 1997); $234 to preserve undeveloped urban fringe open space providing scenic views and wildlife habitat (Breffle, Morey, and Lodder 1998); $353 to reduce the frequency of algal blooms from once every other day to once every five days (Stumborg, Baerenklau, and Bishop, 2001); and $252 to simultaneously increase five ecosystem services—dilution of wastewater, natural purification of water, erosion control, habitat for fish and wildlife, and recreation (Loomis et al. 2000). And as a further indication of their willingness to pay for the goods land conservation provides, citizens continue to pass local and state conservation ballot measures for funding, in amounts over $1.2 billion in 2004, $1.7 billion in 2005, $6.7 billion in 2006, and $2 billion in 2007.

Given these benefits, the public sector acts on society's behalf by developing programs to acquire natural lands and the ecosystem services they provide. To do so, however, administrators of such public land acquisition programs need to develop protocols to identify and target the most ecologically valuable lands and determine the budgetary resources needed to retain them. Most programs encourage land owners to voluntarily sell their ecologically valuable land. Because only a landowner who benefits by selling will participate (unless motivated by a stewardship or environmental goal), the program must offer a market sales price at least as high as the landowner would receive from another buyer. Thus conservation programs often cannot enrol all the ecologically valuable land they would wish to. Therefore, programs need to operate in a manner that ensures they acquire lands that maximizes society's welfareor benefit for their available budget.

Land conservation programs that preserve land with ecological value can be found throughout the United States. At least 38 of the nation's 50 states have statewide land conservation programs (Resources Agency of California, 2004).[1] State and local governments and nonprofit organizations collect a great deal of data and do extensive mapping and analysis to determine parcel and neighborhood characteristics. Yet these targeting strategies seldom incorporate the cost of land acquisition in their efforts to determine which parcel to purchase. For example, the Florida Forever program lists 38 performance measures by which potential acquisition projects are evaluated, but does not address acquisition costs at all. Most frequently, these programs rank the eligible parcels by their conservation benefits and seek those with the highest benefits until the program's budget is expended, i.e., they maximize benefits irrespective of the cost of acquisition.

---

1 These include the Arizona Preserve Initiative (1996), Land for Maine's Future, New York's Open Space Conservation Plan, and the Florida Forever/Florida Preservation 2000 program.

Unfortunately, this strategy may result in lower overall benefits from land conservation. To ensure continued public support and funding, land conservation programs need to use the public's money in the most efficient manner possible and achieve the greatest benefits they can for the available budget. Many studies have shown that incorporating acquisition costs can provide higher benefits. For example, Ando et al. (1998) demonstrate that both economic factors and ecological factors are needed to conserve habitat for endangered species efficiently. Wu, Zilberman, and Babcock (2001) and Ferraro (2003) found similar results. Messer (2006) found that consideration of acquisition costs could increase the conservation benefits of land acquired on a program's budget by an estimated \$3.1 to \$3.9 million or enable the program to achieve the same benefits with a budget savings of \$0.9 to \$3.5 million. Despite this evidence, few programs have included acquisition costs in their land targeting or acquisition protocols.

So we come to the question: Why do these conservation programs ignore acquisition costs when selecting parcels? One possibility is the administrators want to enrol parcels with the highest ecological benefit regardless of their costs, the "Cadillac" parcels. Cadillac parcels are often well known and highly visible to the general public. Conversion of such parcels can cause a public outcry; thus the program administrators may think they need to enrol these parcels first. Alternatively, administrators may seek out the parcels of land most threatened with imminent conversion to a developed use. They may decide to use their limited budget to enrol land parcels that will disappear if not retained now, rather than to acquire those more likely to remain in a natural state (and provide their benefits free of charge). Of course, because these threatened parcels are desirable for a developed use, they also might be the most expensive to acquire. Under this situation, program administrators attempt to conserve parcels which are both highly threatened with conversion and have a high level of benefits (i.e. minimize the expected loss in benefits) regardless of the parcels' costs believing if they did not do so, these benefits would be lost forever. Therefore program administrators may behave no differently even if they included land acquisition costs into their calculations.

Even if program administrators want to include land acquisition costs, obtaining the accurate market values for parcels with significant ecological values may be difficult. Markets for large rural parcels tend to be "thin," i.e., they have few recent and comparable sales. Although worthwhile during an acquisition process, land appraisals can be expensive and time-consuming to prepare and thus less useful for a targeting exercise. When land values are based on assessments done for property tax purposes, they may be skewed due to thin markets and a lack of comparable properties. A parcel's use-value assessment will not reflect the market value of the land. Additionally, while somewhat accurate average land values can be found for a county, they are not useful for determining the value of specific land parcels.

This study proposes that program administrators would target better and use the program's budget more effectively if they could 1) determine the market values of desirable parcels and 2) incorporate these land values along with measures of environmental benefits in a targeting strategy. Thus this analysis seeks to accomplish two objectives. First, it utilizes a hedonic methodology to estimate the marginal value of different land and neighborhood characteristics for large parcels that might be considered for enrolment in a land conservation program. In this case, land and neighborhood characteristics had already been collected to determine the ecological value of parcels. It uses the estimated coefficients to predict the market values (acquisition costs) for land parcels. Second, it incorporates these predicted market values (acquisition costs) along with benefit measures into alternative targeting scenarios to determine the most efficient means of maximizing the benefits to society given a fixed budget. Using a three-county study area in Maryland, we demonstrate how targeting schemes that incorporate predicted market prices in addition to the ecological benefits are more efficient. In addition, while not the primary focus of the chapter, we also compare the acreage and costs of land parcels selected under different targeting scenarios conducted both regionally and at the county level.

Background on Maryland's GreenPrint Program

As of December 2002, already developed lands represent 20 percent of Maryland's total land area and protected lands[2] account for another 19 percent of the State's 6.2 million acres (U.S. Census Bureau 2002). This leaves 61 percent of Maryland lands (3.8 million acres) in private, undeveloped land uses in 2002. One half of the undeveloped land is in agriculture and one half is in forest or natural cover.

In 2001, Maryland instituted the GreenPrint program to specifically target large contiguous land areas designated as its Green Infrastructure (GI). The Maryland Department of Natural Resources used a Green Infrastructure Assessment (GIA) to identify and rank land for inclusion in the two components of its GI: hubs and corridors. Hubs are "unfragmented areas hundreds or thousands of acres in size, and are vital to maintaining the state's ecological health" (Weber 2003). The hubs generally meet minimum parcel requirements of 250 acres and provide habitat for native plants and animals, protect water quality and soils, and regulate climate and temperature (Weber 2003). The average size of the hubs is approximately 2,200 acres. Intensive human land uses, including housing and commercial development, agriculture, and quarries, as well as major roads, are excluded from the hubs.

Corridors are linear strips of natural lands that allow plants and animals unrestricted movement, typically along stream valleys and mountain ridges. Corridors are designed to "allow wildlife safe passage through their natural domain, facilitate seed and pollen transport helping plant life thrive across the state, and keep streams and wetlands healthy by protecting adjacent vegetation" (Maryland Department of Natural Resources [DNR] 2003). The corridors connecting hubs

2 Protected lands include lands publicly owned at the federal, state, and local levels, as well as private preserves and privately owned lands with conservation easements.

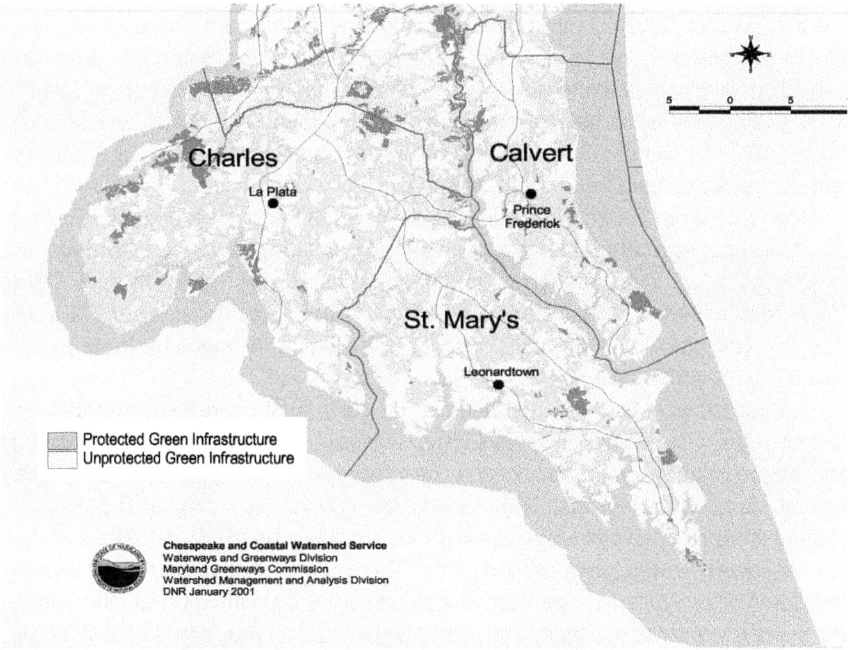

Figure 10.1 Green infrastructure identified and protected in southern Maryland counties

are at least 1,100 feet wide. The GIA uses a least-cost path analysis technique to determine the best ecological paths between hubs. In this case, the cost is measured by the difficulty for wildlife to traverse the landscape along a particular route rather than land acquisition costs. Therefore, the path with the fewest obstacles (for example, roads, development) between two hubs is the least-cost path.

Gaps within the GI are areas of intensive human alternation of the land from its natural state within or near hubs and corridors. These gaps may be targeted for purchase and restoration to natural cover such as forest or wetlands. Buffers added around wetlands, streams, and shorelines within hubs may also contain agriculture or other intensive human land uses.

The Green Infrastructure comprises 2,030,472 acres, or 32 percent of Maryland's total acreage, of which 1,777,475 acres are in hubs and 252,997 acres are in corridors of natural land cover.[3] Altered open areas, including agricultural lands, lawns, quarries, and cleared lands, constitute an additional 375,546 acres in the potential Green Infrastructure land network (Weber 2003). This GI acreage encompasses 63 percent of Maryland's forest land, 87 percent of its unmodified wetlands, and 88 percent of its occurrences of rare, threatened, or endangered

3 Open water is excluded from these calculations.

species (Weber 2003). Four types of ecological habitat are emphasized: large blocks of interior forest, large wetland complexes, rare species and migratory bird habitat, and pristine stream and river segments. Twenty-six percent or 529,771 acres of this land are protected, including state, federal, and locally owned areas. Figure 10.1 depicts the Green Infrastructure for southern Maryland in light gray and the protected land within it in darker gray.

The GreenPrint Program enrolled 21,146 acres of land rich in natural resources. The Maryland Agricultural Land Preservation Foundation used GreenPrint funding to protect 8,625 acres of agricultural lands ranked very high for their Green Infrastructure values. The average cost was $1,542 per acre for these 29,771 acres. The smallest parcel was 82 acres. The largest acquisition was a multiple parcels purchase of over 900 acres.[4]

Failing to account for parcel acquisition costs in the targeting protocol will decrease the GreenPrint program's effectiveness and efficiency unless benefits and acquisition costs are negatively correlated (that is, a parcel's ecological benefits are high when acquisition costs are low or vice versa). The program created comprehensive ecological scores for parcels throughout the state and then ranked parcels within geographic regions. This comprehensive ecological ranking provides for a systematic, scientific method of ecological valuation and determines the benefits provided by any one parcel.[5] The GreenPrint program currently targets ecologically valuable natural lands without considering the costs associated with the parcels' acquisition.[6] Several other targeting schemes are possible: the program could target the least expensive lands, thereby minimizing the total cost of preserving some number of acres or maximizing the number of acres preserved

4 Maryland has had a long history of land preservation programs. GreenPrint was created to specifically protect ecologically important land in a contiguous manner. Maryland began preserving land in 1967, when it established the Maryland Environmental Trust to preserve open space through conservation easement donations. While land remains in private ownership, a conservation easement limits the landowner's right to develop and subdivide his or her land forever. In 1969, the DNR created Program Open Space which has acquired more than 250,000 acres for state and local parks. In 1978, it created the Maryland Agricultural Land Preservation Foundation (MALPF) to purchase development rights from farmland owners. MALPF has preserved nearly 400,000 acres (Maryland Department of Agriculture, 2004). The Maryland Greenways Commission, preserving natural infrastructure through corridors such as streams and mountain ridges, was begun in 1990. In 1997, Maryland also enacted a Smart Growth program including the Rural Legacy and Priority Funding Area initiatives.

5 From an economic perspective, we would like to have people's willingness to pay for different land and neighborhood attributes as a measure of the benefits that certain characteristics provide. However, in the absence of these measures we use the ecological rankings that were developed out of the literature and expert opinion.

6 GreenPrint preserves natural lands through conservation easements in addition to land acquisitions. For simplicity, this manuscript focuses on land acquisition costs. However, a similar approach could be used for purchase of development rights.

for a fixed budget; the program could target specific ecological characteristics that are not valued in the marketplace to obtain a high level of benefits at a low cost; or the program could target the highest benefits per dollar spent. Incorporating costs will allow the GreenPrint program to maximize the aggregate benefits achieved for a given budget when selecting land to preserve.

Land Values

In a competitive private land market,[7] the market value of a land parcel is equal to the net present value of returns to the land. In essence, the value is the stream of net agricultural returns given the parcel's characteristics while in agriculture until it converts to a residential use and then the stream of net residential returns.[8] Land contains a bundle of characteristics that defines its quality and net returns. As mentioned above, to enrol land into the conservation program, administrators must pay the full present value (*PV*) to obtain the land fee simple from an owner willing to sell to the program. Thus program administrators can approximate the cost of enrolling any given parcel into the program by computing the present value, i.e., the market value of the land.

Hedonic models have been used to estimate land values in the agricultural land market for both improved and unimproved parcels (Geoghegan, Lynch, and Bucholtz 2003; Lynch and Lovell 2003; Bastian et al. 2002; Nickerson and Lynch 2001; Faux and Perry 1999; Bockstael 1996; Xu, Mittelhammer, and Barkley 1993; Holway and Burbay 1990; Palmquist and Danielson 1989). They trace out the locus of equilibrium market prices as a function of the attributes of the land parcels. Underlying the hedonic model is an assumption that the buyer maximizes utility, satisfaction, or happiness subject to his or her budget constraint. According to Rosen (1974), each buyer has a willingness to pay (bid function) for particular land attributes. Buyers determine the combination of parcel characteristics and price (willingness to pay) that will leave them the most satisfied. The market has many buyers and many sellers (land parcels) and thus an equilibrium is reached

7 To simplify we consider a competitive private land market that includes agricultural and residential lands only. Forest, commercial, industrial, and institutional lands are excluded from this definition.

8
$$PV = \int_{0}^{t^*} A(a_i, t) e^{-rt} dt + \int_{t^*}^{\infty} R(a_i, u) e^{-ru} du$$

where A is net agricultural returns, i.e., the stream of income from today to the optimal date for development, t^* and R is net residential rents, i.e., the stream of income from development from t^* through infinity. Income (A and R) from any use on a parcel will depend on its characteristics, a_i. The optimal date for development, t^*, usually occurs where the agricultural income equals the residential returns defined as functions of the land parcel characteristics.

Table 10.1 Description of model data

Variable	Description	Mean	Std Dev	Effect
SALEPRICE	Parcel inflation adjusted market value	$228,198	$141,316	
SQFTSTRC	Foundation square footage	1406.08	1369.70	+
houseage	1/Age of Structure	0.19	0.36	+
agesqft	1/Age * SQFTSTRC	506.33	1054.69	-
constrav	% Construction Grade Average	0.26	0.44	+
CONSTGOODP	% Construction Grade Good through Luxury	0.06	0.24	+
basement	% with Basement	0.30	0.46	+
garage	% with Attached or detached garage	0.38	0.49	+
totbaths	Total number of bathrooms	1.25	1.26	+
fireplace	% with Fireplace	0.34	0.47	+
waterfront	% with Waterfront property	0.05	0.22	+
citymiles	Min distance to Washington or Baltimore in miles	49.12	11.70	-
subdivis	% of homes in a subdivision	0.50	0.50	?
calvert	% in Calvert County dummy	0.19	0.39	?
stmarys	% in St. Mary's County dummy	0.40	0.49	?
ssp_land	Parcel in Sensitive Species Project Review Area	0.11	0.32	?
ACRES	Acres	20.11	29.66	-
PerPasture	Land Use: % in Pasture	0.02	0.09	-
PerCrop	Land Use: % in Cropland	0.18	0.30	-
PerForest	Land Use: % in Forest	0.60	0.37	-
PWETLANDS	% of Acres in Vegetated Wetlands	0.07	0.14	-
s_slope_m_h	Soil % Acres with Slope Greater than 8 Percent	0.33	0.40	-
s_erodehigh	Soil % Acres with High Erodibility	0.40	0.45	-
s_erodem	Soil % Acres with Moderate Erodibility	0.31	0.41	-
s_flood	Soil % Acres with Floodplain Soil	0.24	0.36	-

Note: N = 463

between supply and demand of the various characteristic combinations. Hedonic analysis allows us to estimate the marginal willingness to pay for any characteristic assuming all other parcel characteristics stay the same. For example, how much more would one pay for one more acre of wetlands on a property, given the size, location, soil quality, etc. stay exactly the same?

Data

We compiled data 1) to estimate the hedonic model for parcels with recent market transactions, 2) to predict the parcel land market values for all parcels, and 3) to calculate a GreenPrint Desktop Ecological Score for each parcel. Table 10.1 lists the model variables with their descriptions, means, standard deviations, and expected effects on the parcel market value.

The hedonic model was estimated using arms-length transactions for unrestricted parcels greater than 10 acres in Charles, Calvert, and St. Mary's Counties in southern Maryland from 1999 to 2002.[9] Our primary data were collected from the Maryland Department of Planning's MDPropertyView 2002 Database (MDPVD), which contains the State's Department of Assessments and Taxation information for each parcel in the state. The MDPVD supplies information on sales price,[10] assessed value, geographic location, waterfront access, and the houses' structural characteristics.

The spatially referenced parcels (latitude and longitude) from this database can be linked to other state and federal spatially referenced data sets.[11] The Maryland Department of Planning (MDP) also compiles detailed land use data from satellite and aerial photography taken as recently as 2002. We used GIS to extract the land uses from the 2002 coverage. We categorized land use as Urban, Agriculture, Forest, Water, and Wetlands. Urban includes the sub-categories of low-density residential, medium-density residential, high-density residential, commercial, industrial, institutional, extractive, and open urban land uses. Agriculture includes cropland, pasture, orchards, vineyards, and agricultural buildings and storage. Forest includes deciduous, evergreen, and mixed forests as well as brush. Water and Wetlands refer

9 Arms-length signifies a sale to non-family members. All publicly held lands and parcels already enrolled in a preservation program are omitted from the parcel population, as are commercial, exempt, exempt commercial, and industrial land uses. MALPF district parcels are not omitted as their land use is only temporarily restricted.

10 Parcel sales prices are adjusted for inflation using the Consumer Price Index – All Urban Consumers for Washington-Baltimore, MD-DC-VA-WV (Bureau of Labor Statistics 2003) to 1999 dollars.

11 The data set creation relies on the Arc View 3.2 and Arc Geographic Information Systems (GIS) 8.2 software programs to extract and combine data for geographically referenced parcels. A buffer parcel was created to proxy the actual parcel. The buffer is a circular area around the parcel centroid with the total area equal to the land parcel's acreage. Many other methods could be used to extract the parcel characteristics.

to open water and intermittently wet areas, respectively. The land use variables are measured as the percent of total parcel acreage. PERFOREST measures the percent of parcel acreage in forest, PERCROP measures the percent of parcel acreage in cropland, and PERPASTURE measures the percent of parcel acreage in pasture. We omitted the percent of parcel acreage in development; this use usually commands the highest price. Thus the coefficients for these land use variables are estimated relative to the percent of the parcel acreage in development.

The MDP's 1973 soil maps group soils by productivity, erosion potential, permeability, stoniness and rockiness, depth to bedrock, depth to water table, slope, stability, and susceptibility to flooding. Information was extracted with GIS and four variables created to represent the soil characteristics of the land parcels. The slope of the land parcel, S_SLOPE_M_H, is the percent of the parcel with slope greater than 8 percent. Steeper slopes are more difficult to develop or cultivate. The percent of soils with moderate erodibility, S_ERODEM, and with high erodibility, S_ERODEH, are also included. Soil erodibility is not desirable in the market place although it is valued in the GreenPrint program's ranking of ecological characteristics. Finally, S_FLOOD measures the percent of the parcel with floodplain soils. These soils have marginal value for agricultural uses as well as for urban development (MDP 1973).

Two binary variables were created, CALVERT equals 1 if the parcel is in Calvert County and STMARYS equals 1 if the parcel is in St. Mary's County. These variables were included to control for any differences among the three counties on factors that might impact market value, such as tax rates, zoning regulations,[12] school quality, and public services.

Many of the variables described above are also attributes that the GreenPrint program considers in its parcel rankings and thus would be available to program administrators to use to estimate land values. For example, the land use variables, acreage in vegetated wetlands, soil erodibility, distance to Washington, D.C., and waterfront access, are attributes that directly impact the GreenPrint program's ecological and development risk rankings. Interestingly, many of these variables may actually decrease the market value of the parcel, while being valued ecologically by the GreenPrint program. For example, steeper slopes are expected to reduce parcel

12 Zoning regulations can affect land value. However, zoning in this analysis is almost perfectly correlated within the three counties. First, the parcel population is limited to the private, non-commercial market for agricultural and residential land. Commercial, industrial, and exempt land uses are omitted from the study. Second, the parcel population is restricted to those parcels in excess of 10 acres. Third, the improved parcels are separated from the unimproved parcels for modeling. These limitations create a parcel population with very similar zoning regulations within each county. Specifically, 86 percent of the Charles County parcels are zoned at 1 house per 3 acres, 71 percent of the St. Mary's County parcels are zoned at 1 house per 5 acres, and 91 percent of the Calvert County parcels are zoned rural at 1 house per 10 acres. There is almost no variation in the zoning regulations within the Calvert county's parcel population, there is little variation in the other two counties, and initial estimations resulted in insignificant zoning parameters in the improved and unimproved hedonic models.

market value but are desired in lands targeted for GreenPrint acquisition. These variables carry special importance in achieving the goal of greater benefits per dollar spent by the conservation program.

Hedonic Model Results

Our goal was to explain the inflation adjusted market value, SALEPRICE, for 10 acre or larger parcels sold between 1997 and 2002, using the land characteristics defined above. We evaluated the best functional form for the model (the relationship between the parcel characteristics and the sales price), the model's predictive ability, and the existence of different markets (buyers looking for homes or not) to identify the model to produce the market values.

Most variables are assumed to have a linear relationship with the sales price. However, the square footage of the house (SQFTSTRC) and the number of acres (ACRES) may have a nonlinear relationship. For example, square footage may increase the sales price up to some point and then adding another square foot of space has a much smaller impact. Therefore, we estimated two models to determine the best method of incorporating these nonlinear relationships: Model 1 has what is called an inverse semi-log functional form with SQFTSTRC and ACRES transformed by natural logarithm. Model 2 has a nonlinear functional form with the square root of SQFTSTRC and ACRES.[13]

We wanted to ensure our model produces good predictions of the market value of land parcels that have not sold recently. To test the predictions, we withheld some land parcels (10 percent) to validate our estimated coefficients and estimated the models with the other land parcels (90 percent). We then predicted the land value for these 10 percent. The differences between the predicted parcel values and the actual parcel values were calculated to determine how well the model predicts the true parcel values.

We also separated parcels that have houses on them from those without. It could be that parcels without houses attract different buyers and thus have different valuations for the parcel characteristics. For example, a buyer looking to relocate to a larger house may not consider unimproved land a substitute for improved land. Similarly, a farmer who wants to expand operations may not wish to purchase an improved parcel, having no need for the house. We validated this split using a Chow test for structural change (Model 1: $F_{(10,434)} = 1.95$; Model 2: $F_{(10,434)}=1.98$).[14] Based on this

13 The square root transformation allows SQFTSTRC and ACRES to have decreasing positive implicit price curves while allowing greater variation than would be found with the natural log transformation.

14 The Chow statistic is [(RSSR – USSR)/p]/[USSR/(n-2p)] where RSSR is the Restricted Sum of Squared Residuals, USSR is the Unrestricted Sum of Squared Residuals, p is the number of restrictions being tested, and n is the total number of observations in the restricted model. The statistic is distributed as F(p,n-2p).

Table 10.2 Estimated coefficient explaining the value for 10+ acre parcels in three southern Maryland counties

	Model 1: Inverse Semi-log		Model 2: Nonlinear	
	Improved	Unimproved	Improved	Unimproved
Variable	Parameter (StdDev)	Parameter (StdDev)	Parameter (StdDev)	Parameter (StdDev)
INTERCEPT	-44656 (49036)	152219** (65397)	46651 (39944)	257586*** (57382)
SQFTSTRC^#	5988** (2727)	-	1407*** (429)	-
HOUSEAGE	990138*** (258848)	-	146432** (0.191)	-
AGE* SQFT^#	-148593*** (32740)	-	-6292*** (1260)	-
CONSTRAV	79867*** (16927)	-	68729*** (16790)	-
CONSTGOODP	175936*** (24172)	-	163933*** (24056)	-
BASEMENT	34614** (13885)	-	30108** (13460)	-
GARAGE	32086** (14257)	-	31886** (13924)	-
TOTBATHS	11258 (7233)	-	8675 (7076)	-
FIREPLACE	56640*** (16030)	-	54483*** (15754)	-

WATERFRONT	71890*** (24907)	23485 (32221)	73442*** (24416)	24634 (31681)
STMARYS	11894 (13252)	-17430 (14980)	5748 (13004)	-20394 (14736)
ACRES^#	70235*** (8993)	66896*** (8897)	22611*** (2737)	20756*** (2578)
PERPASTURE	-78656* (45204)	64689 (93303)	-82832* (44055)	61842 (91747)
PERCROP	49268** (19957)	19951 (23370)	46711** (19511)	23311 (23016)
S_SLOPE_M_H	-18931 (20838)	-29940 (22399)	-17862 (20300)	-31322 (22012)
S_ERODEHIGH	-62006* (32543)	-221459*** (55873)	-52609* (31858)	-222424*** (54889)
S_ERODEM	-83908** (36757)	-214964*** (58284)	-71406** (35979)	-216284*** (57230)
S_FLOOD	-92954*** (34299)	-304745*** (56085)	-87585*** (33554)	-306282*** (55112)
Adjusted R2	0.58	0.33	0.60	0.35

* indicates rejection of the null hypothesis at the 0.10 significance level; ** at the 0.05 significance level; ***at the 0.01 significance level.
^ SQFTSTRC, ACRES are transformed by natural logarithm in Model 1: Inverse semi-log.
# SQFTSTRC, ACRES are transformed by square root in Model 2: non-linear

statistic, we concluded that conducting separate tests for improved and unimproved parcels is the most appropriate method.

The results of our tests are consistent with the expected effects indicated in Table 10.1. In both model specifications, the statistically significant estimated coefficients are the same (although of different magnitudes) for the improved and unimproved parcels. Table 10.2 presents the coefficients and standard errors for the two models.

Across the improved parcels models, an additional square foot adds to the market value as expected. House age significantly decreases the parcel market value, as newer homes are worth more than older homes. The marginal value of an additional square foot is significantly lower for newer homes than for older homes. This is not unexpected as newer homes have more square footage, on average, than older homes. Average and good-luxury construction grades lead to higher market values. Basements, garages, and fireplaces add value to the sales price of a parcel. Surprisingly, the total number of bathrooms has no significant effect on the market value.

A waterfront location commands a premium based on the market value for improved parcels. Additional pasture land lowers the market value while additional cropland raises it. Highly and moderately erodible soils as well as floodplain soils significantly lower parcel market values while steeper slopes do not have a significant effect. A parcel in St. Mary's County has the same value as those in Calvert or Charles.

In explaining the unimproved parcel prices, waterfront location and county have no significant effect on the market value. Neither do pasture and cropland, nor steeper slopes. As expected, highly and moderately erodible soils as well as floodplain soils significantly lower parcel market values.

Out-of-sample predictions were made to compare the predictive quality of the models. Model 2 has smaller average differences between the actual and predicted market values for the improved parcels and a higher adjusted R^2. Among the unimproved parcels, Model 1 has smaller mean differences between actual and predicted market values but Model 2 has a higher adjusted R^2. Therefore, we decided to use the estimated coefficients from Model 2 to predict the parcel prices in our study. These out-of sample predictions provide the predicted land values used in the targeting schemes a degree of validity to skeptics of hedonic models or regression approaches. Many program administrators and policy makers prefer a more standard approach to real estate valuation (even though in most cases appraisers use regression analysis to provide their valuations). Of course, if one found that the model predicted very poorly, then additional data collection and estimation might be warranted. In some areas, unusual characteristics can have an impact on market prices. For example, proximity to a nuclear power plant might decrease land values throughout the neighborhood or having a view of Mount Vernon might increase the value of all the parcels on the opposite side of the Potomac. In either of these cases, if the program has collected the standard land characteristics and ecological measures, it might need to reconsider both the ecological valuation derived and the estimation of land acquisition costs.

The results from the hedonic model estimations were used to predict parcels' market values in the study area of Charles, Calvert, and St. Mary's Counties, MD. The mean predicted market value was $146,949 for unimproved parcels and $267,611 for improved parcels.

Current GreenPrint Targeting Scheme

Program administrators have developed a comprehensive ecological scoring for all parcels in the state to better target valuable parcels and help them prioritize which parcels to conserve. Maryland's detailed ecological scores provide a ranking scheme for quantifying the ecological benefits of different targeting protocols and enable the examination of different targeting strategies that include economic considerations. GIA identifies the hubs and corridors which are then scored on ecological and development risk indices and are ranked within physiographic regions. The highest ranked are considered for conservation. These identified lands are then assigned Desktop Ecological Scores (DES) to re-rank parcels for acquisition.

The most detailed site comparisons are made at the individual cell level (0.314 acre). This corresponds to the finest resolution in the satellite imagery land use data available. The fine scale ranking is calculated for all cells in the state and is based on the cell's local features score and the cell's landscape significance. According to Weber (2003), the formula for ranking cells by landscape significance is:

- score of cell within hub = 100-[(hub composite ecological percentile)/2.5]
- score of cell within corridor = 80-[(hub composite ecological percentile)/3.334]
- score of cell outside hubs and corridors = 0.

A fine scale development risk ranking is also developed for all cells using many of the parameters collected for the ecological ranking. In addition, a land value surface is included in the development risk ranking. The assessed market value for the land is used to create a land value surface which is included in the development risk rankings as a proxy for development risk (Weber 2003). The parameter data on market land value is created using the 1997–98 MDPVD and the land value surface is interpolated. Implicitly, this method assumes that land parcels have identical characteristics and have an equal gradation in value between them which is probably not the case.

Next, Desktop Ecological Scores are computed. Parameters of importance include the number of acres of the GI on the parcel, the percent of the parcel in the GI, the mean ecological score for the GI piece of the parcel, contiguousness of the parcel with other protected lands (for example, county, state, or federal

Table 10.3 Scoring parameters and weights for desktop ecological scores

Parameter	Excellent Rank	Good Rank	Fair Rank	Poor Rank	Parameter weight
Acres of Green Infrastructure in Parcel	> 65	32.1–65	18–32	<18	2
Percent of Green Infrastructure in Parcel	>90%	69–90%	34–68.9%	<34%	1
Mean Ecological Score for Green Infrastructure in Parcel	>85	76–85	66–75.9	<66	3
Nearby Acres of Protected lands	>434	152–434	5–151	<5	1
Percent Gain in Protection to Hub or Corridor	>10%	2.5–10%	1.0–2.4%	<1%	1

open space and parks, parcels with conservation easements restricting further development), and the percentage increase in GI attained by adding the parcel. Depending on its ranking on a particular parameter, a land parcel is awarded points: 4 for an excellent ranking, 2 for good, 1 for fair, and 0 for poor. The numerical cut-offs for these rankings on the five parameters are listed in Table 10.3. Thus if a parcel has more than 65 acres of GI, it would receive a score of 4 on that parameter. Similarly if a parcel has a mean ecological score between 66 and 75.9 it would receive 1 point. Then each parameter's points are multiplied by the weights in Table 10.3 as certain parameters are deemed more important than others. The sum of the weighted points on all five parameters is the DES for a given parcel. The DES scale is divided into quartiles to distinguish parcels as excellent (DES 21–32), good (DES 15–20), fair (DES 9–14), and least suitable (DES 0–8) prospects for acquisition.

The DES is designed to measure the benefits to society of preserving a given land parcel, and is used in the GreenPrint program to maximize these benefits subject to funding constraints. This is written as

$$\max DES_i * p_i \text{ subject to } \sum_i c_i p_i \leq B,$$

where DES_i is the measure of benefits for parcel i, p_i equals 1 if parcel i is acquired and 0 otherwise, c_i is the cost of acquiring parcel i, and B is available GreenPrint funding (the budget). The program currently makes land acquisitions, beginning with the highest ranked parcels and working downward, until the available funding is exhausted. Ranking and purchasing parcels by benefits only, the GreenPrint program uses what may be termed a "Benefits" targeting protocol.

Results

Because it targets parcels by benefits only, the GreenPrint program may not be allocating its scarce funding resources optimally. In this study, we present alternative targeting strategies for comparison with the program's Benefits targeting approach. The first alternative targeting scheme is built on maximizing the total acreage subject to budget constraints:

$$\max \sum_i ACRES_i * p_i$$
$$s.t. \sum c_i p_i \leq B$$

where $ACRES_i$ is parcel i 's acreage, p_i equals 1 if parcel i is acquired and 0 otherwise, c_i is the cost of acquiring parcel i, and B is available GreenPrint funding. This approach minimizes the costs, or $\min \sum_i (c_i / ACRES_i) * p_i$, for a given budget constraint, where (c_i /$ACRES_i$) is the parcel's market value (cost) per acre. The program administrator ranks the parcels from lowest to highest market value per acre and enrols them until the budget constraint is reached. This strategy is termed "Acreage" targeting.

The second alternative targeting scheme focuses on a specific benefits metric deemed ecologically important, highly erodible soils. The hedonic model contained this variable, S_ERODEHIGH, and it had a negative impact on market value. Targeting this ecologically important characteristic may help select ecologically relevant parcels with low costs. The targeting protocol's optimization can be written as

$$\max \sum_i S\_ERODEHIGH_i * p_i$$
$$s.t. \sum c_i p_i \leq B$$

where S_ERODEHIGH is the percent of parcel i with highly erodible soil, p_i equals 1 if parcel i is acquired and 0 otherwise, c_i is the cost of acquiring parcel i, and $B$is available GreenPrint funding. This strategy is termed "Erodible Soils" targeting.

Supplementing the analysis described above, we also compared the GreenPrint Benefits targeting protocol with another strategy termed "Benefits per Dollar." This scheme optimizes the summation of the DES scores for the parcels divided by the acquisition cost or (DES/c_i) or

$$\max \sum_i DES / c_{ii} * p_i$$
$$s.t. \sum_i c_i p_i \leq B$$

In this case, the program administrator seeks parcels which provide a high level of benefits for a low cost. Taking this approach requires an assumption that the DES score is a cardinal measure—i.e. parcels are ranked such that the distance between a DES score of 32 and a DES score of 31 is the same as the distance between a DES score of 16 and a DES score of 15. Thus if parcel 1's DES score is 32 and parcel 20's is 16, the benefits of conserving parcel 1 must be twice as large ecologically as conserving parcel 20. Both the fine scale development risk and the fine scale ecological rankings are based on ranking parcels such that parcel 1 might be better than parcel 2 but we do not know "how much" better, this assumption about the DES score thus may overstate the degree of cardinality. If the DES scores are not cardinal, we could be over or under-stating the amount of extra benefits we will generate using a benefit per dollar approach.

To perform our analyses, we calculated the predicted price (c_i) and the DES for every parcel at least 10 acres in size with designated agricultural or residential land. Those parcels with an excellent ranking on the DES (scores ranging from 21 to 32) were evaluated for inclusion in the targeting scenarios. Targeting was limited to parcels within Calvert, Charles, and St. Mary's Counties and included both improved and unimproved land parcels. An improved parcel's full market value was used in the rankings for the parcel's land acquisition cost, including the value of the structure on the parcel. Given one of the goals of the Greenprint program is reclamation and restoration, the program could purchase a property with a housing structure and then remove it. If a conservation easement approach was used and only the right to develop was acquired, the value of the structure would not be considered relevant. We considered two budget constraints, $16 million and $25 million,[15] in our first analysis, in which we treated the three counties as a single region and reported overall results. In the second analysis, we divided a $16 million program budget evenly among the three counties and reported separate results for each.

Regional Targeting Scenarios

Table 10.4 presents the outcomes for the tri-county region of the three targeting strategies—Benefits maximization (DES maximization), Acreage maximization (cost minimization), and Erodible Soils maximization—under program budgets of $16 million and $25 million. The number of parcels targeted under each scenario is displayed in the first row of the table. Total Acres summarizes the extent of the targeting schemes' reach in land area. The Mean Predicted Parcel Market Value per Acre can be compared across packages to assess the relative costs of acquiring one more acre. The Mean Percent of Parcel with Highly Erodible Soils measures the degree of highly erodible soils among the targeted parcels.

15 Under each projected budget, the targeted parcels included full parcels for which sufficient budgeting was available to purchase the entire parcel. If a parcel could not be purchased in entirety, the next ranked parcel that could be purchased was selected.

Table 10.4 Overall targeting packages for GreenPrint for three counties: Benefits, Acreage and Erodible soils

Targeting type	Benefits		Acreage		Erodible soils	
Projected budget	*$16 million*	*$25 million*	*$16 million*	*$25 million*	*$16 million*	*$25 million*
# of Parcels	50	89	31	55	71	104
Total Acres	9,222	13,971	16,790	23,943	5,911	10,484
Mean Predicted Parcel Market Value	$318,903	$280,640	$515,040	$454,001	$225,049	$237,410
Mean Parcel Market Value per Acre	$1,729	$1,788	$951	$1,043	$2,703	$2,355
Mean % of Parcel with Highly Erodible Soils	26.5%	34.4%	39.7%	39.2%	100.0%	96.3%
DES Score 30–32	54.0%	30.0%	6.0%	5.0%	1.4%	2.0%
DES Score 26–29	46.0%	59.0%	50.0%	51.0%	28.2%	28.0%
DES Score 21–25	0.0%	0.0%	44.0%	44.0%	70.4%	70.0%

Table 10.5 Overall alternative targeting strategy for three counties: benefits or benefits per dollar

Targeting scheme	*Benefits*	*Benefits/per dollar*	*Benefits*	*Benefits/per dollar*	*Benefits*	*Benefits/per dollar*
	$5 million		$16 million		$25 million	
Parcels	4	44	32	19	41	175
Mean Predicted Per Acre Price	$6,936	$826	$2,825	$1,059	$3,016	$1,172
Mean DES	32	27	30	26	30	26
Total Acres Enrolled	871	6,019	4,953	15,287	7,400	21,648

Given a $16 million budget, the Acreage protocol includes the most acreage (16,790 acres), as expected. The Benefits protocol includes more acreage (9,222 acres) than the Erodible Soils protocol (5,911 acres), which enrolled smaller parcels. DES rankings give a large weight to larger parcels, thus larger parcels have higher benefits score all else being equal. Benefits targeting enrols 50 parcels, compared to 71 parcels under Erodible Soils targeting. Acreage targeting enrols only 31 parcels; it enrolled parcels with the largest average parcel size (542 acres). The Acreage scheme also has the highest mean parcel market value and the lowest per acre cost (at $951, compared to $1,729 for the Benefits targeting and $2,703 for the Erodible Soils targeted parcels). As expected, the mean percent of the parcel with highly erodible soils is highest (at 100 percent) in the Erodible Soils package. Acreage targeted parcels average nearly 40 percent with erodible soils and Benefits targeted parcels only 26.5 percent.

The Benefits protocol has the greatest number and proportion of parcels with top ranking on the DES: 54 percent of its parcels are scored between 30 and 32, compared to 6 percent and 1.4 percent of the parcels targeted in the Acreage and Erodible Soils approaches, respectively. The remaining parcels under Benefits targeting are scored between 26 and 29, while half of the Acreage parcels and about 28 percent of the Erodible Soils parcels fall in this middle scoring category. The final category contains parcels with DES scores of 21 to 25. Forty-four percent of the Acreage targeted parcels and 70 percent of the Erodible Soils parcels have these DES scores. Clearly the Benefits targeting approach enrols the top ranked parcels. Somewhat surprisingly, the Acreage targeted parcels are more likely to have higher DES scores than the Erodible Soils targeted parcels. This suggests that optimizing on one ecological metric may create a relative deficit in others at least in the case of erodible soils.

Given a $25 million budget, the three targeting strategies yield outcomes that mirror those reported above. The Acreage protocol again includes the most acreage (23,943 acres), followed by the Benefits (13,971 acres) then the Erodible Soils (10,484 acres) protocols. Benefits targeting enrols 89 parcels, compared to 104 (smaller) parcels under Erodible Soils targeting. Acreage targeting still enrols the fewest parcels (55) and has the largest average parcel size (435 acres). The Acreage per acre cost is $1,043, an increase of $92 over the per acre cost in the $16 million budget. This compares to $1,788 for the Benefits targeted parcels (an increase of only $59 over the per acre cost in the smaller budget) and $2,355 ($348 less per acre than the comparable cost in the smaller budget) for the Erodible Soils targeted parcels. The mean percent of the parcel with highly erodible soils remains high, at over 96 percent, in the Erodible Soils scheme. Acreage targeted parcels average about 39 percent with erodible soils and Benefits targeted parcels are close behind, at nearly 35 percent.

The Benefits protocol again has the greatest number and proportion of parcels with the top DES scores: 30 percent of these parcels are scored 30 or higher—but this is a drop from the 54 percent scoring in this category under the smaller budget. However, results for the other targeting strategies are similar to those from the smaller budget analysis: 5 percent and 2 percent of the Acreage and Erodible Soils targeted parcels, respectively, are in the top DES category. The remaining parcels under Benefits targeting receive scores between 26 and 29 on the DES, as do about half of the Acreage parcels and 28 percent of the Erodible Soils parcels. The 21–25 DES category comprised 44 percent of the Acreage targeted parcels and 70 percent of the Erodible Soils parcels. While the Benefits targeting approach still enrols more top rated parcels than the other approaches, it begins to enrol a higher percentage of lower ranked parcels as the budget increases. On the other hand, the distributions for Acreage and Erodible Soils targeted parcels remain almost exactly the same under the two budget scenarios. The difference among the three targeting schemes is greater when the budget is smaller: Having a big enough budget to enrol all excellent parcels makes the incorporation of acquisition costs or variations in the targeting schemes less important than under a situation of constrained budgets.

The difference in the cost per acre and the number of acres enrolled can be seen starkly in Table 10.5, where a comparison is presented of targeting by Benefits and by Benefits per Dollar of acquisition costs. For small budgets such as $5 million, the Benefits targeting approach enrols 871 acres at an average cost of almost $7,000 per acre. If instead program administrators had maximized the benefits for each dollar of acquisition costs, they could have enrolled over 6,000 acres at a cost of $826 per acre. Although the mean DES score is higher for the parcels targeted by the Benefits strategy (32) than for those in the Benefits per Dollar approach (27), the additional 5,000 acres acquired through the latter approach would seem to provide a great deal of overall ecological benefits to society. Even with a much less constrained budget of five times that amount, or $25 million, a program administrator taking acquisition costs into consideration would trade off an average DES score of 30 and 7,400 acres for an average DES score of 26 and 21,650 acres, almost three times more acreage enrolled. Focusing just on benefits results in a per acre acquisition cost of $3,016, compared to $1,172 with a Benefits per Dollar approach.

County-Specific Targeting Scenarios

Table 10.6 presents the outcomes of the Benefits, Acreage, and Erodible Soils targeting strategies for the three southern Maryland counties separately. These results demonstrate how the impact of the targeting schemes changes under a scenario in which counties, rather than the state or region, are responsible for identifying and preserving lands under GreenPrint. In this scenario, the total GreenPrint budget of $16 million was split equally among the counties, and findings were compared to the results of the regional approach using the $16 million budget (reported previously in Table 10.4).

For the Benefits targeting scheme, the total number of parcels enrolled drops to 48 from 50 parcels in the regional selection process. In addition, the total number of acres decreases by 283, to a total of 8,939 acres. The mean per acre value of

Table 10.6 Disaggregate targeting practices for GreenPrint for three counties with $16 million budget: Benefit, acreage, and erodible soils

	Benefit			Acreage			Erodible Soils		
	Calvert	*Charles*	*St. Mary's*	*Calvert*	*Charles*	*St. Mary's*	*Calvert*	*Charles*	*St. Mary's*
# of Parcels	16	16	16	11	12	10	17	31	24
Total Acres	3,056	3,014	2,869	4,286	6,232	5,559	2,221	1,388	2,257
Mean Predicted Parcel Market Value	$328,663	$333,036	$328,557	$482,021	$439,717	$532,963	$312,676	$170,393	$221,742
Mean Parcel Market Value per Acre	$1,721	$1,768	$1,832	$1,237	$847	$959	$2,393	$3,807	$2,358
Mean % of Parcel with Highly Erodible Soils	2.8%	57.5%	21.4%	1.5%	41.2%	40.5%	18.8%	100.0%	99.2%
DES Score 30–32	50.0%	56.0%	62.5%	27.3%	0.0%	0.0%	12.0%	0.0%	4.0%
DES Score 26–29	44.0%	44.0%	37.5%	45.40%	67.0%	40.0%	29.0%	26.0%	21.0%
DES Score 21–25	6.0%	0.0%	0.0%	27.30%	33.0%	60.0%	59.0%	74.0%	75.0%

the properties is higher in Charles and St. Mary's, which is surprising as these are usually lower cost counties than Calvert. The mean percent of parcels with highly erodible soils is higher in Charles but lower in both Calvert and St. Mary's, compared to the comparable percent in the regional analysis. St. Mary's has a higher percent of its parcels with the highest possible DES scores (63 percent) compared to Calvert at 50 percent and Charles at 56 percent. Unlike what occurred in the regional selection process, the county-level selection reveals parcels in the lowest DES category: 6 percent of the Calvert parcels have scores below 26. Thus unless equity is a major priority of the GreenPrint program, selecting parcels regionally or selecting among the least constrained parcel set results in better outcomes.

The Acreage targeting method for each of the counties targets a comparable numbers of parcels. However, far fewer acres are enrolled under this local selection strategy—a total of 16,077 acres compared to the 16,790 acres of the regional selection. The average price per acre also increases somewhat in Calvert ($1,237 per acre) and St. Mary's ($959 per acre) compared to the $951 of the regional selection process. On the other hand, Charles is able to enrol parcels with an average market value of $847 per acres. This suggests that a regional targeting package would allocate greater funding for Charles County acreage and thus would be able to enrol more acres. Twenty-seven percent of the parcels enrolled in Calvert County place in the highest range of DES scores, and Charles County enrols a higher percent of parcels (67 percent) in the middle range of DES scores than occurs in the regional approach (50 percent). However, 60 percent of St. Mary's enrolled parcels fall in the low range of DES scores, compared to 44 percent of the regionally-selected parcels. These results indicate again that the regional-level targeting packages have more parcels to select from and therefore may achieve higher metrics. In this case, it depends on how much weight is given to enrolling low cost parcels and more acres relative to the distribution of the DES scores.

With the Erodible Soil targeting strategy, the counties enrol one additional parcel (for a total of 72 parcels) and only 45 fewer acres, relative to the regional targeting scenario. Calvert and St. Mary's parcels are less expensive than those selected via the regional targeting; but at $3,807 per acre, the market price average of parcels in Charles County is more than $1,000 per acre higher than the regional per acre average price of $2,703. On the other hand, both Calvert and St. Mary's enrol higher percentages of more valued land (12 and 4 percent, respectively, fall into the highest DES category) than occurs with the regional approach (at 1.4 percent). At the lower end, Charles and St. Mary's have slightly higher percentages of parcels with DES scores in the 21–25 range (74 and 75 percent, respectively) compared to the 70 percent in the regional case. These results indicate again that the county-level targeting packages may be less optimal than the regional-level targeting packages.

The Benefits, Acreage, and Erodible Soils targeting strategies perform better at the regional level than when restricted to specific counties. Regional targeting can maximize the use of appropriate optimization metrics across the entire area. By contrast, the three counties have constrained parcel sets, and thus fewer choices. Economic theory suggests, and our results support the notion, that the regional targeting strategies are more effective at reaching the optimal goal than the county-specific constrained approaches and supports statewide administration of the program over local administration. More generally, this observation supports large-scale, comprehensive land conservation programs to maximize ecological benefits while most efficiently allocating public funds.

Targeting Suggestions based on Hedonic Model Estimation Results

Interestingly, beyond the inclusion of the acquisition costs into the targeting schemes, the hedonic results for both the improved and unimproved parcels offer insight on the relative costs of targeting various land characteristics for acquisition. The insignificance of waterfront location on the market value for an unimproved parcel suggests that targeting these parcels may be useful for increasing ecological benefits. Unimproved parcels with waterfront area may have significant barriers to development, such as floodplain soils or wetlands, site-level attributes that deter construction but could provide water quality and soil erosion protection. Since a waterfront location has a positive effect on market value for improved parcels, programs should avoid these while more efficiently targeting waterfront acreage through unimproved parcels.

Among improved parcels, those with higher percentages of pasture land have lower market values than comparable parcels without pasture land. Pasture land may be more highly valued ecologically as this land is less intensively developed than cropland. It also might be less costly to restore to a natural state. Conversely, improved parcels with high percentages of cropland are more expensive all else the same, and should not be targeted. Thus, pasture and forest appear to be better options for providing ecosystem services in this region. Interestingly, for the unimproved parcels, no land use had a significant impact on the market price. Therefore pasture, forest, and cropland are equivalent from a monetary standpoint.

The negative coefficients on the soil characteristics for both the improved and unimproved parcels suggest that land conservation programs should target land parcels with highly erodible soils and floodplains. As the percent of these ecologically valuable characteristics increases, the market price decreases, so parcels with these desirable characteristics would have lower acquisition costs than similar parcels without these characteristics. However, one needs to be somewhat cautious in focusing only on one parameter, given the results above that parcels with highly erodible soils were smaller in size and thus cost more per acre.

Conclusions

We acknowledge that land conservation programs may have reasons to acquire Cadillac parcels (public visibility) and expensive parcels facing significant development risks (expected loss of benefits). Yet even in these circumstances, land acquisition costs should be considered. By incorporating land acquisitions costs into their targeting schemes, programs would be able to preserve more acres for the same budgetary resources or achieve the same ecological benefits at a lower cost. This is especially true when ecological values are positively correlated with land values—i.e., when those parcels with the highest ecological values are also those with the highest costs. In addition, the benefits of incorporating land acquisition costs into the targeting schemes increase as budget resources become more constrained. Programs with large budgets may find little differences between targeting schemes if they can enrol all desirable parcels. However, most programs have much more limited scope and thus the acquisition costs matter. Resources for land conservation are scarce despite the passage of many conservation funding initiatives. The more constrained the budget, the more important considering acquisition costs becomes.

Incorporating land values however can be challenging for these types of programs. Markets are thin and there are few comparable properties with which to compare parcels. In addition, property tax assessment may be skewed by use-value or preferential tax programs. Given these challenges, we suggest that programs estimate hedonic models to predict market values for representative properties. As mentioned above, few of the programs incorporate the cost of the parcels in their targeting schemes despite more than two decades of recommendations to do so by the academic community.

Because most programs collect data on land and neighborhood characteristics, they should be able to obtain market sales prices for recent arms' length sales with a little extra effort. These price data can be used to estimate hedonic models in order to obtain the parameters needed to predict prices for those parcels that have not recently sold. We found that models should be estimated separately for parcels with homes and those without, and that the square footage of the house and the number of acres should be entered into the model nonlinearly. Overall, the models predict land values for the parcels well.

We incorporated these predicted land values in various ways and found the three sets of targeting strategies perform differently under different situations and constraints. The Benefits scenarios clearly target the parcels with the greatest DES scores but at a higher per acre cost. The Acreage scenarios target the greatest amount of acreage for conservation but with a lower overall DES score. The Erodible Soils scenarios target those parcels with the highest mean percentage of highly erodible soils. In some sense, we were surprised that targeting erodible soils did not enrol a higher acreage. The hedonic model suggested that parcels with erodible soils would be less expensive all else the same; however these parcels were also smaller, and smaller parcels generally cost more per acre as a rule. Therefore using a single metric, such as erodible soils, may not be a perfect solution in all cases.

We also compared the Benefits targeting to a Benefits per Dollar approach. We found that factoring in the benefits per dollar of acquisition cost results in substantially more acreage being enrolled while maximizing the overall benefits. Maximizing benefits per dollar instead of just benefits resulted in almost three times more acreage enrolled by programs with larger budgets, and over six times more acreage enrolled by smaller-budgeted programs. The additional enrolled acreage would surely provide a great deal of overall ecological benefits to society. The only drawback of this approach is one must assume that the rank ordering is cardinal rather than ordinal.

As many programs already have collected GIS data similar to those used in this study, these land conservation programs can conduct similar analyses to make well-informed decisions. Given that the GreenPrint DES calculation heavily weights areas of highly erodible soils and areas of wetlands, these program managers may utilize the Acreage targeting schemes among parcels with excellent rankings on the DES, in order to maximize the acreage targeted and preserved, or assume that the measures of ecological benefits are cardinal. Both these types of targeting allow the greatest amount of land with the highest ecological benefits value to be enrolled.

The study also highlights the benefits of developing land targeting strategies from an unconstrained parcel choice set. The optimal targeting schemes are developed across larger regions—even across the entire state—rather than in smaller isolated pockets such as counties. Of course, political or equity consideration may also be important to implementation strategies.

Future work for direct implementation of this conservation targeting technique can include improvement of the hedonic model. The inclusion of additional data, especially more ecological characteristics of the land parcels, would strengthen the model. Incorporating partial parcels or conservation easements into the strategy would be useful where there may not be sufficient funds to target an entire parcel. Finally, calculation of the cardinal fine-scale ecological scores and willingness to pay measures related to specific ecological attributes would enable researchers to develop benefit/cost ratios utilizing the willingness to pay for specific ecological attributes for the benefits and the predicted parcel market values for the costs.

References

Ando, A., Camm, J., Polasky, S. and Solow, A. 1998. Species distributions, land values, and efficient conservation. *Science*, 279, 2126–8.

Bastian, C., McLeod, D., Germino, M., Reiners, W. and Blasko, B. 2002. Environmental amenities and agricultural land values: A hedonic model using geographic information systems data. *Ecological Economics*, 40(3), 337–49.

Bockstael, N. 1996. Modeling economics and ecology: The importance of a spatial perspective. *American Journal of Agricultural Economics*, 78, 1168–80.

Breffle, W., Morey, E. and Lodder, T. 1998. Using contingent valuation to estimate a neighborhood's willingness to pay to preserve undeveloped urban land. *Urban Studies*, 35(4), 715–27.

Bureau of Labor Statistics. 2003. *Consumer Price Index – All Urban Consumers* [Online: U.S. Department of Labor]. Available at: http://data.bls.gov [accessed 1 March 2010].

Faux, J. and Perry, G. 1999. Estimating irrigation water value using hedonic price analysis: A case study in Malheur County, Oregon. *Land Economics*, 75(3), 440–52.

Ferraro, P.J. 2003. Assigning priority to environmental policy interventions in a heterogeneous world. *Journal of Policy Analysis and Management*, 22, 27–43.

Geoghegan, J., Lynch, L. and Bucholtz, S. 2003. Capitalization of open spaces into housing values and the residential property tax revenue impacts of agricultural easement programs. *Agricultural and Resource Economics Review*, 32(1), 33–45.

Holway, J. and Burby, R. 1990. The effects of floodplain development controls on residential land values. *Land Economics*, 66(3), 259–71.

Loomis, J., Kent, P., Strange, L., Fausch, K. and Covich, A.2000. Measuring the total economic value of restoring ecosystem services in an impaired river basin: Results from a contingent valuation survey. *Ecological Economics*, 33, 103–17.

Lynch, L. and Lovell, S. 2003. Local land markets and agricultural preservation programs, in *Government Policy and Farmland Markets: The Maintenance of Farmer Wealth*, edited by C.B. Moss and A. Schmitz. Ames: Iowa State Press, 285–302.

Maryland Department of Agriculture. 2004. *Maryland Agricultural Land Preservation Foundation* http://www.mda.state.md.us/malpf.php.(accessed 14 June 2005)

Maryland DNR. 2003. *Maryland's Green Infrastructure* [Online: Maryland Department of Natural Resources]. Available at: http://www.dnr.state.md.us/greenways/greenprint/ [accessed 1 October 2003]. Also at http://www.dnr.maryland.gov/greenways/gi/gi.html and http://www.greenprint.maryland.gov/

Maryland Department of State Planning. 1973. *Natural Soil Groups Technical Report.* Baltimore: Maryland Department of State Planning.

Maryland Greenways Commission. 2001. Green infrastructure identified and protected in southern Maryland *as part of the Maryland Atlas of Greenways, Water Trails, and Green Infrastructure.* Annapolis: Maryland Department of Natural Resources and the Chesapeake Bay and Watershed Programs. http://dnr.maryland.gov/greenways/ (accessed 9 February 2004).

Messer, K.D. 2006. The conservation benefits of cost-effective land acquisition: A case study in Maryland *Journal of Environmental Management*, 79, 305–15.

Nickerson, C. and Lynch, L. 2001. The effect of farmland preservation programs on farmland prices. *American Journal of Agricultural Economics*, 83(2), 341–51.

Palmquist, R. and Danielson, L. 1989. A hedonic study of the effects of erosion control and drainage on farmland values. *American Journal of Agricultural Economics*, 71(1), 55–62.

Pate, J. and Loomis, J. 1997. The effect of distance on willingness to pay values: A case study of wetlands and salmon in California. *Ecological Economics*, 20, 199–207.

Resources Agency of California. 2004. *Preserving California's Natural Heritage: State Land Conservation Summary, Selected Funding Sources* [Online]. Available at: http://ceres.ca.gov/planning/conservation_guidebook [accessed5 January 2005].

Rosen, S. 1974. Hedonic prices and implicit markets: Product differentiation in pure competition. *The Journal of Political Economy*, 82(1), 34–55.

Stumborg, B., Baerenklau, K. and Bishop, R. 2001. Nonpoint source pollution and present values: A contingent valuation study of Lake Mendota. *Review of Agricultural Economics*, 23(1), 120–32.

Tri-County Council for Southern Maryland (2004). *Regional Map of Southern Maryland Counties*. http://www.tccsmd.org/[accessed 10 November 2004].

U.S. Census Bureau. 2002. *Statistical Abstract of the United States.* Washington, D.C.: U.S. Government Printing Office.

Weber, T. 2003. *Maryland's Green Infrastructure Assessment: A Comprehensive Strategy for Land Conservation and Restoration.* Annapolis: Maryland Department of Natural Resources, Watershed Services Unit, Landscape and Watershed Analysis Division.

Wu, J.J., Zilberman, D. and Babcock, B. 2001. Environmental and distributional impacts of conservation targeting strategies. *Journal of Environmental and Ecological Economics*, 41, 333–50.

Xu, F., Mittelhammer, R. and Barkley, P. 1993. Measuring the contributions of site characteristics to the value of agricultural land. *Land Economics*, 69(4), 359–69.

Chapter 11
A Case Study of Wisconsin's Knowles–Nelson Stewardship Program

W. David Clutter

Communities throughout the nation face considerable challenges as they attempt to preserve water quality and quantity, protect representative samples of biological diversity, and provide recreational opportunities for all citizens to enjoy. Since the establishment of Yellowstone National Park in 1872, federal, state, and local governments have served as the primary conduit for protecting and conserving our nation's critical lands, waters, and wildlife (Endicott 1993). However, particularly in the past 40 years, nonprofit conservation organizations have played an increasingly important role in conserving land and waters that improve quality of life and, in many cases, support local economies (Wisconsin Department of Natural Resources [WDNR] 2006). As a result many government agencies are beginning to recognize the growing influence and important function provided by nonprofit conservation organizations, such as The Nature Conservancy and local land trusts. Navigating the often complex nature of natural resource protection, government agencies and nonprofit conservation organizations both realize the benefits of collaborating. These types of public–private partnerships are moving away from what were once primarily ad hoc activities and projects toward more systemic partnerships and programs (Endicott 1993).

Today, through a range of public–private conservation initiatives, a number of states around the country provide grant funding to nonprofit conservation organizations and local municipalities in order to encourage local involvement and to leverage additional resources for land and water conservation. As this collaborative trend continues, it is important to understand the factors that influence implementation of these types of statewide public–private conservation programs. In this study, data were gathered through interviews, surveys, and a Delphi study approach regarding a Wisconsin-specific case: the nonprofit component of the Knowles–Nelson Stewardship Program's Local Assistance Subprogram. More specifically, this study investigates the implementation of the Stewardship Program, with the goal of understanding those factors that promote successful partnerships for land conservation.

To date, little research has focused on the factors that influence implementation of statewide public–private conservation grant programs, such as Wisconsin's Knowles–Nelson Stewardship Program. As will be demonstrated in the results section, this study corroborates themes identified in the implementation literature and provides practical information for land trust organizations, agency staff and administrators, and advisory council members, as well as legislators interested in forwarding state land conservation goals. The results of this research can be used to guide implementation efforts of similar public–private conservation initiatives and to structure new and emerging initiatives.

An Overview of Wisconsin's Stewardship Programs

In 1989 the Wisconsin Legislature authorized a statewide land and easement acquisition program that provided $250 million through general obligation bonding over 10 years (aka "Stewardship I"). The state's second program, Stewardship II (2000–2010) and today known as the Warren Knowles–Gaylord Nelson Stewardship 2000 Program, provides $60 million annually to meet the goals of the program (Hotynski 2005). In an attempt to keep pace with inflation and provide the same buying power as the program had in 1990, the most recent program reauthorization (2010–2020) increased the annual amount to $105 million.

The goal of the Warren Knowles–Gaylord Nelson Stewardship Program is to protect Wisconsin's most valuable land and water resources while providing diverse outdoor recreational opportunities. This program seeks to accomplish these goals by enabling the Wisconsin Department of Natural Resources (WDNR) to acquire land or an interest in land (e.g., purchase of development rights) and to support conservation efforts of nonprofit conservation organizations and local units of government through matching grant provisions. The Stewardship Program has four major components:

1. Land and easement acquisition for conservation and outdoor recreation purposes.
2. Local assistance grants to acquire land, conservation easements, and development projects that support nature-based outdoor recreation activities.
3. Property development grants to support recreational facilities on state properties; and
4. Conservation of hardwood forests within the Baraboo Hills through easements and acquisitions.

As specified by statute, nonprofit conservation organizations (NCOs) are eligible for all elements of the Stewardship Program. As in most states, an NCO is defined as "a charitable trust or other nonprofit association whose purposes include the acquisition of property for conservation purposes and that is described in section 501(c)(3) of the Internal Revenue Code and is exempt from federal income tax under section 501(a) of the Internal Revenue Code" (Assistance to Nonprofit Conservation Organizations 2008). For the purposes of this paper, that part of the Stewardship's Local Assistance Subprogram that provides matching funds to

NCOs will be referred to as the "nonprofit component of the Stewardship." While seeking to catalyze cooperation and engage partners like local governments and NCOs, this statewide program serves as one of Wisconsin's primary sources of land acquisition funding for conservation and outdoor recreation. The nonprofit component of the Stewardship was introduced by an NCO advocate and modeled after a statewide program developed in California. Approximately $8 million of the current $60 million annual allocation available to the WDNR is shared with nonprofit conservation organizations in the form of matching grants.

The Bureau of Community Financial Assistance (CFA), located within the Division of Customer and Employee Services, administers all grant and loan programs within the WDNR, including the nonprofit component of the Stewardship. Housed within the Division of Land, the Bureau of Facilities and Lands provides real estate services for the Stewardship Program (e.g., appraisal review). The Natural Resources Board (NRB), whose members are appointed by the Governor, sets policy for the state DNR. Within the NRB, the Stewardship Subcommittee, comprised of representatives from nonprofits and local units of government appointed by the WDNR Secretary, provides policy recommendations to Department staff.

Over the past 17 years of the Stewardship Program, administrators, agency staff, nonprofit participants, special committee members, and nonprofit advocates have accumulated a body of knowledge about implementation of this type of public–private conservation grant program. This study uses their expert opinion to identify and describe the range of factors that influence the efficacy of implementing these programs. However, before these data are presented, it is important to review the literature on policy implementation to identify how the success (or failure) of the Knowles–Nelson Stewardship Program might be assessed.

Understanding Policy Implementation

Before policy implementation can be understood it must first be defined. However, as one discovers from a review of the literature, defining policy implementation is not entirely straightforward. For Goggin et al. (1990), implementation is simply the carrying out of public policies. Mazmanian and Sabatier elaborate on this concept: "Implementation is the carrying out of a basic policy decision, usually incorporated in a statute but which can also take the form of important executive orders or court decisions. Ideally, that decision identifies the problem(s) to be addressed, stipulates the objective(s) to be pursued, and, in a variety of ways, 'structures' the implementation process" (1983: 20–21). Matland (1995) discusses several possible definitions of successful implementation, including one originally provided by Ingram and Schneider (1990): "agencies comply with the directives of the states; agencies are held accountable for reaching specific indicators of success; goals of the statute are achieved; local goals are achieved, or there is an improvement in the political climate around the program" (1995: 154).

In 1973, Pressman and Wildavsky released their book *Implementation* and initiated a flurry of research on policy implementation (Talen 1996). The policy implementation literature spans a broad range of topics including but not limited to: the importance of coordination (Pressman and Wildavsky 1973), implementation as a system of games (Bardach 1977), the importance of clear and consistent mandates (Mazmanian and Sabatier 1983), the degree of political leadership (Daniere 1995), and so on. Over the past 30 years, three generations of policy implementation literature have emerged (Goggin et al. 1990), most of which focus on implementing some type of federal policy (e.g., Clean Air Act).

This first generation of literature viewed implementation from the perspective of policy-generating actors and tended to be exploratory and inductive, with the goal of creating new theory (Winter 2003). For example, Pressman and Wildavsky (1973) turned from a focus on how a bill becomes a law and instead targeted how a law is implemented as a program (Goggin et al. 1990: 14). Mazmanian and Sabatier, in their 1983 book entitled *Implementation and Public Policy*, exemplify the second generation of implementation research. Their primary contribution was the "development of analytical frameworks to guide research on the complex phenomenon of policy implementation" (Goggin et al. 1990: 14). The third generation research focused on developing a more quantitative and statistical approach to studying policy implementation and attempted to "shed new light on implementation behavior by explaining why that behavior varies across time, policies, and units of government" (Goggin et al. 1990: 17).

Five years after Goggin and his colleagues developed their "Communication Model", Matland attempted to synthesize the implementation literature through his Ambiguity-Conflict Model of Policy Implementation. Matland notes that the literature often makes "long lists of variable that may affect implementation," (ibid., p. 153) but that these variables are at times contradictory to one another. He believes that these contradictory recommendations occur "because the underlying antecedent characteristics of a policy are analyzed insufficiently" (ibid., p. 53). Furthermore, he suggests that the implementation literature lacks theoretical structure and that by focusing on a policy's level of conflict and ambiguity "testable predications can be made as to how the implementation process will unfold" (ibid., p. 170). Matland suggests that researchers should pay more attention to the "conditions under which these variables are important and the reasons we should expect them to be important" (Matland 1995: 153). To better characterize the underlying antecedent characteristics of different policy types, Matland developed the ambiguity-conflict matrix (see Table 11.1).

Matland's conflict-ambiguity model sought to identify "the type of implementation process" and "the central principle determining outcomes for this type of implementation" (ibid p. 159). By focusing on a policy's level of ambiguity and conflict, he suggests that his model "provides an analytical tool for identifying which of several differing models in the literature best describes the implementation process" (ibid p. 156). In short, this model allows one to more accurately identify key relevant factors that affect implementation of a given policy type. The conflict-

Table 11.1 Matland's ambiguity-conflict matrix: policy implementation process

Low-Conflict, Low-Ambiguity *Administrative Implementation* Resources E.g., Smallpox Eradication	**High-Conflict, Low-Ambiguity** *Political Implementation* Power E.g., School Busing
Low-Conflict, High-Ambiguity *Experimental Implementation* Contextual Conditions E.g., Headstart Program	**High-Conflict, High-Ambiguity** *Symbolic Implementation* Coalition Strength E.g., Community Action Agencies

ambiguity model characterizes four implementation process types: *administrative implementation; political implementation; experimental implementation; and, symbolic implementation.*

The central guiding principle for *administrative implementation* (low-conflict, low-ambiguity) is a need to secure necessary *resources*. Matland suggests that these types of policies and programs are "programmed decisions," with desired outcomes "virtually assured" if "sufficient resources are appropriated for the program" (ibid., p. 160). *Political implementation* on the other hand (high-conflict, low-ambiguity) depends on "having sufficient power to force one's will on the other participants or having sufficient resources to be able to bargain an agreement on means" (ibid., p. 164). In these situations policy goals tend to be explicit, but the allocation of resources may be contested or they lie outside of the implementing agency's control.

With *experimental implementation* (low-conflict, high-ambiguity) there is general agreement on the need to pursue some form of policy in response to a problem or need, but it is unclear as to which policy or program should be employed. For these policy situations, policy or program design depends on the mix of actors involved and success implementation is a function of "the resources and actors present in the microimplementing environment" (ibid., p. 166). Finally, in this most complex of the implementation scenarios, *symbolic implementation* (high-conflict, high-ambiguity), policy goals are unclear and resources are highly contested. In these situations outcomes are "determined by the coalition of actors at the local level who control the available resources" (ibid., p. 168).

Research Methods

This study employed a descriptive, single-case design utilizing the Delphi Method as a means to harness opinion from a wide range of participants. The Delphi technique is "a method for structuring a group communication process so that the process is effective in allowing a group of individuals, as a whole, to deal with a complex problem" (Linstone and Turoff 1975: 3). This allows for soliciting expert opinion on complex issues while maintaining participant anonymity.

Interviews were conducted with five individuals (identified from publications and local experts) with considerable knowledge and experience with the Stewardship Program. These interviews focused upon the history of the nonprofit component of the Stewardship Program and how it has functioned over the years, while identifying other individuals who are/were deeply involved in implementing and/or guiding policy. As a means to assess the extent to which the program was currently being implemented, representatives from the Stewardship Advisory Committee, the Governor's Blue Ribbon Task Force on the Stewardship, and past and present WDNR staff and administrators were presented with open-ended and semi-structured questions, as well as a Likert-scale questionnaire.

The next step in the analysis was to undertake the Delphi process to identify the range of factors that most affect program implementation. The first of three Delphi instruments was used to open the discussion and encourage participants to list a range of factors that they felt influenced implementation of the nonprofit component of the Stewardship. A second Delphi instrument asked participants to review and rate the range of factors identified from the first Delphi instrument. A third and final Delphi instrument asked participants to rank the most important factors that have positive effects. Throughout the three Delphi iterations, participants were asked to add additional factors that they thought might affect program implementation.

Following the work of the Delphi panel, interviews were conducted with ten stakeholders in an effort to seek clarification and/or additional information on comments provided during the course of the study. Participants included state employees (past and present), nonprofit representatives, and Stewardship Advisory Committee members. Three of these ten did not participate in the Delphi study but served in key capacities that informed Stewardship policy (i.e., an academic and Governor's Task Force appointee involved with statewide conservation planning and implementation, a planner with intimate knowledge of the program, and a second Governor's Task Force appointee). Documentation and archival records were also drawn upon, including *Report to the Governor by the Blue Ribbon Task Force on the Stewardship Program, A Staff Evaluation of the Knowles–Nelson Stewardship Program* and *Stewardship Program Re-Authorization Recommendations of the Stewardship Subcommittee to the Wisconsin Natural Resources Board.*

Results

The results of this study reveal a richness of respondent perspectives on factors that affect implementation of statewide public–private conservation programs.

Table 11.2 Assessment of program implementation

Mazmanian and Sabatier's six conditions of effective implementation	Participant response scores (mean value: 1 to 5)
Enabling legislation is clear and consistent	(4.6)
Enabling legislation achieves policy goals and gives implementing officials sufficient jurisdiction over target groups	(4.6)
Enabling legislation maximizes probability that implementing officials and target groups will perform as desired	(4.4)
Agency leaders possess significant managerial and political skill and are committed to statutory goals	(4.0)
Program is supported by organized constituency groups and a few key legislators throughout implementation	(4.4)
Statutory objectives are not undermined over time by conflicting public policies or changes in socioeconomic conditions	(4.0)

Factor rankings from the Delphi process were generally consistent among study participants; however the results did expose some differences based upon cohort—that is, agency versus nonprofit staff. Study results, represented in a series of tables and narrative format, reflect expert opinion from pre-Delphi interviews, Delphi study outcomes, follow-up interviews, and documentation and literature used to corroborate, clarify, and present the data within the context of an existing theory.

Results of the pre-Delphi survey are presented in Table 11.2 above. A Likert-scale questionnaire was used to assess current program implementation against Mazmanian and Sabatier's (1983) conditions of successful implementation. A mean of 5 is the strongest score, indicating a high level of agreement among respondents that the Stewardship Program is meeting the condition, while a mean closer to 1 is a weaker score. Scores were consistently high, suggesting the nonprofit component of the Stewardship is being implemented reasonably well at this time. Mazmanian and Sabatier note it is not imperative that all six conditions be met at the highest levels to implement a policy effectively, although the first two conditions "must always be met at least moderately well" (1983: 42).

In the third and final Delphi, participants were asked to select the seven (7) issues that, in their opinion, are most critical to implementing public-private conservation grant programs similar to the nonprofit component of Stewardship. They were asked to assign a value of '7' to the most important, '6' to the next most important, and so until the seventh (the least important of the seven) is assigned a value of '1.' Ordered rankings of the 17 factors they identified as having positive

Table 11.3 Factors that affect program implementation positively

Final rankings by Delphi participants		Total	Mean	Std. Dev.
1	Strong NCO organizational capacity	119	5.41	2.15
2	Use of good planning documents	64	2.91	2.79
3	NCO assistance to build land trust capacity	63	2.86	2.12
4	Allowance of land donations as match	61	2.77	2.45
5	Commitment of agency to program	59	2.68	2.97
6	Effective program administration	54	2.45	2.15
7	Encouragement of partnerships by agency leadership	46	2.09	2.41
8	Placement and effectiveness of agency Community Service Specialists in regions	40	1.82	2.22
9	NCO partnerships and reauthorization	32	1.45	2.28
10	Sharing of funding and expertise	25	1.14	1.93
11	Flexible codes and policies	24	1.09	1.54
12	Statutory authority to protect diverse land	16	0.73	1.78
13	Resolution of program issues by Stewardship Advisory Council	12	0.55	1.41
14	Thorough grant guidelines for NCOs	9	0.41	1.33
15	Project quality and appeal to agency	6	0.27	0.88
16	Use of pre-review process	4	0.18	0.50
17	Combining of grants and land purchase into land division	3	0.14	0.47

effects on implementation are presented in Table 11.3. Participants were asked *not* to rank factors on how well they are currently performed or implemented; rather, they were asked to think about the key factors that they felt were necessary to implement programs similar to the nonprofit component of Stewardship, and to use their knowledge of and experience with similar state or federal programs to inform their choices.

The factor consistently ranked first by a significant majority of respondents was the need for strong organizational capacity of the participating nonprofit conservation organizations. Clearly, with this type of public–private conservation program, implementation will falter without a nonprofit partner with the capacity

Table 11.4 Factors that affect program implementation positively, by cohort

Rankings by NCOs	Mean	Rankings by agency	Mean
Strong NCO organizational capacity	5.5	Strong NCO organizational capacity	5.2
Encouragement of partnerships by agency leadership	3.3	Use of good planning documents	4.1
Commitment of agency to program	3.2	NCO assistance to build land trust capacity	3.1
Allowance of land donations as match	2.8	Effective administration	2.9
NCO assistance to build land trust capacity	2.7	Allowance of land donations as match	2.6
NCO partnerships and reauthorization	2.0	Placement and effectiveness of CSSs in regions	2.3
Effective administration	2.0	Commitment of agency to program	2.1
Use of good planning documents	1.9	Flexible codes and policies	1.3
Placement and effectiveness of CSSs in regions	1.3	Sharing of funding and expertise	1.0
Sharing of funding and expertise	1.3		

to secure deals and raise the required matching funds. The next five factors were all ranked within six points of one another: use of good planning documents, assistance from NCOs to build land trust capacity, administrative allowance of land donations as match, commitment of agency staff to the program, and effective management by administrator. Beyond land trust capacity, results focus on strategic conservation, a mechanism for building land trust capacity (i.e., Gathering Waters Conservancy), administrative rules that encourage land trust involvement, and a committed and highly functioning agency to implement the program.

A review of the data reveals some differences in the factor rankings based upon cohort—namely, the interests of the nonprofit community versus the agency's perspective. In a sense, these cohorts represent what Sabatier and Jenkins-Smith (1993) identify as "advocacy coalitions." The most significant differences between the 12 NCO participants and 10 agency participants occurred in two areas: encouragement of partnerships by agency leadership and use of good planning documents (see Table 11.4). In the case of agency leadership, nonprofits felt that the Secretary of the WDNR, particularly at the outset of the program, played a critical role in encouraging partnerships with private nonprofit conservation organizations. By contrast, many of the agency staff identified the use of good

Table 11.5 Factors that affect program implementation negatively, by cohort

Ranking by NCOs	Mean	Ranking by agency	Mean
Excessive interference by legislature	4.4	Understaffing of agency grants/ lands programs	3.6
Public access requirements on protected lands	4.2	Property tax consequences to landowners	3.4
Anything that delays project approval	4.2	Excessive interference by legislature	3.2
Lengthy appraisal process	4.2	Public access requirements on protected lands	3.2
Excessive number of rules and statutes	4.1	Complicated grant application process	3.1
Discouragement of applications by NCOs due to public access reqs	3.7	Conflict between agency bureaus	3.1
Landowner disagreement with appraised value of land	3.4	Anything that delays project approval	3.0
Unacceptability of agency as easement co-holder	3.4	Excessive number of rules and statutes	3.0
Understaffing of agency grants/ lands program	3.3	Lengthy appraisal process	2.9
Complicated grant application process	3.3	Discouragement of applications by NCOs due to public access reqs	2.8

planning documents as vital to implementation. Despite other minor differences, however, scores between these two groups were relatively consistent.

With regard to issues that negatively affect implementation, there was less agreement among participants and greater variability of scores when contrasting agency and nonprofit participant responses (see Table 11.5). Though the negative effects were not ranked as part of the final Delphi, this information provides perspectives relevant to this study's conclusions.

When considering factors that negatively affect implementation, NCO participants seemed to focus primarily on two main areas: legislative involvement and program delays. Among the legislative factors cited were excessive interference by the legislature, public access requirements on protected lands, and passage of too many rules and statutes. Regarding delay factors, they listed lengthy and disputed appraisal processes and other administrative issues that take time and threaten land deals.

By contrast, agency representatives viewed agency capacity (i.e., inadequate staffing) and property tax consequences to landowners as the top factors threatening implementation. With regard to property tax consequences, if a landowner in Wisconsin chooses to encumber his or her property with a conservation easement, the change in land classification (e.g., from agricultural use to recreational land) can actually increase the property tax—clearly a disincentive. Other negative factors include a complicated grant application process and conflicts between agency bureaus that can create roadblocks. For instance, the Bureau of Community Financial Assistance, where the nonprofit component of the Stewardship is located, maintains a focus on working with external partners (e.g., land trusts) to help them achieve their goals. The Bureau of Facilities and Lands, particularly the real estate section, is focused on efficient and effective real estate processes—but many land trusts lack the capacity to effectively and efficiently close deals. Therefore some of the administrative processes proposed by one bureau conflict with those of the other.

Table 11.6 presents the main themes identified through the Delphi process, listing the key factors cited by respondents as having positive effects on implementation of public–private conservation grant programs and their aggregate scores.

Finding #1: Strong NCO Organizational Capacity is Necessary

Overwhelmingly, Delphi participants identified strong NCO organizational capacity as a central feature for successful implementation of the Stewardship Program. The primary capacity-related issues named by participants were staff competence and experience, particularly related to real estate skills and the ability to raise the required matching funds. This factor comports with Matland's view of implementing policies that are generally low in conflict and highly ambiguous—that is to say, a recognition that "outcomes will depend largely on which actors are active and most involved" (1995: 165). Though Matland's actors extend beyond the nonprofit organizations involved in this program—for instance to include other implementation actors such as agency personnel—it is clear that Delphi participants felt that nonprofit capacity is a central feature with regard to implementation success.

Capacity building was reinforced during the 2000 reauthorization of the Stewardship program, as legislation was introduced and enacted (Chapter 23, § 23.0955) that allowed Gathering Waters Conservancy (and several other state-wide nonprofits) the opportunity to apply for a segregated pool of funding that supports their organizational mission of building capacity for Wisconsin land trusts. One could certainly interpret these "capacity building grants" as helping to maximize the probability that target groups will perform as desired.

Finding #2: There Must be Agency Commitment to the Concept of Funding NCOs

A number of study participants, particularly those working for nonprofits, reported that agency program staff were focused, great to work with, and extremely important to successful implementation of the Stewardship Program. There were numerous references to a key agency staff person that served as an advocate for nonprofits, as well as a critical program facilitator. In addition, one participant noted that agency leadership at the highest levels "set the tone for increased

Table 11.6 Summary of key findings from the Delphi analyses

Strong organizational capacity of nonprofit conservation organizations	182
• NCO organizational capacity (119)	
• External, nonprofit organization helping to build land trust capacity, e.g., Gathering Waters Conservancy (63)	
Agency commitment to the concept of an NCO program	105
• Commitment of key agency staff to the concept of funding NCOs (59)	
• Agency leadership at highest level encouraging partnerships with NCOs (46)	
Statutes and codes that encourage and enable NCOs to achieve goals	101
• Statutes and codes that allow NCOs to use donations to match (61)	
• Flexible codes and policies that enable NCOs to achieve goals (24)	
• Statutes and codes that allow NCOs to protect diverse landscapes (16)	
Strong organizational capacity of implementing agency	94
• Highly effective and responsive Community Financial Assistance (54)	
• Placement and effectiveness of Regional Community Services Specialists (40)	
Use of good planning documents as a basis for protection efforts	64
Effective Nonprofit Partnerships and Coalitions	57
• Partnerships/coalitions that work together on program reauthorization (32)	
• Partnerships sharing funding and expertise (25)	

partnership involvement," advocated for involving land trusts and local units of government, and provided the authority to help to tamp down internal conflicts that could threaten program implementation. This sentiment is in keeping with Mazmanian and Sabatier's third condition (sympathetic agencies) and fourth condition (leadership with managerial and political skill and commitment to goals). Furthermore, a number of study participants, commitment at the staff level was equally if not more important than commitment by agency leaders. Goggin et al. suggest that "the first essential characteristic of contribution is competency, or skill, which is a function of the individual's capacity to interact effectively with his or her environment. The second ingredient is motivation, or will" (1990:

130). This finding also supports Matland's view on the importance of the actors involved with implementing programs.

Finding #3: Statutes must Encourage and Enable NCOs to Achieve Conservation Goals

Study participants familiar with the statutory basis of the Stewardship Program stressed the importance, especially early on, of having code that was flexible, clear, and consistently applied. In other words, the code allowed NCOs leeway in how to use their resources to protect land, raise matching funds, and accomplish other goals, but also established a structure for tight program administration. Effective statutes and codes are written in such a way as to provide this flexibility and structure, as well as to reduce conflict, build productive partnerships, and encourage participation.

Mazmanian and Sabatier's first condition of effective implementation is a clear fit with this finding, replete with overlapping language. Condition 1 states that "the enabling legislation or other legal directive (that) mandates policy objectives" should be "clear and consistent or at least provide substantive criteria for resolving goal conflicts" (1983: 41). This factor is also consistent with their second and third conditions in that the inherent flexibility provided by statute and code represents both a "sound theory identifying the principal factors and causal linkages affecting policy objectives" (Condition 2), and supportive decision rules that maximize the "probability that implementing officials and target groups will perform as desired" (Condition 3) (ibid., p. 41).

Finding #4: Strong Agency Organizational Capacity is Key

Consistent with Mazmanian and Sabatier's third condition of effective implementation, which speaks to the importance of implementing agencies having "sufficient financial resources" and "adequate hierarchical integration" (1983: 41), study participants stressed the importance of having highly trained real estate and grants staff in the CFA, adequate staffing levels, timely program administration and support from agency leadership. In addition, participants identified structural elements such as a central program coordinator (i.e., grants manager) and "program delivery at the local level" (i.e., Community Services Specialists located in each of the agency's five regions).

Goggin et al. define organizational capacity with respect to a state implementing agency simply as the government's ability to "get its act together" so as "to institute the structure, the routines, and the coordinated efforts of talented people sufficient to convert a policy message into a set of real achievements" (1990: 118). They suggest that "capacity is improved when the individuals hired to get the job done are sufficiently numerous, qualified, and favorably disposed toward the call to action," noting that agency capacity "requires possession of the requisite financial resources for the program," including "those targeted directly to clients and those spent in the process of implementation" (1990: 120).

Finding #5: Multi-nonprofit Partnerships and Coalitions are Useful

Study participants identified the importance of partnerships between and among nonprofits, as well as other agencies, on land protection projects and priorities; however, more comments centered on the role of coalitions in helping to reauthorize the Stewardship Program. Gathering Waters Conservancy was identified as an NCO that facilitated many of these coalitions and partnerships, with a specific focus on program reauthorization in 2000 and again in 2007. One participant noted that a variety of "nonprofits, involving land trusts, statewide organizations, and hook-and-bullet groups" worked "on the political side in working to get Stewardship reauthorized." Although study participants did not rank partnerships as highly as other factors affecting implementation, it is clear that reauthorization is critical to program sustainability and thus implementation. Without reauthorization, for instance, program implementation would have ended over eight years ago. As Mazmanian and Sabatier state in their fifth condition of effective implementation, a program must be "actively supported by organized constituency groups and by a few key legislators (or a chief executive) throughout the implementation process" (1983: 41).

Finding #6: Quality Planning Documents are Important

The Land Legacy Report, a document that identifies priority natural resources and outdoor recreational opportunities for protection over the next 50 years, was a directive to the WDNR from a Governor appointed board. Though there are general criteria that nonprofits are encouraged to pursue for acquisition and easement projects, NCOs will generally receive a higher ranking if their target lands have been identified within the Land Legacy document. This reflects Mazmanian and Sabatier's first condition of effective implementation which speaks to the issue of good planning documents, that is to say, a directive that "mandates policy objectives which are clear and consistent" (1983: 41).

Other Relevant Issues Affecting Implementation

Throughout the Delphi process and during interviews, study participants mentioned specific individuals and organizations that play key roles in coordinating implementation goals. For instance, Community Services Specialists (i.e., CSS—regionally-based agency personnel charged with assisting nonprofits and local units of government) were consistently identified as critical, front-line players important to the success of the program. Gathering Waters Conservancy, a statewide land trust service provider, was identified not only for its role in helping to build the capacity of land trusts, but as a key partner and advocate for the reauthorization of the Stewardship Program. Finally, a significant number of individuals cited the agency grants manager (located within the CFA) as playing a critical role in the successful implementation of the nonprofit component of the Stewardship. This person was lauded for coordinating complex systems of policy and working closely with external partners, as well as handling legal and administrative responsibilities within the agency. As one study participant put it, the grants manager "was the DNR staff person most responsible for the success of this program." And one Delphi participant provided a unique perspective on the roles of both Gathering Waters and the agency grants manager, describing Gathering Waters as the "external coordinator" and the agency grants manager as the "internal coordinator."

Finally, probably the most glaring omission by participants involved in the Delphi process—but identified during the interviews—was the $8 million annual allocation available to nonprofits for land and easement acquisition. In the recent program reauthorization, the allocation increased to $12 million annually. Perhaps this factor was simply assumed by participants; however, clearly, without funding available for land acquisition the program would simply not exist. As for Mazmanian and Sabatier, they state that "money is obviously critical" to implementing a policy or program (1983: 26). Taken together with the importance of land trust and agency capacity, these results comport to Matland's "low-conflict, high-ambiguity" quadrant in his conflict-ambiguity matrix (i.e., experimental implementation) where resources and actors are central to successful implementation.

Policy Implications

Public–private conservation initiatives are becoming a valuable tool in protecting natural lands, waters, and wildlife. The Knowles–Nelson Stewardship Program, specifically the nonprofit component, is an excellent example of this type of public-private conservation initiative. By using a Wisconsin-specific case, this research identifies key factors that affect implementation of statewide public–private conservation grant programs. Through a pre-Delphi survey, a Delphi process, interviews, and documentation, this research also offers support of the Mazmanian and Sabatier's theories on implementation.

The results of this research provide clear implications for implementing policy related to statewide public–private conservation grant programs. First, all actors (e.g., legislators, agency and nonprofit staff and administrators) should focus on building and maintaining nonprofit capacity and effective coalitions, while making sure to secure the financial resources necessary to implement this type of policy/program.

Second, in addition to maintaining high levels of organizational capacity, the agency must also secure highly talented individuals that are committed to the concept of a public–private program. Agency staff must be given program oversight and administrative flexibility, and be placed strategically within the agency and allocated by region in order to work closely and creatively with the nonprofits. Ultimately, these types of public–private programs seem to live or die by the talents, efforts, and commitment of the participating clients (e.g., nonprofits) and street-level bureaucrats (i.e., agency staff and administrators).

Third, if the goal of a given program is to engage client organizations, such as land trusts, individuals involved in drafting statutes and/or administrative rules must provide flexibility and understand the mission and capacities of client organizations. For example, allowing land trusts to use donated land or easements as match provides an excellent way of helping a land trust meet its match requirement, while providing an enormous benefit to conservation in Wisconsin (i.e., more land protected in the end). By contrast, mandating that land trusts provide unfettered public access to eased lands (i.e., land owned almost exclusively by private landowners) will likely have a chilling effect on private landowners considering a conservation easement, potentially reducing the amount of protected land within the state.

Fourth, the use of good planning documents is tied to the ultimate outcomes of any land and water conservation effort, that is, protecting what it is we intend to protect. Land conservation, particularly today when natural resources are being lost at an extremely fast pace, must be strategic and targeted. Without tying our acquisition and easement efforts to thoughtful, long-range planning, we're simply throwing money away. Scattershot conservation will not achieve the ultimate goals of water, habitat, and biodiversity protection.

Fifth, involving a diverse advisory council(s) can provide additional expertise and innovative thinking. Particularly with a large, statewide public–private conservation program like the Stewardship, it is imperative to engage a diversity of interests. Having representation from the land trust community, local units of government, and academia, in addition to agency staff and representatives, provides a sharing of knowledge and expertise critical to identifying key problem areas and solutions to those problems.

Finally, study participants identified the importance of having a committed and highly qualified "internal coordinator" working inside the implementing agency that has significant program oversight and administrative flexibility and serves as an advocate for client organizations (e.g., nonprofit conservation organizations); effective "local coordinators" placed by the agency throughout the state to serve local client organizations; and an "external coordinator" that builds nonprofit capacity and facilitates ongoing coalitions.

In closing, by using a case study of Wisconsin's Knowles–Nelson Stewardship Program, this research has identified the factors that affect implementation of statewide public–private conservation grant programs. This study's results should be of value to local and state governments that pursue a public–private approach to land conservation. These results can guide implementation efforts of similar public–private conservation initiatives and structure new and emerging initiatives.

References

Assistance to Nonprofit Conservation Organizations, Wisc. Stat. Ch. 23 §23.0955(1). 2008.

Bardach, E. 1977. *The Implementation Game: What Happens After a Bill Becomes a Law.* Cambridge, MA: MIT Press.

Daniere, A.G. 1995. Transportation planning and implementation in cities of the Third World: The case of Bangkok. *Environment and Planning C: Government and Policy*, 13, 25–45.

Endicott, E. 1993. *Land Conservation through Public/Private Partnerships.* Washington D.C.: Island Press.

Goggin, M., Bowman, A., Lester, J., and O'Toole, L.J. 1990. *Implementation Theory and Practice: Toward a Third Generation.* Glenview, IL: Scott, Foresman/Little, Brown Higher Education.

Hotynski, R. 2005. *Warren Knowles–Gaylord Nelson Stewardship Program*, Informational Paper 57. Madison, WI: Wisconsin Legislative Fiscal Bureau.

Ingram, H. and Schneider, A., 1990. Improving Implementation Through Framing Smarter Statutes. *Journal of Public Policy*, 10: 67–88.

Linstone, H.A. and Turoff, M. (eds). 1975. *The Delphi Method: Techniques and Applications*. London; Amsterdam; Don Mills; Ontario; Sydney; Tokyo: Addison-Wesley Publishing Company.

Matland, R.E. 1995. Synthesizing the Implementation Literature: The Ambiguity-Conflict Model of Policy Implementation. *Journal of Public Administration Research and Theory*, Vol. 5, No. 2: 145–74.

Mazmanian, D.A. and Sabatier, P.A. 1983. *Implementation and Public Policy.* Glenview, IL: Scott, Foresman.

Pressman, J.L. and Wildavsky, A.B. 1973. *Implementation: How Great Expectations in Washington are Dashed in Oakland.* Berkeley, CA: University of California Press.

Sabatier, P.A. and Jenkins-Smith, H.C. 1993. *Policy Change and Learning: An Advocacy Coalition Approach.* Boulder; San Francisco; and Oxford: Westview Press.

Talen, E. 1996. Do plans get implemented? A review of evaluation in planning. *Journal of Planning Literature*, 10, 248–59.

Winter, S. 2003. Implementation perspectives: Status and reconsideration, in *Handbook of Public Administration*, edited by B.G. Peters and J. Pierre. London; Thousand Oaks, CA: Sage Publications, 212–22.

Wisconsin Department of Natural Resources. 2006. *Wisconsin Land Legacy Report: An Inventory of Places to Meet Wisconsin's Future Conservation and Recreation Needs*. Madison, WI: Author.

Chapter 12

Conclusion: Evaluating the Prospects for Integrating Land Conservation and Growth Management

Timothy S. Chapin and Christopher Coutts

Within the last several decades, urban planning has experienced a number of revolutions, almost all of which have strengthened and professionalized the discipline. Some of these revolutions have revolved around the technology employed by planners, as computerized mapping capabilities in the form of geographic information systems are now found in most planning offices, and the volume and quality of data available to planners has increased exponentially. There has also been a major shift in the view towards community involvement, as quality public participation, collaboration by key stakeholders, and consensus building are emphasized more than ever.

While urban planning has evolved in numerous ways, many of the concepts central to the discipline remain. As discussed in this book, one of these fundamental ideas is the need to balance conservation and development, simultaneously protecting rural landscapes while promoting development in more urban places, and installing grey infrastructure (water/sewer, roads, etc.) without compromising the quality of green infrastructure (greenways, water bodies, habitat lands, etc.). As we noted in the introduction to this volume, Ebenezer Howard's Garden Cities concept offers perhaps the best articulation of the need to balance undeveloped and developed landscapes, even going so far as to articulating an urban form that reflects this balance.

While Howard's ideas have had a substantial influence on the discipline, with many growth management and smart growth programs able to trace their lineage back to the Garden Cities concept, the tension between conservation and development remains. There remain marked concerns that development outcomes are economically, environmentally, and socially unsustainable. The environmental community continues to express real alarm about the ability of natural systems to service and sustain the diverse animal and plant life found in undeveloped areas.

The foremost example within Florida of the conservation and development tension is the Everglades, a remarkably complex, eerily beautiful, and environmentally unique ecosystem that covers as much as half of the state's landmass. Decades of intrusion into the Everglades by agricultural uses and sprawling suburban development, supported by federal and state policies, have altered the flows of water in this river of grass and contributed to the loss of many animal and plant species and the listing of numerous others. Within the last twenty years the evidence of environmental damage became so clear that there has been a substantial push to reclaim and restore the Everglades. Within the last decade the federal government, the state of Florida, affected local governments, and large landowners (including the sugar industry) have come together to develop a Comprehensive Everglades Restoration Plan, or CERP. CERP is designed to restore portions of the Everglades to their natural state, at substantial public cost. The CERP approach also calls for stronger state and local policies for managing development in and around the Everglades and more clearly delineating urban and undeveloped lands.

Like Florida's experience with the Everglades, many communities in the United States—and throughout the globe—are beginning to rethink their approaches for managing growth and more successfully balancing conservation and development. As detailed in this book, one of the key strategies for promoting land conservation is the acquisition of land, or the development rights linked to the land, by the public sector. Andy McLeod's work in this volume describes Florida's experience with its Preservation 2000 and Florida Forever programs, one of the latest and most successful land acquisition programs on the planet. Other states, including Maryland (see Szobota and Lynch, Chapter 10), Wisconsin (see Clutter, Chapter 11), and Pennsylvania (see Daniels, Chapter 3), have pursued a similar strategy. These programs are purchasing sensitive lands, buying development rights on agricultural properties, and investing in green infrastructure systems, usually at substantial expense but with great effectiveness given their funding levels.

Despite their successes, however, these land acquisition programs have generally remained disassociated from the planning and growth management processes in these locations. Even in Florida, where state-mandated, local comprehensive planning is integral to almost any land use decision, the Florida Forever program operates outside of the local comprehensive planning process and with few connections to these planning documents. It is this disconnect that contributes to Daniels and Lapping's conclusion that "land preservation must take place within the comprehensive planning process to work toward smart growth goals" (see Chapter 2).

The evidence presented in this book suggests that the potential for better linking public land acquisition programs to growth management efforts is limited by several key theoretical and structural challenges. There is good news to report, though, in that efforts to forge these links appear more prevalent than ever, and the chapters in this volume indicate that these links can be strengthened through partnerships with nonprofit organizations, through innovative state and local policy, and through better targeting schemes for acquiring lands. Below we highlight the key challenges and opportunities that emerged from the work of the contributors.

Challenges to Balancing Conservation and Development

Perhaps the single most salient conclusion from these collected chapters is that the goal of balancing conservation and development is not easily achieved. Littered throughout this volume are programs or places that have tried, usually unsuccessfully, to balance the desire for environmental protection/farmland preservation with growth and development of their urban areas. While there are numerous examples of successful farmland preservation programs, too often these programs are small, poorly resourced, and subject to changing political winds (see Chapter 3). Similarly, Florida's experience with the innovative, but ultimately doomed Rural Land Stewardship Areas (RLSA) program illustrates that land development can trump conservation efforts unless sufficient safeguards are in place for the protected lands (see Chapter 5).

Why do conservation efforts struggle in the face of development pressure? Conservation efforts struggle in large part because of difficulties in measuring the economic value of ecosystem services provided by undeveloped lands. While the federal government and some states are attempting to develop models for measuring the value of these services and then developing a scheme for paying for them, for most landowners the greatest economic value for the property lies in developing it. Unfortunately, current methods for targeting land for acquisition usually do not take into account the realities of land markets. Evidence from Maryland's GreenPrint program (Chapter 10) suggests that land conservation program managers need to understand these market realities when targeting land for acquisition, which can yield more efficient use of limited program funds.

This volume also highlights a troublesome problem for proponents of linking land acquisition and growth management efforts. An analysis of the Portland, Oregon land market found that land acquisition programs might actually accelerate development on surrounding properties, in large part by driving up the price of adjacent properties or properties with views of these protected spaces (see Chapter 6). This finding is reinforced by the experience of Collier County, Florida, as it pursued a rural lands stewardship program (see Chapter 5). The protection of large swaths of environmentally sensitive lands enabled and accelerated the development of exurban communities far from existing development. In these places, as elsewhere, land preservation programs can successfully protect some lands, but with the unintended consequence of encouraging development on adjacent or nearby lands.

A final challenge to balancing conservation and development rests in public and legislative attitudes on these issues. Surveys of Florida citizens indicate that the public at large considers land conservation and growth management as distinct activities (see Chapter 9). Land conservation is embraced by younger, racially/ethnically diverse, and more liberal constituents, while growth management's base of support rests in older, educated, and more wealthy residents. There are similar schisms at the legislative level in Florida, as decades of support for the largest state-funded land acquisition program in the nation has eroded in recent years, ultimately hobbling the Florida Forever program (see Chapter 4).

Opportunities for Linking Conservation and Growth Management

Despite these challenges, there remains substantial opportunity for linking conservation efforts to growth management regimes. These opportunities rest in part on the existence of several programs that have attempted to connect conservation and development. States and local governments should look to these existing programs for inspiration, and ideas on program/policy design, and to take stock of the lessons that can be learned from these efforts.

Programs such as Florida Forever (Chapter 3) or the RLSA program in Florida (Chapter 6), inspired by the need to conserve and protect land in a very fast-growing state, offer other states and local governments models upon which to build better programs for balancing conservation and development. Although smaller in scale, Wisconsin's Knowles–Nelson Stewardship program (Chapter 11) demonstrates the important role of nonprofits in identifying lands suitable for purchase and for leveraging resources—financial and human—to acquire these lands. Maryland's GreenPrint program (Chapter 10) is yet another notable state-level effort to protect important environmental and agricultural lands in a state experiencing development pressure in exurban areas. There are also several excellent farmland preservation programs, many of which have been successful in linking conservation and growth management (Chapter 3). The mechanisms that appear to work best in these farmland preservation efforts are public/private partnerships, local-level public support, and a growth management approach in which urban growth boundaries are coupled with agricultural-only zoning in rural areas.

Another opportunity for forging the link between land conservation and growth management is the growing recognition of the public health benefits associated with these strategies. There is growing evidence of the importance of land conservation in improving the health outcomes in communities, and some conservation programs may already be delivering health benefits without lauding their role in doing so (see Chapter 7). Smart growth proponents have latched onto the physical and psychological benefits of well-planned communities, arguing for a development agenda that promotes mixed-use, multi-modal communities that promote physical activity and socialization. Moving forward this public health "common ground" should be used as justification for implementing sustainable land use practices and pursuing land conservation, both as part of a comprehensive growth management strategy as envisioned by Daniels and Lapping (see Chapter 2).

A Partnership Agenda for Governments, Nonprofits, and the Private Sector

As with any public endeavor—especially one as impactful and permanent, and with the ability to instigate such powerful reactions—planning to manage development is only as effective as the players involved. It is important to recognize that the local political structure plays a key role in shaping growth management policies and the degree to which land conservation occurs. For example, evidence indicates that professional managers and larger councils are useful tools for insulating governments from the influence of local growth machines and promoting growth management and conservation agendas (see Chapter 7). This volume underscores the important role of the public sector, and key actors within the public sector, in promoting a balanced set of policies and then seeing these policies implemented.

There is evidence throughout this volume that points to a partnership model for successfully achieving land conservation and growth management. Wisconsin's Knowles–Nelson Stewardship program was designed to promote these partnerships across public, nonprofit, and private interests, and the growing capacity of these actors has contributed to the success of that program (see Chapter 11). Florida's experiences with its land conservation programs and RLSA program also points to the need for meaningful, productive partnerships between the public and private sectors if efforts to balance conservation and development are to be successful.

Conclusion

In closing, this volume began with the goal of documenting some of the leading practices of local and state governments undertaking work at the nexus of land conservation and growth management. Beyond documenting these practices, which is valuable and useful as other places look to develop and implement policy at this nexus, it is clear that much work remains to be done. While Florida, Pennsylvania, Oregon, Wisconsin, Maryland, and the local areas discussed in this book are likely better off for these efforts, no single policy or program offers a perfect mix of sound design, desired impact, implementation ease, and political sustainability.

Urban planning has evolved to a point at which there is a widespread belief that development practices must be more sensitive to protecting and preserving natural landscapes. The protection of these lands is necessary not solely for aesthetic purposes or for an intangible well-being, but for an ability to continue to expand or develop new urban settlements. While conservation could certainly happen without land development, the reverse is not true. Conservation sustains the natural resources on which humans depend for their health, and for the ability to expand human settlements. For these reasons growth management is inextricably linked to conservation. Again harkening back to Howard's Garden Cities concept, sustainable urban and natural landscapes require a balance between conservation and development, and it is our hope that this volume contributes to this discussion and points the way to better public policies and programs, and to stronger partnerships for achieving this balance.

Index

References to illustrations are in **bold**

agricultural productivity 34
 California 40
 and conservation 123
agricultural zoning
 Baltimore County 49
 benefits 45
 counties 48
 densities 44
 Lancaster County 49, **52**
 Marin County 48, 49
airborne pollution, and conservation 123–4
amenity value, open spaces 103, 104
American Farmland Trust 9, 18
Askew, Reubin, Governor 57

Baltimore County (MD)
 agricultural zoning 49
 farmland preservation 46
Bloxham, William, Governor 56
Boulder, greenbelt 16
Britain, new town planning 1
Broward, Napoleon Bonaparte, Governor 56
Bush, Jeb, Governor 60, 81, 82

California
 agricultural output 40
 farmland preservation 40
 land preservation 17
Carroll County (MD), farmland preservation 19
Chapin, Tim 3, 4
Chattanooga, greenways and trails 16
Chittenden County (VT), farmland loss 35
citrus industry, Florida, decline 79
cluster development, and farmland preservation 19
Clutter, David 4
Collier County (FL)
 Audubon Society 81
 Eastern Collier Property Owners Group 81, 82
 RLSA program 80–1, 84, 85, 86–9
  adoption 86
  Ave Maria 88, 89, 95
  boundary 86
  criticisms of 89
  DCA role 93
  Immokalee 86, 89
  natural resource index 88
  preservation-development tension 86, 89
  Review Committee 89
  St. Lucie County RLSA, comparison 90–1
  stewardship sending/receiving areas 87, 88
  success factors 86–9, 94
 Rural Lands Assessment Area Oversight Committee 82
conservation
 and agricultural production 123
 and airborne pollution 123–4
 development, tension 219
 and health 121–2, 135–6
 infrastructure approach, diagram **127**
 land preservation, distinction 128
 and mental health 125
 and physical activity 124–5
 and safety 125–6
 and social capital 125
 and water 122–3
conservation easements 11–12, 18, 37, 39
 acquisitions 11
 durability 11
 examples 11

guides 12, 21
Pacific Forest Trust 21
tax benefits 11–12
Vermont Land Trusts 21
conservation medicine 120
Coutts, Christopher 4
Crist, Charlie, Governor 66, 68, 69, 70, 75

Daniels, Tom 3, 18
Delphi technique 205–6, 207–8
development, and land preservation 1–2, 94–6, 221, 223
tension 219
development rights 11
costs 49
purchase 45, 46–7
disease, and sprawl 126

ecosystems
and health 120–1, 126
and land preservation 120
services 173–4
willingness to pay for 174
environment, and health 119–20
environmental
goods provision, and the political market 143–8
interests, and open space preservation 146
estate taxes, reduction 12
Everglades
Comprehensive Everglades Restoration Plan 220
environmental damage 219–20

Farm and Ranchland Protection
Act (1996) 36–7
Program 47
farmers
average age 36
federal subsidies 35
farmland
acreage 35
cropland 35
environmental benefits 34
loss
Chittenden County 35
Florida 35
Wisconsin 35
farmland preservation 18–20, 34–53
and agricultural output 49–50
Baltimore County 46
California 40
Carroll County 19
and cluster development 19
counties 44–51
acres preserved 45, 48
agricultural zoning 48
expense 51
farmland changes 46
flaws 50–1
funds, sources 47
lessons learned 52–3
population changes 46, 50
program costs 47–8, 49
program structure 46–7
strengths 49–50
urban growth boundaries 48
development rights, purchase 36, 38–9
funds
federal 37
public 20
shortage of 3 7–8
and growth management 38, 51
guidebooks 18–19
identifying suitable land 19
justification for 35–7
Lancaster County 19, 44, 49
Marin County 46
Maryland 19, 36
Montgomery County 46, 49
New Jersey 20
New York 19, 36, 45
Pennsylvania *see under* Pennsylvania
pros and cons 18
purposes 18
Rural Legacy Program 19–20
Sonoma County 46, 49
and sprawl containment 34
state programs 39–40
strategies 37
voluntary transactions 38
see also conservation easements
Farmland Preservation Report 18
farms, gross sales 35

Feiock, Richard 4
Florida
1000 Friends of 58, 68
Annual Policy Survey 163
Bert Harris Act (1995) 81
CARL program 57, 58, 61, 62, 64
citrus industry, decline 79
Conservation and Recreational Lands Trust Fund 160
Department of Community Affairs 81, 85, 86, 87, 89, 91–2, 93–4, 118
Departmental of Environmental Protection program 61–3, 74
environmentalism 57
farmland loss 35
Florida Natural Areas Inventory 62
greenways and trails 16
Growth Management Act (1985) 65, 118, 149, 160–1
growth management study 163–71
citizen attitudes 164, 165–9
data 163–4
implications 170–1
summary results 169–70
variables 165
health planning 119
housing growth 68
Internal Improvement Trust Fund 61–2
Land Conservation Act (1972) 160
land preservation 17, 55–76
Babcock Ranch 67–8
and development 2
funds 57–8, 160
and growth 64–6
mega-projects 67–8
milestones 57
tradition 56–61
uncertainties 55
US Sugar/River of Grass 67, 68
Nature Conservancy 70, 72–3, 160
optional sector planning, process 85–6
population growth 68
RLSA 3–4, 79–86, 92–3
acreage requirements 85
assessment 94–6
complexity 95, 96
contradictions 80
county programs 92–3
demise 94–5
development of regional impact, process 85
goals 79–80, 84–5
Growth Management Study Commission 82–3
implementation 86
legislation 84–6
limitations, DCA role 93–4
multi-county schemes 85
origins 80–3
stewardship credits 85
stewardship sending/receiving areas 84–5
see also Collier County; St. Lucie County
stamp tax revenue 66–7
Trust for Public Land 70, 73
water management districts 63
wetlands, loss 56
see also Collier County RLSA; Everglades; Florida Communities Trust RLSA; St. Lucie County
Florida Communities Trust
acquisition applications
by jurisdiction 150
comparison of governments 151–2, 153
funded/unfunded 129, 132–4
funds 64
growth management plan 149–50
health questionnaire 129–34, **129**
land acquisitions, logit model 152
open space acquisitions 4, 117, 134–5, 136, 148–50
purchases 64
acreage 149
purpose 60, 63–4, 118–19
Florida Forever 55, 79, 149, 220
achievements 55–6, 71
acquisitions 63, 67, 71–2
management 73–4
Act (1999) 66, 73
Amendment 5: 60, 69
backers 69
benefits 75–6

challenges 71–5
Coalition 69, 71
extension 69
financing 56
funds
allocations 60, 70, 118
decrease 69, 70
future 74–5
opposition to 70
greenways and trails 60, 61, 70
large landscapes, prioritization 65
performance measures 174
priority list 69, 72
programs 61–71
project rankings 62
Rural Family Lands Protection Program 74
scope 56
success 61
see also Preservation 2000
Forest Legacy Program 21
forestland preservation 20–1
Forest Legacy Program 21

garden cities 1
Garden Cities model
green spaces/developed land, symbiosis 1, 2, 219
USA 1
Graham, Bob, Governor 57
green infrastructure
definition 127
and health 127–8
Green Infrastructure Assessment, Maryland 176, 177
greenbelts 1, 93
GreenPrint Program (MD) 4, 17, 173, 176–98
acreage 178
background 176–9
corridors 176–7
data 180, 181–3
Desktop Ecological Scores 187–8
Green Infrastructure 176
acreage 177–8
Assessment 176, 177
map **177**
hedonic model
data 180
results 183–7
variables 180, 181
hubs 176
land acquisition costs
need for 178, 196–7
problems with 197
land values 179, 181
calculation 179fn7
and zoning regulations 182fn12
purpose 176
site comparisons 187
targeting schemes
alternative 189–90
county-specific 193–6
current 187–8
and hedonic model results 196
regional 190–3
greenways and trails 15–16, 23, 124
Chattanooga 16
definition 15
Florida 16
Florida Forever 60, 61, 70
land preservation 14
Preservation 2000 58
growth management
agricultural zoning 44
citizen attitudes to
and community 163
demographic factors 162
gender differences 162
homevoter hypothesis 162
and political orientation 162
and social class 161–2
study 163–71
variables 161–3
see also Florida, growth management study; smart growth
development rights, purchase 44
and farmland preservation 38, 51
counties 44–51
and housing affordability 50–1
and land preservation 219–22, 223
programs, purpose 33
urban growth boundaries 48
Oregon 44

health
  and conservation 121–2, 135–6
  and ecology 121
  and ecosystems 120–1, 126
  and environment 119–20
  and green infrastructure 127–8
  promotion, process 120
health ecology 121
hedonic analysis
  land values 179, 181
  Maryland counties 173, 181
  open spaces value 103
    Portland 106–9
Higgins, Harrison 3
housing affordability, and growth management 50–1
Howard, Ebenezer 219
  Garden Cities of Tomorrow 1
Hurricane Katrina 123

Kirk, Claude, Governor 57
Knowles–Nelson Stewardship Program (WI)
  components 202
  implementation evaluation
    Delphi technique 205–6, 207–8
    documentation 206
    effectiveness conditions 207
    interviews 206
    negative factors 210–11
    policy implications 215–16
    positive factors 208–9
    results 206–15
    success factors 211–15
  nonprofit conservation organizations 202–3, 222
  as partnership model 223

Lake Tahoe
  region 16
  Regional Planning Agency 17
Lancaster County (PA)
  agricultural output 50
  agricultural zoning 49
    map **52**
  farmland preservation 19, 44, 49
    preserved farms, map **52**
  urban growth areas, map **52**
Land Evaluation and Site Assessment 19
land market, and open space preservation 102
land preservation
  acquisition costs, neglect of 175
  Cadillac parcels 175
  California 17
  conservation, distinction 128
  and development 1–2, 94–6, 221, 223
    tension 219
  and ecosystems 120
  farmland 18–20
  Florida, *see under* Florida
  forestland 20–1
  greenways and trails 14
  and growth management 219–22, 223
  literature 9–14, 23
  Maryland 17
  meaning 10
  natural areas 16–17
  need for 9
  parklands 14–15
  Philadelphia 15
  private 8
  proactivity, need for 23
  programs, USA 173, 174
  public financing of 13–14
  research needs 21–2, 22, 23
  rural 16–21
  and smart growth 8, 10, 220
  urban/suburban 14–16
  see also open space preservation
Land Trust Alliance 12
land trusts 9, 13, 14
land use conversion
  analysis, open spaces value, Portland 109–12
  factors 104–5
  identification 105
land use regulations, ineffectiveness 9–10
land values
  determining 179
  hedonic analysis 179, 181
Land and Water Conservation Fund 15
Lapping, Mark 3
Last Great Places campaign 17
Lee, SeJin 4

Letchworth Garden City 1
Lexington City, urban growth boundaries 44
Lynch, Lori 4

McLeod, Andrew 3, 220
Marin County (CA)
  agricultural zoning 48, 49
  farmland preservation 46
Martinez, Bob, Governor 58
Maryland
  Agricultural Land Preservation Foundation, acreage 178
  counties, hedonic analysis 173
  Department of Natural Resources 176
  Department of Planning 181
  Environmental Trust 12
  farmland preservation program 19, 36
  Greenways Commission 15–16
  land area
    developed 176
    protected 17, 176
    undeveloped 176
  Rural Legacy Program 7, 19
  Transferable Development Rights 20
  see also GreenPrint Program
mental health, and conservation 125
Molotch, Harvey 146
Montgomery County, farmland preservation 46, 49
Mormino, Gary 56–7

National Recreation and Parks Association 14
Nature Conservancy 17, 201
New Hampshire Forests, Society for the Protection of 21
New Jersey
  farmland preservation 20
  Pinelands, preservation area 16–17
New Urbanism movement, USA 1
New York, farmland preservation 19, 36, 45
Nimbyism, and open space preservation 146–7

Olmsted, Frederick Law, Central Park (NY), design 14
open space preservation
  criteria 112
  and environmental interests 146
  and land market 102
  and local politics 145–6
  and Nimbyism 146–7
  and political institutions 147–8
  and the political market 148–50
  Portland *see under* Portland
  priorities 101–2
  and urban growth machine 146–7
  see also land preservation
open spaces
  active versus passive uses 128
  amenity value 103, 104
  and land market dynamics 105
  and property values 103–4
  value, hedonic analysis 103
Oregon
  urban growth boundaries 44
  see also Portland

Pacific Forest Trust, conservation easements 21
Pennsylvania
  Bureau of Farmland Protection 41
  farmland preservation 41–4
    acres preserved 42
    flaws 43–4
    fund sources 42
    land trusts 42
    program costs 42
    program structure 41–2
    strengths 42–3
  population growth 44
Philadelphia, land preservation 15
physical activity, and conservation 124–5
policy implementation
  conflict-ambiguity model 204–5
  definitions 203–4
  literature review 203–5
political institutions, and open space preservation 147–8
political market, the
  environmental goods provision 143–8
  and open space preservation 148–50, 153–4

Portland
    land market 4
    open space preservation 105–12
        acreage 106
        ballot measures 106
        criteria 113
        hedonic analysis 106–9
        land conversion **111**
        land use conversion analysis 109–12
    parkland acquisition 14–15
Preservation 2000: 58–9, 64, 73, 74, 79, 118, 149, 220
    acreage preserved 59
    annual expenditure 59
    establishment 160
    greenways and trails 58
    see also Florida Forever
Project for Public Spaces 15
property rights 38
property values, and open spaces 103–4

Reed, Nathaniel P. 58
RLSA programs *see under* Collier County; Florida; St. Lucie County
Rural Legacy Program
    farmland preservation 19–20
    Maryland 7, 19

safety, and conservation 125–6
St. Lucie County (FL)
    population 89
    RLSA program 86, 89–92
        acreage 90
        Collier County RLSA, comparison 90–1
        DCA objections 91–2
        demise 90, 92
        development of regional impact, process 92
        preservation-development tension 90
        properties 90, 91, 92
        stewardship sending/receiving areas 90
        Towns, Villages, and Countryside concept 91, 92
smart growth 219
    case studies, need for 22
    dumb growth, comparison 7
    elements 7, 23
    and land preservation 8, 10, 220
    national network 119
    planning for 22–3
    and sprawl containment 8
social capital, and conservation 125
Song, Yan 4
Sonoma County, farmland preservation 46, 49
sprawl
    containment 44
        and farmland preservation 34
        and smart growth 8
    disbenefits 7–8, 9, 34
    and disease 126
Szobota, Karen Palm 4

Transferable Development Rights 16–17, 39, 80, 82
    Montgomery County, Maryland 20
Transportation Equity Act (1998) 16
Trust for Public Lands 101

urban growth boundaries 48
    lack of 50
    Lexington City 44
    Oregon 44
urban growth machine, and open space preservation 146–7
urban planning, developments 219
USA
    land preservation programs 173, 174
    New Urbanism movement 1
    population growth 33–4, 53

Vermont Land Trusts, conservation easements 21

water, and conservation 122–3
Welwyn Garden City 1
Wetland Reserve Program 39
Whyte, William H. 12, 15
Wisconsin
    Bureau of Community Financial Assistance 203

Department of Natural Resources
202
annual allocation 203
farmland loss 35
Natural Resources Board 203
see also Knowles–Nelson Stewardship
Program

World Health Organization
Ecosystems and Human Well-Being
120, 126
Ottawa Charter for Health Promotion
120

Yellowstone National Park 201

For Product Safety Concerns and Information please contact our EU representative GPSR@taylorandfrancis.com
Taylor & Francis Verlag GmbH, Kaufingerstraße 24, 80331 München, Germany

www.ingramcontent.com/pod-product-compliance
Ingram Content Group UK Ltd.
Pitfield, Milton Keynes, MK11 3LW, UK
UKHW021506240926
475702UK00035B/510

* 9 7 8 0 7 5 4 6 7 9 4 1 7 *